The
Parallel
Chronological
Gospels

An Orderly Account of the Life of Jesus Christ

Advantage™
INSPIRATIONAL

John A. Olubobokun

The Parallel Chronological Gospels by John A. Olubobokun, Ph. D.
Copyright © 2011 by John A. Olubobokun
All Rights Reserved.
ISBN 13: 978-1-59755-262-2

Published by: ADVANTAGE BOOKS™
                       Longwood, Florida
                       www.advbookstore.com

Scripture taken from the Holy Bible, King James Version (KJV), public domain

Library of Congress Control Number: 2011932309

Cover design by Pat Theriault

First Printing: August 2011
11 12 13 14 15 16 17 10 9 8 7 6 5 4 3 2 1
Printed in the United States of America

All praise, honour and glory now and forever
to my Lord and Saviour Jesus Christ,
who commissioned me, and enabled me to finish this work!

Foreword

Some of my earliest memories are of reading the Bible and marvelling at the life and ministry of Jesus Christ. However, the more I read, the more I wondered exactly when and where the events occurred during His life. Many times it seemed I would read an account in one gospel, then read what appeared to be the same account in another gospel, yet it was presented in different detail and context. My perplexity convinced me of the need to some day put things in order. Approximately seven years ago, unable to find anything in print, and unaware that others may have already done so, my need translated into a personal project.

An in depth study of the gospel of John, helped me see, as had several others before me, that John focused on the Judean ministry of Jesus, and may have written to fill in the gaps in the accounts of the synoptic writers. That study led to a more detailed study and analysis of the synoptic gospels, and gave further impetus to the project I had already begun. Using Mark's gospel as a template, and utilizing many resources, years of compiling and re-compiling, and a trip to Israel in 2005, have resulted in a work that where appropriate, puts all four gospels side by side in columns (parallel), and the life of Jesus Christ in chronological order.

The sequence of events in parallel columns are highlighted in vertical hierarchy, so that anyone can follow without confusion about the timing, location , and context of such events. Readers may choose to read only the highlighted portions of parallel passages, or read the entire account in each gospel side by side. To reduce *white space* and improve readability, otherwise parallel columns with no entries in more than three rows have been converted into fewer columns, but kept shaded, to connect them to the preceding or following text. Furthermore, the major activities of Jesus' life - preaching, teaching, and healing (Matthew 4:23, 9:35) - are clearly numbered and footnoted throughout.

In compiling The Parallel Chronological Gospels, I have closely followed the King James version (KJV) of the Bible, but have changed archaic words to modern, easy-to-understand synonyms. The result is a unique *modified* King James Version (mKJV) that is refreshingly quite readable and easy to understand.

A compilation such as this is not an exact science. While many of the events in Jesus' life can be timed and located with certainty, some unfortunately cannot. There are things we will not know with certainty until we see Him and "know even as *we are* known" (1Corinthians 13:12). Until then, logic and best guesses must suffice. This work is nonetheless a sincere attempt at presenting the gospels in a logical, easy-to-read, and more understandable format. Imperfect as it may be, it has revolutionized my reading, and comprehension of the gospels. I sincerely hope that it will do the same for you.

Enjoy!

Grace, mercy and peace…

John A. Olubobokun, Ph.D.

(December 2010)

Table of Contents

1: From the beginning to John's ministry

1.01 An orderly account Luke 1:1-4

Luke 1:1-4

1 Forasmuch as many have undertaken to set forth in order a declaration of those things which are most surely believed among us,

2 Even as they delivered them to us, which from the beginning were eyewitnesses, and ministers of the word;

3 It seemed good to me also, having had perfect understanding of all things from the very first, to write to you in order, most excellent Theophilus,

4 That you may know the certainty of those things, in which you have been instructed.

1.02 Pre-incarnate Jesus John 1:1-5, 9-13

John 1:1-5, 9-13

1 In the beginning was the Word, the Word was with God, and the Word was God.

2 The same Word was in the beginning with God.

3 All things were made by him; and without him nothing was made that was made.

4 In him was life; and the life was the light of men.

5 And the light shines in darkness; and the darkness did not comprehend it.

9 That was the true Light, which lights every man that comes into the world.

10 He was in the world, and the world was made by him, and the world did not know him.

11 He came to his own, and his own did not receive him.

12 But as many as received him, to them he gave power to become the sons of God, even to those that believe on his name:

13 Who were born, not of blood, nor of the will of the flesh, nor of the will of man, but of God.

1.03 Gabriel announces God's plan to Zacharias (Jerusalem) Luke 1:5-25

Luke 1:5-25

5 In the days of Herod, the king of Judea, there was a certain priest named Zacharias, of the course of Abia: and his wife was of the daughters of Aaron, and her name was Elisabeth.

6 And they were both righteous before God, walking in all the commandments and ordinances of the Lord blameless.

7 And they had no child, because Elisabeth was barren, and they both were now quite old.

8 And it happened, that while he executed the priest's office before God in the order of his course,

9 According to the custom of the priest's office, his lot was to burn incense when he went into the temple of the Lord.

10 And the whole multitude of people were praying outside at the time of incense.

11 And there appeared to him an angel of the Lord standing on the right side of the altar of incense.

12 And when Zacharias saw him, he was troubled, and afraid.

13 But the angel said to him, Do not be afraid, Zacharias: for your prayer is heard; and your wife Elisabeth shall bear you a son, and you shall call his name John.

14 And you shall have joy and gladness; and many shall rejoice at his birth.

15 For he shall be great in the sight of the Lord, and shall drink neither wine nor strong drink; and he shall be filled with the Holy Ghost, even from his mother's womb.

16 And he will turn many of the children of Israel to the Lord their God.

17 And he shall go before him in the spirit and power of Elijah, to turn the hearts of the fathers to the children, and the disobedient to the wisdom of the just; to make ready a people prepared for the Lord.

18 And Zacharias said to the angel, How shall I know this? For I am an old man, and my wife is also quite old.

19 And the angel answering said to him, I am Gabriel, who stands in the presence of God; I was sent to speak to you, and to show you these glad tidings.

20 Look, you shall be dumb, and not able to speak, until the day that these things shall have happened, because you did not believe my words, which shall be fulfilled in their season.

21 And the people waited for Zacharias, and marvelled that he stayed so long in the temple.

22 And when he came out, he could not speak to them: and they perceived that he had seen a vision in the temple: for he made signs to them, and remained speechless.

23 And it happened, that, as soon as the days of his ministry were accomplished, he went back home.

24 And after those days his wife Elisabeth conceived, and hid herself five months, saying,

25 This is how the Lord has dealt with me in these days that he has looked on me, to take away my reproach among men.

1.04 Gabriel announces God's plan to Mary (Nazareth) Luke 1:26-38

Luke 1:26-38

26 Six months later the angel Gabriel was sent from God to a city of Galilee, named Nazareth,

27 To a virgin engaged to a man whose name was Joseph, of the house of David; and the virgin's name was Mary.

28 And the angel came to her, and said, Hail, you that are highly favoured, the Lord is with you: blessed are you among women.

29 And when she saw him, she was troubled at his saying, and thought to herself what manner of greeting this was.

30 And the angel said to her, Do not be afraid, Mary: for you have found favour with God.

31 Look, you shall conceive in your womb, and give birth to a son, and shall call his name JESUS.

32 He shall be great, and shall be called the Son of the Highest: and the Lord God shall give him the throne of his father David:

33 And he shall reign over the house of Jacob for ever; and his kingdom shall not end.

34 Then Mary said to the angel, How shall this be, seeing I have never had sexual relations with a man?

35 And the angel answered and said to her, The Holy Spirit shall come upon you, and the power of the Highest shall overshadow you: therefore also that holy child who shall be born by you shall be called the Son of God.

36 And, look, your cousin Elisabeth, has also conceived a son in her old age: and this is the sixth month with her, who was called barren.

37 For with God nothing shall be impossible.

38 And Mary said, Look I am the handmaid of the Lord; may it happen to me according to your word. And the angel departed from her.

1.05 Elizabeth's speech to Mary (Hill country of Judea) Luke 1:39-45

Luke 1:39-45

39 And Mary arose in those days, and went into the hill country with haste, into a city of Judea;

40 And entered into the house of Zacharias, and greeted Elisabeth.

41 And it happened that when Elisabeth heard Mary's greeting, the babe leaped in her womb; and Elisabeth was filled with the Holy Spirit:

42 And she spoke out with a loud voice, and said, Blessed are you among women, and blessed is the fruit of your womb.

43 And why has this happened to me, that the mother of my Lord should come to me?

44 For, look as soon as I heard your greeting, the babe leaped in my womb for joy.

45 And blessed is she who has believed: for there shall be a performance of those things the Lord has told her.

1.06 Mary's speech Luke 1:46-56

Luke 1:46-56

46 And Mary said, My soul does magnify the Lord,

47 And my spirit has rejoiced in God my Saviour.

48 For he has regarded the low estate of his handmaiden: for, look, from now on all generations shall call me blessed.

49 For he who is mighty has done great things to me; and holy is his name.

50 And his mercy is on those who fear him from generation to generation.

51 He has showed strength with his arm; he has scattered the proud in the imagination of their hearts.

52 He has put down the mighty from their seats, and exalted those of low degree.

53 He has filled the hungry with good things; and the rich he has sent empty away.

54 He has helped his servant Israel, in remembrance of his mercy;

55 As he spoke to our fathers, to Abraham, and to his seed for ever.

56 And Mary stayed with her about three months, and returned to her own house.

1.07 John's birth, naming, and Zacharias' prophecy (Judea) Luke 1:57-80

Luke 1:57-80

57 Now Elisabeth's full time came that she should give birth; and she gave birth to a son.

58 And her neighbours and her cousins heard how the Lord had showed great mercy upon her; and they rejoiced with her.

59 And it happened, that on the eighth day they came to circumcise the child; and they called him Zacharias, after his father.

60 And his mother answered and said, Not so; but he shall be called John.

61 And they said to her, None of your relatives are called by this name.

62 And they made signs to his father, what he would have him called.

63 And he asked for a writing table, and wrote, His name is John. And they all marvelled.

64 And his mouth was opened immediately, and his tongue loosed, and he spoke, and praised God.

65 And fear came on all who lived around them: and all these sayings were broadcast throughout all the hill country of Judea.

66 And all those that heard them stored them in their hearts, saying, What manner of child shall this be! And the hand of the Lord was with him.

67 And his father Zacharias was filled with the Holy Spirit, and prophesied, saying,

68 Blessed be the Lord God of Israel; for he has visited and redeemed his people,

69 And has raised up a horn of salvation for us in the house of his servant David;

70 As he spoke by the mouth of his holy prophets, which have been since the world began:

71 That we should be saved from our enemies, and from the hand of all that hate us;

72 To perform the mercy promised to our fathers, and to remember his holy covenant;

73 The oath which he swore to our father Abraham,

74 That he would grant us, that we being delivered out of the hand of our enemies might serve him without fear,

75 In holiness and righteousness before him, all the days of our life.

76 And you, child, shall be called the prophet of the Highest: for you shall go before the face of the Lord to prepare his ways;

77 To give knowledge of salvation to his people by the remission of their sins,

78 Through the tender mercy of our God; whereby the dayspring from on high has visited us,

79 To give light to those that sit in darkness and in the shadow of death, to guide our feet into the way of peace.

80 And the child grew, and became strong in spirit, and was in the deserts till the day of his showing to Israel.

1.08 Explanation of Mary's pregnancy to Joseph (Nazareth) Matthew 1:18-25

Matthew 1:18-25

18 Now the birth of Jesus Christ happened this way: When his mother Mary was engaged to Joseph,

before they came together, she was found with child of the Holy Spirit.

19 Then Joseph her husband, being a just man, and not willing to make her a public example, thought to put her away privately.

20 But while he thought on these things, look, the angel of the Lord appeared to him in a dream, saying, Joseph, son of David, do not be afraid to take Mary as your wife: for what is conceived in her is of the Holy Spirit.

21 And she shall give birth to a son, and you shall call his name JESUS: for he shall save his people from their sins.

22 Now all this was done, that the Lord's word through the prophet might be fulfilled, saying,

23 Look, a virgin shall be with child, and shall give birth to a son, and they shall call his name Emmanuel, meaning, God with us.

24 When Joseph awoke from sleep, he did as the angel of the Lord told him, and took Mary as his wife:

25 And did not have sexual relations with her till she had given birth to her firstborn son: and he called his name JESUS.

1.09 Jesus' birth (Bethlehem) Luke 2:1-7

Luke 2:1-7

1 And it happened in those days, that a decree went out from Caesar Augustus, that all the world should be taxed.

2 (And this taxation first happened when Cyrenius was governor of Syria.)

3 And all went to be taxed, every one to his own city.

4 And Joseph also went up from Galilee, out of the city of Nazareth, into Judea, to Bethlehem, the city of David; (because he was of the house and lineage of David:)

5 To be taxed with Mary his espoused wife, whose pregnancy was advanced.

6 And so it was, that, while they were there, her due date arrived.

7 And she gave birth to her firstborn son, and wrapped him in swaddling clothes, and laid him in a manger; because there was no room for them in the inn.

1.10 Jesus' genealogy through Joseph Matthew 1:1-17

Matthew 1:1-17

1 The book of the generation of Jesus Christ, the son of David, the son of Abraham.

2 Abraham fathered Isaac; and Isaac fathered Jacob; and Jacob fathered Judas and his brethren;

3 And Judas fathered Phares and Zara of Thamar; and Phares fathered Esrom; and Esrom fathered Aram;

4 And Aram fathered Aminadab; and Aminadab fathered Naasson; and Naasson fathered Salmon;

5 And Salmon fathered Booz of Rachab; and Booz fathered Obed of Ruth; and Obed fathered Jesse;

6 And Jesse fathered David the king; and David the king fathered Solomon of her that had been the wife of Urias;

7 And Solomon fathered Roboam; and Roboam fathered Abia; and Abia fathered Asa;

8 And Asa fathered Josaphat; and Josaphat fathered Joram; and Joram fathered Ozias;

9 And Ozias fathered Joatham; and Joatham fathered Achaz; and Achaz fathered Ezekias;

10 And Ezekias fathered Manasses; and Manasses fathered Amon; and Amon fathered Josias;

11 And Josias fathered Jechonias and his brethren, about the time they were carried away to Babylon:

12 And after they were brought to Babylon, Jechonias fathered Salathiel; and Salathiel fathered Zorobabel;

13 And Zorobabel fathered Abiud; and Abiud fathered Eliakim; and Eliakim fathered Azor;

14 And Azor fathered Sadoc; and Sadoc fathered Achim; and Achim fathered Eliud;

15 And Eliud fathered Eleazar; and Eleazar fathered Matthan; and Matthan fathered Jacob;

16 And Jacob fathered Joseph the husband of Mary, of whom was born Jesus, who is called Christ.

17 So all the generations from Abraham to David are fourteen generations; and from David until the carrying away into Babylon are fourteen generations; and from the carrying away into Babylon to Christ are fourteen generations.

1.11 Angels proclaim Jesus' birth (Near Bethlehem) Luke 2:8-14

Luke 2:8-14

8 In the same country, there were shepherds out in the field, watching over their flock at night.

9 Suddenly the angel of the Lord appeared to them, and the glory of the Lord shone round about them: and they were very afraid.

10 And the angel said to them, Do not be afraid: Look, I bring you good tidings of great joy, which shall be to all people.

11 For to you is born this day in the city of David a Saviour, who is Christ the Lord.

12 And this shall be a sign to you; You shall find the babe wrapped in swaddling clothes, lying in a manger.

13 And suddenly there was with the angel a multitude of the heavenly host praising God, and saying,

14 Glory to God in the highest, and on earth peace, good will toward men.

1.12 Shepherds visit Jesus then spread the news (Bethlehem) Luke 2:15-20

Luke 2:15-20

15 And it happened that, as the angels had gone back to heaven, the shepherds said to each other, Let us now go to Bethlehem, and see what has happened, which the Lord has made known to us.

16 And they came quickly, and found Mary, and Joseph, and the babe lying in a manger.

17 And when they had seen it, they broadcast what was told them concerning this child.

18 And all those that heard it wondered at the things which the shepherds said.

19 But Mary kept all these things, and pondered them in her heart.

20 And the shepherds returned, glorifying and praising God for all the things that they had heard and

seen, as the angels had told them.

1.13 Jesus' circumcision (Bethlehem) Luke 2:21

Luke 2:21
21 On the eighth day on which the child was circumcised, his name was called JESUS, which was the name the angel gave him before he was conceived in the womb.

1.14 Simeon and Anna (Jerusalem) Luke 2:22-40

Luke 2:22-40
22 And when the days of her purification according to the law of Moses were accomplished, they brought him to Jerusalem, to present him to the Lord;
23 (As it is written in the law of the Lord, Every male that opens the womb shall be called holy to the Lord;)
24 And to offer a sacrifice according to what is said in the law of the Lord, A pair of turtledoves, or two young pigeons.
25 And, look, there was a man in Jerusalem, whose name was Simeon; he was just and devout, waiting for the consolation of Israel: and the Holy Spirit was upon him.
26 And it was revealed to him by the Holy Spirit, that he should not see death, before he had seen the Lord's Christ.
27 And he came by the Spirit into the temple: and when the parents brought in the child Jesus, to do for him according to the law,
28 He took him up in his arms, and blessed God, and said,
29 Lord, now let your servant depart in peace, according to your word:
30 For my eyes have seen your salvation,
31 Which you have prepared before the face of all people;
32 A light to lighten the Gentiles, and the glory of your people Israel.
33 And Joseph and his mother marvelled at those things which were spoken about him.
34 And Simeon blessed them, and said to Mary his mother, Look, this child is set for the fall and rising again of many in Israel; and for a sign which shall be spoken against;
35 (Yes, a sword shall pierce through your own soul also,) that the thoughts of many hearts may be revealed.
36 And there was one Anna, a prophetess, the daughter of Phanuel, of the tribe of Aser: she was of a great age, and had lived with a husband seven years from her virginity;
37 And she was a widow of about eighty-four years, who did not depart from the temple, but served God with fastings and prayers night and day.
38 And she coming in that instant also gave thanks to the Lord, and spoke of him to all those who looked for redemption in Jerusalem.
39 And when they had performed all things according to the law of the Lord, they returned into

Galilee, to their own city Nazareth.

40 And the child grew, and became strong in spirit, filled with wisdom: and the grace of God was upon him.

1.15 Visit of the wise men (Jerusalem and Bethlehem) Matthew 2:1-12

Matthew 2:1-12

1 Now when Jesus was born in Bethlehem of Judea in the days of Herod the king, look, there came wise men from the east to Jerusalem,

2 Saying, Where is he who is born King of the Jews? For we have seen his star in the east, and have come to worship him.

3 When Herod the king had heard these things, he was troubled, and all Jerusalem with him.

4 And when he had gathered all the chief priests and scribes of the people together, he demanded from them where Christ was to be born.

5 And they said to him, In Bethlehem of Judea: for thus it is written by the prophet,

6 And you Bethlehem, in the land of Judah, are not the least among the princes of Judah: for out of you shall come a Governor, that shall rule my people Israel.

7 Then Herod, when he had privately called the wise men, enquired of them diligently what time the star appeared.

8 And he sent them to Bethlehem, and said, Go and search diligently for the young child; and when you have found him, bring me word again, that I may come and worship him also.

9 When they had heard the king, they departed; and, lo, the star, which they saw in the east, went before them, till it came and stood over where the young child was.

10 When they saw the star, they rejoiced with exceeding great joy.

11 And when they had come into the house, they saw the young child with Mary his mother, and fell down, and worshipped him: and when they had opened their treasures, they presented him with gifts; gold, and frankincense, and myrrh.

12 And being warned of God in a dream that they should not return to Herod, they departed into their own country another way.

1.16 Flight to Egypt and Herod's massacre of children (Bethlehem) Matthew 2:13-18

Matthew 2:13-18

13 And when they had departed, look, the angel of the Lord appeared to Joseph in a dream, saying, Arise, and take the young child and his mother, and flee to Egypt, and stay there until I bring you word: for Herod will seek the young child to destroy him.

14 When he arose, he took the young child and his mother by night, and went to Egypt:

15 And was there until the death of Herod: that it might be fulfilled which was spoken of the Lord by the prophet, saying, Out of Egypt have I called my son.

16 Then Herod, when he saw that he had been mocked by the wise men, was intensely angry, and sent, and killed all the children that were in Bethlehem, and in all the surrounding areas, from two years old

and under, according to the time which he had diligently enquired of the wise men.

17 Then was fulfilled what was spoken by Jeremiah the prophet, saying,

18 In Rama there was a voice heard, lamentation, and weeping, and great mourning, Rachel weeping for her children, and would not be comforted, because they are no more.

1.17 Return to Israel (Nazareth) Matthew 2:19-23

Matthew 2:19-23

19 But when Herod was dead, an angel of the Lord appeared in a dream to Joseph in Egypt,

20 Saying, Arise, and take the young child and his mother, and go into the land of Israel: for those wanting to kill the young child are dead.

21 And he arose, and took the young child and his mother, and came to the land of Israel.

22 But when he heard that Archelaus reigned in Judea in place of his father Herod, he was afraid to go there: notwithstanding, being warned of God in a dream, he turned aside to the parts of Galilee:

23 And he came and dwelt in a city called Nazareth: that it might be fulfilled which was spoken by the prophets, He shall be called a Nazarene.

1.18 Childhood of Jesus (Nazareth) and His visit to the Temple (Jerusalem) Luke 2:41-52

Why is this in Matt

Luke 2:41-52

41 Now his parents went to Jerusalem every year at the feast of the Passover.

42 And when he was twelve years old, they went up to Jerusalem according to the custom of the feast.

43 And when the feast was over, as they returned, the child Jesus stayed behind in Jerusalem; and Joseph and his mother did not know it.

44 But they, supposing him to have been in the company, travelled for a day; and they sought him among their family members and acquaintances.

45 And when they did not find him, they turned back again to Jerusalem, seeking him.

46 And it happened, that after three days they found him in the temple, sitting in the midst of the doctors, both hearing them, and asking them questions.

47 And all that heard him were astonished at his understanding and answers.

48 And when they saw him, they were amazed: and his mother said to him, Son, why have you dealt with us this way? Look, your father and I have sought you, worrying.

49 And he said to them, How is it that you were looking for me? Do you not know that I must be about my Father's business?

50 And they did not understand the saying which he spoke to them.

51 And he went down with them, and came to Nazareth, and was subject to them: but his mother kept all these sayings in her heart.

52 And Jesus increased in wisdom and stature, and in favour with God and man.

1.19 The voice crying in the wilderness (Judean Wilderness) Mark 1:1-6, Luke 3:1-6, Matthew 3:1-6, John 1:6-8, 19-23

Mark 1:1-2	Luke 3:1-3	Matthew 3:1-2	John 1:6
1 The beginning of the gospel of Jesus Christ, the Son of God;			
	1 Now in the fifteenth year of the reign of Tiberius Caesar, Pontius Pilate being governor of Judea, and Herod being tetrarch of Galilee, and his brother Philip tetrarch of Ituraea and of the region of Trachonitis, and Lysanias the tetrarch of Abilene,		
	2 Annas and Caiaphas being the high priests, the word of God came to John the son of Zacharias in the wilderness.		
		1a In those days John the Baptist came,	6 There was a man sent from God, whose name was John.
	3 And he came into all the country about Jordan, preaching the baptism of repentance for the remission of sins;	1b preaching in the wilderness of Judea,	
		2 And saying, Repent: for the kingdom of heaven is at hand.	
2 As it is written in the			

prophets, Look, I send my messenger before your face, who shall prepare your way ahead of you.			

John 1:7-8, 19-22

7 The same came for a witness, to bear witness of the Light, that all men through him might believe.

8 He was not that Light, but was sent to bear witness of that Light.

19 And this is the record of John, when the Jews sent priests and Levites from Jerusalem to ask him, Who are you?

20 And he confessed, and did not deny; but confessed, I am not the Christ.

21 And they asked him, What then? Are you Elijah? And he said, I am not. Are you that prophet? And he answered, No.

22 Then they said to him, Who are you? That we may give an answer to those who sent us. What do you say of yourself?

Mark 1:3-4	Luke 3:4-6	Matthew 3:3	John 1:23
3 The voice of one crying in the wilderness, Prepare the way of the Lord, make his paths straight.	4 As it is written in the book of the words of Isaiah the prophet, saying, The voice of one crying in the wilderness, Prepare the way of the Lord, make his paths straight.	3 For this is he who was spoken of by the prophet Isaiah, saying, The voice of one crying in the wilderness, Prepare the way of the Lord, make his paths straight.	23 He said, I am the voice of one crying in the wilderness, Make straight the way of the Lord, as said the prophet Isaiah.
4 John did baptize in the wilderness, and preached the baptism of repentance for the remission of sins.	5 Every valley shall be filled, and every mountain and hill shall be brought low; and the crooked shall be made straight, and the rough ways shall be made smooth;		
	6 And all flesh shall see the salvation of God.		

Mark 1:5-6	Matthew 3:5-6, 4
5 And all the land of Judea, and those of Jerusalem went out to him, and were all baptized by him in the river Jordan, confessing their sins.	5 Then Jerusalem, and all Judea, and all the region round about Jordan, went out to him 6 And were baptized by him in Jordan, confessing their sins.
6 And John was clothed with camel's hair, and with a belt of skin about his waist; and he did eat locusts and wild honey;	4 And John himself was clothed in camel's hair, with a leather belt around his waist; and his food was locusts and wild honey.

1.20 John's message Luke 3:7-14, Matthew 3:7-10

Luke 3:7-14	Matthew 3:7-10
7 Then he said to the multitude that came to be baptized by him, O generation of vipers, who warned you to flee from the wrath to come?	7 But when he saw many of the Pharisees and Sadducees come to his baptism, he said to them, O generation of vipers, who warned you to flee from the wrath to come?
8 Bring forth therefore fruits worthy of repentance, and do not begin to say within yourselves, We have Abraham as our father: for I say to you, That God is able from these stones to raise up children to Abraham.	8 Bring forth therefore fruits worthy of repentance: 9 And do not think or say within yourselves, We have Abraham as our father: for I say to you, that God is able from these stones to raise up children to Abraham.
9 And now also the axe is laid to the root of the trees: every tree therefore which does not produce good fruit is cut down, and cast into the fire.	10 And now also the axe is laid to the root of the trees: therefore every tree which does not produce good fruit is hewn down, and cast into the fire.

Luke 3:10-14
10 And the people asked him, saying, What shall we do then?
11 He answered and said to them, He who has two coats, let him give to him who has none; and he who has food let him do likewise.
12 Then tax collectors also came to be baptized, and said to him, Master, what shall we do?
13 And he said to them, Exact no more than what you have been appointed.
14 And the soldiers in like manner asked him, saying, And what shall we do? And he said to them, Do not do violence to any man, neither accuse any falsely; and be content with your wages.

1.21 John testifies of Jesus Mark 1:7-8, Luke 3:15-18, Matthew 3:11-12, John 1:24-28

Mark 1:7-8	Luke 3:15-18	Matthew 3:11-12	John 1:24-28
	15 And as the people were in expectation,		

	and all men wondered in their hearts about John, whether he was the Christ, or not;		
			24 And those that were sent were of the Pharisees.
			25 And they asked him, saying, Why then do you baptize if you are not that Christ, nor Elias, nor that prophet?
7 And preached, saying, There comes one mightier than I after me, the latchet of whose shoes I am not worthy to stoop down and unloose. 8 I indeed have baptized you with water: but he shall baptize you with the Holy Spirit.	16 John answered, saying to all of them, I indeed baptize you with water; but one mightier than I is coming, the latchet of whose shoes I am not worthy to unloose: he shall baptize you with the Holy Spirit and with fire:	11 I indeed baptize you with water to repentance: but he who comes after me is mightier than I, whose shoes I am not worthy to carry: he shall baptize you with the Holy Spirit, and with fire:	26 John answered them, saying, I baptize with water: but there stands one among you, whom you do not know; 27 He is the one, who coming after me is preferred before me, whose shoe's latchet I am not worthy to unloose.
	17 Whose fan is in his hand, and he will thoroughly purge his floor, and will gather the wheat into his barn; but the chaff he will burn with unquenchable fire.	12 Whose fan is in his hand, and he will thoroughly purge his floor, and gather his wheat into the garner; but he will burn up the chaff with unquenchable fire.	
	18 And many other things in his exhortation he preached to the people.		
			28 These things were done in Bethabara

			beyond Jordan, where John was baptizing.

2: Jesus' baptism to His early ministry

2.01 Jesus baptized (Jordan river) Mark 1:9-11, Luke 3:21-22, Matthew 3:13-17

Mark 1:9-11	Luke 3:21-22	Matthew 3:13-17
9 And it happened in those days, that Jesus came from Nazareth of Galilee, and was baptized of John in Jordan.	21 Now when all the people were baptized, it happened, that Jesus also being baptized, and praying, the heaven was opened,	13 Then Jesus came from Galilee to Jordan to John, to be baptized by him.
		14 But John forbade him, saying, I have need to be baptized by you, and are you coming to me?
		15 And Jesus answering said to him, Permit it to be so now: for it is fitting for us to fulfil all righteousness. Then he permitted him.
10 And straightaway coming up out of the water, he saw the heavens opened, and the Spirit like a dove descending upon him:	22 And the Holy Spirit descended in a bodily shape like a dove upon him, and a voice came from heaven, which said, You are my beloved Son; in you I am well pleased.	16 And Jesus, when he was baptized, went up straightaway out of the water: and, lo, the heavens were opened to him, and he saw the Spirit of God descending like a dove, and resting upon him:
11 And there came a voice from heaven, saying, You are my beloved Son, in whom I am well pleased.		17 And look a voice from heaven, saying, This is my beloved Son, in whom I am well pleased.

2.02 Jesus' genealogy through Mary Luke 3:23-38

Luke 3:23-38

23 And Jesus himself began his ministry at about thirty years of age, being (as was supposed) the son of Joseph, who was the son of Heli,

24 Who was the son of Matthat, who was the son of Levi, who was the son of Melchi, who was the son

of Janna, who was the son of Joseph,

25 Who was the son of Mattathias, who was the son of Amos, who was the son of Naum, who was the son of Esli, who was the son of Nagge,

26 Who was the son of Maath, who was the son of Mattathias, who was the son of Semei, who was the son of Joseph, who was the son of Judah,

27 Who was the son of Joanna, who was the son of Rhesa, who was the son of Zorobabel, who was the son of Salathiel, who was the son of Neri,

28 Who was the son of Melchi, who was the son of Addi, who was the son of Cosam, who was the son of Elmodam, who was the son of Er,

29 Who was the son of Jose, who was the son of Eliezer, who was the son of Jorim, who was the son of Matthat, who was the son of Levi,

30 Who was the son of Simeon, who was the son of Judah, who was the son of Joseph, who was the son of Jonan, who was the son of Eliakim,

31 Who was the son of Melee, who was the son of Mean, who was the son of Mattatha, who was the son of Nathan, who was the son of David,

32 Who was the son of Jesse, who was the son of Obed, who was the son of Booz, who was the son of Salmon, who was the son of Naasson,

33 Who was the son of Aminadab, who was the son of Aram, who was the son of Esrom, who was the son of Phares, who was the son of Judah,

34 Who was the son of Jacob, who was the son of Isaac, who was the son of Abraham, who was the son of Thara, who was the son of Nachor,

35 Who was the son of Saruch, who was the son of Ragau, who was the son of Phalec, who was the son of Heber, who was the son of Sala,

36 Who was the son of Cainan, who was the son of Arphaxad, who was the son of Sem, who was the son of Noe, who was the son of Lamech,

37 Who was the son of Mathusala, who was the son of Enoch, who was the son of Jared, who was the son of Maleleel, who was the son of Cainan,

38 Who was the son of Enos, who was the son of Seth, who was the son of Adam, who was the son of God.

2.03 Jesus tempted (Judean wilderness) Mark 1:12, 13, Luke 4:1-13, Matthew 4:1-11

Mark 1:12-13	Luke 4:1-2	Matthew 4:1-2
12 And immediately the Spirit drove him into the wilderness.	1 And Jesus being full of the Holy Spirit returned from Jordan, and was led by the Spirit into the wilderness,	1 Then was Jesus led up of the Spirit into the wilderness to be tempted of the devil.
13 And he was there in the wilderness forty days, tempted	2 Being forty days tempted of the devil. And in those days he	2 And after fasting forty days and forty nights, he was hungry.

of Satan; and was with the wild beasts; and the angels ministered to him.	did eat nothing: and when they were ended, he was hungry.	

Luke 4:3-13	Matthew 4:3-11
3 And the devil said to him, If you are the Son of God, command this stone to become bread.	3 And when the tempter came to him, he said, If you are the Son of God, command that these stones become bread.
4 And Jesus answered him, saying, It is written, That man shall not live by bread alone, but by every word of God.	4 But he answered and said, It is written, Man shall not live by bread alone, but by every word that proceeds out of the mouth of God.
9 And he brought him to Jerusalem, and set him on a pinnacle of the temple, and said to him, If you are the Son of God, cast yourself down from here:	5 Then the devil took him up to the holy city, and set him on a pinnacle of the temple,
10 For it is written, He shall give his angels charge over you, to keep you: 11 And in their hands they shall bear you up, lest at any time you dash your foot against a stone.	6 And said to him, If you are the Son of God, cast yourself down: for it is written, He shall give his angels charge concerning you: and in their hands they shall bear you up, lest at any time you dash your foot against a stone.
12 And Jesus answering said to him, It is said, You shall not tempt the Lord your God.	7 Jesus said to him, It is written again, You shall not tempt the Lord your God.
5 And the devil, taking him up into a high mountain, showed him all the kingdoms of the world in a moment of time.	8 Again, the devil took him up into an exceeding high mountain, and showed him all the kingdoms of the world, and their glory;
6 And the devil said to him, All this power I will give you, and their glory: for it is delivered to me; and to whomever I will I give it. 7 Therefore if you will worship me, all shall be yours.	9 And said to him, All these things I will give you, if you will fall down and worship me.
8 And Jesus answered and said to him, You get behind me, Satan: for it is written, You shall worship the Lord your God, and he is the only one you shall serve.	10 Then Jesus said to him, Go away from here, Satan: for it is written, You shall worship the Lord your God, and he is the only one you shall serve.
13 And when the devil had ended all the temptation, he departed from him for a season.	11 Then the devil left him, and, look, angels came and ministered to him.

2.04 We beheld His glory John 1:14-18

John 1:14-18

14 And the Word became flesh, and dwelt among us, (and we beheld his glory, the glory as of the only begotten of the Father,) full of grace and truth.

15 John bore witness of him, and cried, saying, This was he of whom I spoke, He who comes after me is preferred before me: for he was before me.

16 And of his fullness have all we received, and grace for grace.

17 For the law was given by Moses, but grace and truth came by Jesus Christ.

18 No man has seen God at any time; the only begotten Son, which is in the bosom of the Father, he has declared him.

2.05 Jesus returns to John John 1:29-34

John 1:29-34

29 The next day John saw Jesus coming to him, and said, Look the Lamb of God, who takes away the sin of the world.

30 This is he of whom I said, After me comes a man which is preferred before me: for he was before me.

31 And I did not know him: but I came baptizing with water, so that he should be made manifest to Israel.

32 And John bore record, saying, I saw the Spirit descending from heaven like a dove, and it stayed upon him.

33 And I did not know him: but he who sent me to baptize with water, said to me, The person you see the Spirit descending, and remaining on, is the one who baptizes with the Holy Spirit.

34 And I saw, and bore record that this is the Son of God.

2.06 Calls first disciples (Bethabara beyond Jordan) John 1:35-51

John 1:35-51

35 Again the next day, John stood with two of his disciples;

36 And looking upon Jesus as he walked, he said, Look the Lamb of God!

37 And the two disciples heard him speak, and they followed Jesus.

38 Then Jesus turned, and saw them following, and said to them, What do you want? They said to him, Rabbi, (which is to say, being interpreted, Master,) where do you live?

39 He said to them, Come and see. They came and saw where he lived, and stayed with him that day: for it was about the tenth hour (4 p.m.).

40 One of the two who heard John speak, and followed him, was Andrew, Simon Peter's brother.

41 He first found his own brother Simon, and said to him, We have found the Messiah, which is, being interpreted, the Christ.

42 And he brought him to Jesus. And when Jesus looked at him, he said, You are Simon the son of

Jona: You shall be called Cephas, which is by interpretation, A stone.

43 The following day Jesus intending to go to Galilee, found Philip, and said to him, Follow me.

44 Now Philip was of Bethsaida, the city of Andrew and Peter.

45 Philip found Nathanael, and said to him, We have found him, of whom Moses in the law, and the prophets, did write, Jesus of Nazareth, the son of Joseph.

46 And Nathanael said to him, Can any good thing come out of Nazareth? Philip said to him, Come and see.

47 Jesus saw Nathanael coming to him, and said of him, Look an Israelite indeed, in whom is no guile!

48 Nathanael said to him, Where do you know me from? Jesus answered and said to him, Before Philip called you, when you were under the fig tree, I saw you.

49 Nathanael answered and said to him, Rabbi, you are the Son of God; you are the King of Israel.

50 Jesus answered and said to him, Because I told you, I saw you under the fig tree, you believe? You shall see greater things than these.

51 And he said to him, Very Truly, I say to you, Hereafter you shall see heaven open, and the angels of God ascending and descending upon the Son of man.

2.07 Performs first miracle (Cana, Galilee), and first stay in Capernaum John 2:1-12

John 2:1-12

1 And on the third day of the week, there was a marriage in Cana of Galilee; and the mother of Jesus was there:

2 And Jesus and his disciples were invited to the marriage.

3 And when the wine ran out, Jesus' mother said to him, They have no wine.

4 Jesus said to her, Woman, what have I to do with you? My hour has not yet come.

5 His mother said to the servants, Whatever he says to you, do it.

6 And there were set there six water pots of stone, after the manner of the purifying of the Jews, containing two or three quarter barrels each.

7 Jesus said to them, Fill the water pots with water. And they filled them up to the brim.

8 And he said to them, Draw out now, and take to the master of ceremony. And they took it.

9 When the master of ceremony had tasted the water that was made wine, and did not know where it came from: (but the servants which drew the water knew;) the master of ceremony called the bridegroom,

10 And said to him, Every man at the beginning serves good wine; and when men have well drunk, then that which is cheap: but you have kept the good wine until now.

11 This beginning of miracles Jesus did in Cana of Galilee, and manifested his glory; and his disciples believed on him.

12 After this he went down to Capernaum, he, and his mother, and his siblings, and his disciples: and they stayed there a few days.

2.08 First cleansing of the temple and reception in Jerusalem (Jerusalem) John 2:13-25

John 2:13-25

13 And the Jews' Passover was at hand, and Jesus went up to Jerusalem,

14 And found in the temple those that sold oxen and sheep and doves, and the money changers:

15 And when he had made a scourge of small cords, he drove them all out of the temple, and the sheep, and the oxen; and poured out the changers' money, and overthrew the tables;

16 And said to those who sold doves, Take these things from here; do not make my Father's house a house of merchandise.

17 And his disciples remembered that it was written, The zeal of your house has eaten me up.

18 Then the Jews answered and said to him, What sign will you show us, seeing that you do these things?

19 Jesus answered and said to them, Destroy this temple, and in three days I will raise it up.

20 Then the Jews said, Forty six years was this temple under construction, and will you raise it up in three days?

21 But he spoke of the temple of his body.

22 When therefore he had risen from the dead, his disciples remembered that he had said this to them; and they believed the scripture, and his words..

23 Now when he was in Jerusalem at the Passover, in the feast day, many believed in his name, when they saw the miracles which he did.

24 But Jesus did not commit himself to them, because he knew all men,

25 And did not need anyone to testify of man: for he knew what was in man.

2.09 Meeting with Nicodemus (Judea) John 3:1-21

John 3:1-21

1 There was a man of the Pharisees, named Nicodemus, a ruler of the Jews:

2 The same came to Jesus by night, and said to him, Rabbi, we know that you are a teacher come from God: for no man can do these miracles that you do, except God is with him.

3 Jesus answered and said to him, Very Truly, I say to you, Except a man is born again, he cannot see the kingdom of God.

4 Nicodemus said to him, How can a man be born when he is old? Can he enter the second time into his mother's womb, and be born?

5 Jesus answered, Very Truly, I say to you, Except a man be born of water and of the Spirit, he cannot enter into the kingdom of God.

6 That which is born of the flesh is flesh; and that which is born of the Spirit is spirit.

7 Do not marvel that I said to you, You must be born again.

8 The wind blows where it wants, and you hear its sound, but cannot tell where it is coming from, and where it is going: so is everyone who is born of the Spirit.

9 Nicodemus answered and said to him, How can these things be?

10 Jesus answered and said to him, Are you a master of Israel, and do not know these things?

11 Very Truly, I say to you, We speak what we do know, and testify of what we have seen; and you do not receive our witness.

12 If I have told you earthly things, and you do not believe, how shall you believe, if I tell you of heavenly things?

13 And no man has ascended up to heaven, but he who came down from heaven, even the Son of man who was in heaven.

14 And as Moses lifted up the serpent in the wilderness, even so must the Son of man be lifted up:

15 That whoever believes in him should not perish, but have eternal life.

16 For God so loved the world, that he gave his only begotten Son, that whoever believes in him should not perish, but have everlasting life.

17 For God did not send his Son into the world to condemn the world; but that the world through him might be saved.

18 He who believes on him is not condemned: but he who does not believe is condemned already, because he has not believed in the name of the only begotten Son of God.

19 And this is the condemnation, that light has come into the world, and men loved darkness rather than light, because their deeds were evil.

20 For every one that does evil hates the light, neither comes to the light, lest his deeds should be reproved.

21 But he who does truth comes to the light, that his deeds may be made manifest, that they are done in God.

2.10 Co-ministry with John (Judea) John 3:22-36

John 3:22-36

22 After these things Jesus and his disciples came into the land of Judea; and there he stayed with them, and baptized.

23 And John also was baptizing in Aenon near to Salim, because there was much water there: and the people came, and were baptized.

24 For John had not yet been thrown into prison.

25 Then there arose a question between some of John's disciples and the Jews about purifying.

26 And they came to John, and said to him, Rabbi, he who was with you beyond Jordan, to whom you bore witness, Look, the same baptizes, and all men come to him.

27 John answered and said, A man can receive nothing, except it has been given him from heaven.

28 You yourselves bear me witness, that I said, I am not the Christ, but that I am sent ahead of him.

29 He who has the bride is the bridegroom: but the friend of the bridegroom, who stands and hears him, rejoices greatly because of the bridegroom's voice: my joy is therefore fulfilled.

30 He must increase, but I must decrease.

31 He who comes from above is above all: he who is of the earth is earthly, and speaks of the earth: he who comes from heaven is above all.

32 And what he has seen and heard, he testifies to; and no man receives his testimony.

33 He who has received his testimony has certified that God is true.

34 For he whom God sent speaks the words of God: for God gives him the Spirit without measure.

35 The Father loves the Son, and has given all things into his hand.

36 He who believes on the Son has everlasting life: and he who does not believe the Son shall not see life; but the wrath of God rests on him.

2.11 Herod imprisons John Mark 6:17-20, Luke 3:19-20, Matthew 14:3-5

Mark 6:17-20	Luke 3:19-20	Matthew 14:3-5
17 For Herod himself had sent and laid hold upon John, and bound him in prison for Herodias' sake, his brother Philip's wife: for he had married her.	19 But Herod the tetrarch, being reproved by him for Herodias his brother Philip's wife, and for all the evils which Herod had done,	3 For Herod had laid hold of John, and bound him, and put him in prison for Herodias' sake, his brother Philip's wife.
	20 Added yet this above all, that he shut up John in prison.	

Mark 6:18-20	Matthew 14:4-5
18 For John had said to Herod, It is not lawful for you to have your brother's wife.	4 For John said to him, It is not lawful for you to have her.
19 Therefore Herodias had a quarrel against him, and wanted to have killed him; but she could not:	5 And when he would have put him to death, he feared the multitude, because they considered him as a prophet.
20 For Herod feared John, knowing that he was a just and holy man, and observed him; and when he heard him, he did many things, and heard him gladly.	

2.12 Jesus leaves Judea for Galilee Mark 1:14a, Matthew 4:12, John 4:1-4

John 4:1-3
1 Therefore when the Lord knew how the Pharisees had heard that Jesus made and baptized more disciples than John,
2 (Though Jesus himself did not baptize, but his disciples,)
3 He left Judea, and departed again into Galilee.

Mark 1:14a	Matthew 4:12	John 4:4
14 Now after John was put in prison, Jesus came to Galilee,	12 Now when Jesus had heard that John was cast into prison, he left for Galilee;	
		4 And he needed to go through Samaria.

2.13 Samaritan woman at Jacob's well (Samaria) John 4:5-42

John 4:5-42

5 Then he came to a city of Samaria, which is called Sychar, near to the parcel of ground that Jacob gave to his son Joseph.

6 Now Jacob's well was there. Jesus therefore, being wearied with his journey, sat on the well: and it was about the sixth hour (12 noon).

7 There came a woman of Samaria to draw water: Jesus said to her, Give me a drink.

8 (For his disciples were gone away unto the city to buy meat.)

9 Then the woman of Samaria said to him, How is it that you, being a Jew, asks drink of me, a woman of Samaria? For the Jews have no dealings with the Samaritans.

10 Jesus answered and said to her, If you knew the gift of God, and who it is that said to you, Give me a drink; you would have asked of him, and he would have given you living water.

11 The woman said to him, Sir, you have nothing to draw with, and the well is deep: from where then would you get that living water?

12 Are you greater than our father Jacob, who gave us the well, and drank from it himself, and his children, and his cattle?

13 Jesus answered and said to her, Whoever drinks of this water shall thirst again:

14 But whoever drinks of the water that I shall give him shall never thirst; but the water that I shall give him shall be in him a well of water springing up into everlasting life.

15 The woman said to him, Sir, give me this water, so that I do not thirst, neither come here to draw.

16 Jesus said to her, Go, call your husband, and come here.

17 The woman answered and said, I have no husband. Jesus said to her, You have said well, I have no husband:

18 For you have had five husbands; and he whom you now have is not your husband: in that you answered truthfully.

19 The woman said to him, Sir, I perceive that you are a prophet.

20 Our fathers worshipped in this mountain; and you say, that in Jerusalem is the place where men ought to worship.

21 Jesus said to her, Woman, believe me, the hour comes, when you shall neither in this mountain, nor in Jerusalem, worship the Father.

22 You worship who you do not know: we know who we worship: for salvation is of the Jews.

23 But the hour is coming, and now is, when the true worshippers shall worship the Father in spirit

and in truth: for the Father seeks such to worship him.

24 God is a Spirit: and those who worship him must worship him in spirit and in truth.

25 The woman said to him, I know that Messiah is coming, who is called Christ: when he comes, he will tell us all things.

26 Jesus said to her, I who speak to you am he.

27 At this point his disciples came, and marvelled that he talked with the woman: yet no man said, What are you looking for? Or, Why do you talk with her?

28 The woman then left her water pot, went into the city, and said to the men,

29 Come, see a man, who told me all things that I ever did: is this not the Christ?

30 Then they went out of the city, and came to him.

31 In the meantime his disciples urged him, saying, Master, eat.

32 But he said to them, I have meat to eat that you do not know of.

33 Therefore the disciples said to one another, Has any man brought him anything to eat?

34 Jesus said to them, My meat is to do the will of him who sent me, and to finish his work.

35 Do not say, There are yet four months, and then comes harvest? Look, I say to you, Lift up your eyes, and look on the fields; for they are white already to harvest.

36 And he who reaps receives wages, and gathers fruit to life eternal: that both he who sows and he who reaps may rejoice together.

37 And herein is that saying true, One sows, and another reaps.

38 I sent you to reap that on which you bestowed no labour: other men laboured, and you have entered into their labours.

39 And many of the Samaritans of that city believed on him for the saying of the woman, who testified, He told me all that I ever did.

40 So when the Samaritans had come to him, they begged him to stay with them: and he stayed there two days.

41 And many more believed because of his own word;

42 And said to the woman, Now we believe, not because of what you said: for we have heard him ourselves, and know that this is indeed the Christ, the Saviour of the world.

2.14 Jesus relocates to Galilee (Galilee) John 4:43-45, Mark 1:14-15, Luke 4:14-15

John 4:43-45
43 Now after two days he departed from there, and went to Galilee.
44 For Jesus himself testified, that a prophet has no honour in his own country.
45 Then when he had come to Galilee, the Galileans received him, having seen all the things that he did at Jerusalem at the feast: for they also went to the feast.

Mark 1:14b-15	Luke 4:14-15
	14 And Jesus returned in the power of the Spirit

	into Galilee: and his fame went through all the region round about.
	15 And he taught in their synagogues, being glorified of all.
14b preaching the gospel of the kingdom of God,	
15 And saying, The time is fulfilled, and the kingdom of God is at hand: repent, and believe the gospel.	

3: Arrival in Galilee to first tour of Galilee

3.01 Jesus heals a nobleman's son (Cana) John 4:46-54

John 4:46-54

[1] **46** So Jesus came again into Cana of Galilee, where he made the water wine. And there was a certain nobleman, whose son was sick at Capernaum.

47 When he heard that Jesus had come out of Judea into Galilee, he went to him, and begged him that he would come down, and heal his son: for he was at the point of death.

48 Then Jesus said to him, Except you see signs and wonders, you will not believe.

49 The nobleman said to him, Sir, come down before my child dies.

50 Jesus said to him, Go your way; your son will live. And the man believed the word that Jesus had spoken to him, and he went his way.

51 And as he was now going down, his servants met him, and told him, saying, Your son lives.

52 Then he asked them the hour when he began to amend. And they said to him, Yesterday at the seventh hour (1 p.m.) the fever left him.

53 So the father knew that it was at the same hour, in the which Jesus said to him, Your son will live: and he himself believed, as did his whole house.

54 This is again the second miracle that Jesus did, when he had come out of Judea into Galilee.

3.02 First rejection in Nazareth (Nazareth) Luke 4:16-30

Luke 4:16-30

16 And he came to Nazareth, where he had been brought up: and, as was his custom, , he went into the synagogue on the Sabbath, and stood up to read.

17 And he was given the book of the prophet Isaiah. And when he had opened the book, he found the place where it was written,

18 The Spirit of the Lord is upon me, because he has anointed me to preach the gospel to the poor; he has sent me to heal the brokenhearted, to preach deliverance to the captives, and recovering of sight to

---

[1] Healing Miracle 1 (of 37). Nobleman's son. Joh 4:46-54.

the blind, to set at liberty those who are bruised,

19 To preach the acceptable year of the Lord.

20 And he closed the book, and he gave it back to the minister, and sat down. And the eyes of all those in the synagogue were fastened on him.

21 And he began to say to them, This day is this scripture fulfilled in your ears.

22 And all bore him witness, and wondered at the gracious words which proceeded out of his mouth. And they said, Is not this Joseph's son?

23 And he said to them, You will surely say this proverb to me, Physician, heal yourself:: Whatever we have heard done in Capernaum, do also here in your country.

24 And he said, Truly I say to you, No prophet is accepted in his own country.

25 But I tell you a truth, many widows were in Israel in the days of Elijah, when the heaven was shut up three years and six months, when great famine was throughout all the land;

26 But to none of them was Elijah sent, except to Zarephath, a city of Sidon, to a woman that was a widow.

27 And many lepers were in Israel in the time of Elisha the prophet; and none of them were cleansed, except Naaman the Syrian.

28 And all those in the synagogue, when they heard these things, were filled with wrath,

29 And rose up, and thrust him out of the city, and led him to the brow of the hill on which their city was built, that they might throw him down headlong.

30 But he passing through their midst went his way,

3.03 Moves to Capernaum Matthew 4:13-17

Matthew 4:13-17

13 And leaving Nazareth, he came and lived in Capernaum, which is upon the sea coast, in the borders of Zebulon and Naphtali:

14 That it might be fulfilled which was spoken by Isaiah the prophet, saying,

15 The land of Zebulon, and the land of Naphtali, by the way of the sea, beyond Jordan, Galilee of the Gentiles;

16 The people who sat in darkness saw great light; and to those who sat in the region and shadow of death light has sprung up.

17 From that time Jesus began to preach, and to say, Repent: for the kingdom of heaven is at hand.

3.04 Calls Simon and his partners (Sea of Galilee) Mark 1:16-20, Luke 5:1-11, Matthew 4:18-22

Mark 1:16-18	Luke 5:1-3	Matthew 4:18-20
16 Now as he walked by the sea of Galilee, he saw Simon and Andrew his brother casting a	1 And it happened, that, as the people pressed upon him to hear the word of God, he stood by	18 And Jesus, walking by the sea of Galilee, saw two brothers, Simon called Peter, and Andrew

net into the sea: for they were fishermen.	the lake of Gennesaret,	his brother, casting a net into the sea: for they were fishermen.
17 And Jesus said to them, You come after me, and I will make you become fishers of men.	2 And saw two ships standing by the lake: but the fishermen were gone out of them, and were washing their nets.	19 And he said to them, Follow me, and I will make you fishers of men.
18 And straightaway they forsook their nets, and followed him.	3 And he entered into one of the ships, which was Simon's, and requested that he thrust out a little from the land. And he sat down, and taught the people out of the ship.	20 And they straightaway left their nets, and followed him.

Luke 5:4-9
4 Now when he had finished speaking, he said to Simon, Launch out into the deep, and let down your nets for a draught.
5 And Simon answering said to him, Master, we have toiled all night, and have caught nothing: nevertheless at your word I will let down the net.
6 And when they had done this, they netted a great multitude of fishes: and their net began to break.
7 And they called to their partners, in the other ship, to come and help them. And they came, and filled both ships, so that they began to sink.
8 When Simon Peter saw it, he fell down at Jesus' knees, saying, Depart from me; for I am a sinful man, O Lord.
9 For he was astonished, as were all those with him, at the draught of fishes they had caught:

Mark 1:19-20	Luke 5:10-11	Matthew 4:21-22
19 And when he had gone a little further from there, he saw James the son of Zebedee, and John his brother, who also were in the ship mending their nets.	10 And so also were James, and John, the sons of Zebedee, which were partners with Simon. And Jesus said to Simon, Do not be afraid; from henceforth you shall catch men.	21 And going on from there, he saw other two brothers, James the son of Zebedee, and John his brother, in a ship with Zebedee their father, mending their nets; and he called them.
20 And straightaway he called them: and they left their father Zebedee in the ship with the hired servants, and went after him.	11 And when they had brought their ships to land, they forsook all, and followed him.	22 And immediately they left the ship and their father, and followed him.

3.05 Heals a man with an unclean spirit (Synagogue in Capernaum) Mark 1:21-28, Luke 4:31-37

Mark 1:21-28	Luke 4:31-37
21 And they went to Capernaum; and straightaway on the Sabbath day he entered the synagogue, and taught.	31 And came down to Capernaum, a city of Galilee, and taught them on Sabbaths.
22 And they were astonished at his doctrine: for he taught them as one that had authority, and not as the scribes.	32 And they were astonished at his doctrine: for he spoke with power.
23 And there was in their synagogue a man with an unclean spirit; and he cried out,	33 And in the synagogue there was a man, who had a spirit of an unclean devil, and cried out with a loud voice,
24 Saying, Let us alone; what have we to do with you, Jesus of Nazareth? Have you come to destroy us? I know who you are, the Holy One of God.	34 Saying, Leave us alone; what have we to do with you, Jesus of Nazareth? Have you come to destroy us? I know who you are; the Holy One of God.
25 And Jesus rebuked him, saying, Keep quiet, and come out of him. 26 And when the unclean spirit violently shook him, and cried with a loud voice, he came out of him.	35 And Jesus rebuked him, saying, Keep quiet, and come out of him. And when the devil had thrown him down before them, he came out of him, and did not hurt him.
27 And they were all amazed, so much so that they questioned among themselves, saying, What is this? What new doctrine is this? For with authority he commands even the unclean spirits, and they obey him.	36 And they were all amazed, and spoke among themselves, saying, What sort of word is this! for with authority and power he commands the unclean spirits, and they come out.
28 And immediately his fame spread abroad throughout all the region round about Galilee.	37 And his fame went out into every place of the country round about.

3.06 Heals Simon's mother-in-law (Capernaum) Mark 1:29-31, Luke 4:38-39, Matthew 8:14-15

Mark 1:29-34	Luke 4:38-41	Matthew 8:14-17
29 And as soon as they came out of the synagogue, they entered the house of Simon and	38a And he went out of the synagogue, and entered into Simon's house.	14a And when Jesus came into Peter's house, he saw his wife's mother laid up, and sick of a

---

[2] Healing Miracle 2 (of 37). Man with an unclean spirit in the Synagogue. Mr 1:21-28, Lu 4:31-37.

[3] Healing Miracle 3 (of 37). Peter's mother-in-law. Mr 1:29-31, Lu 4:38-39, Mt 8:14-15.

Andrew, accompanied by James and John.		fever.
30 But Simon's mother-in-law lay sick of a fever, and immediately they told him about her condition.	38b And Simon's mother-in-law was running a high fever; and they asked him to help her.	14b he saw his wife's mother laid up, and sick of a fever.
31 And he came and took her by the hand, and lifted her up; and immediately the fever left her, and she ministered to them.	39 And he stood over her, and rebuked the fever; and it left her: and immediately she arose and ministered to them.	15 And he touched her hand, and the fever left her: and she arose, and ministered to them.

3.07 Heals many (Capernaum) Mark 1:32-34, Luke 4:40-41, Matthew 8:16-17

Mark 1:32-34	Luke 4:40-41	Matthew 8:16, 17
[4]32 And at evening, when the sun had set, they brought to him all that were diseased, and those that were possessed with devils.	40 Now when the sun was setting, all those who had any sick with various diseases brought them to him; and he laid his hands on every one of them, and healed them.	16 When it was evening, they brought to him many that were possessed with devils: and he cast out the spirits with his word, and healed all those who were sick:
33 And all the city was gathered together outside the door.		
34 And he healed many that were sick with various diseases, and cast out many devils; and did not allow the devils to speak, because they knew him.	41 And devils also came out of many, crying out, and saying, You are Christ the Son of God. And he rebuking them did not allow them to speak: for they knew that he was Christ.	
		17 That it might be fulfilled which was spoken by Isaiah the prophet, saying, Himself took our infirmities, and bore our sicknesses.

---

[4] Healing Miracle 4 (of 37). Multitudes (after Peter's mother-in-law). Mr 1:32-34, Lu 4:40-41, Mt 8:16-17.

3.08 Begins first tour of Galilee (Capernaum) Mark 1:35-39, Luke 4:42-44, Matthew 4:23-25

Mark 1:35-38	Luke 4:42-43
35 And in the morning, rising up a great while before day, he went out, and went to a solitary place, and there prayed.	42 And when it was day, he departed and went into a deserted place: and the people looked for him, and came to him, and tried to persuade him, not to depart from them.
36 And Simon and those that were with him went to look for him.	
37 And when they had found him, they said to him, everyone is look for you.	
38 And he said to them, Let us go into the neighbouring towns, that I may preach there also: for this is why I came.	43 And he said to them, I must preach the kingdom of God to other cities also: for this is why I was sent.

Mark 1:39	Luke 4:44	Matthew 4:23
39 And he preached in their synagogues throughout all Galilee, and cast out devils.	44 And he preached in the synagogues of Galilee.	[5]23 And Jesus went about all Galilee, teaching in their synagogues, and preaching the gospel of the kingdom, and healing all types of sickness and all types of diseases among the people.

Matthew 4:24-25
24 And his fame went throughout all Syria: and they brought to him all sick people that had various diseases and torments, and those which were possessed with devils, and those which were lunatic, and those that were paralyzed; and he healed them.
25 And great multitudes of people followed him from Galilee, and from Decapolis, and from Jerusalem, and from Judea, and from beyond Jordan.

3.09 Heals a leper; His fame spreads (Galilee) Mark 1:40-45, Luke 5:12-16, Matthew 8:1-4

---

[5] Healing Miracle 5 (of 37). First preaching tour of Galilee. Mr 1:35-39, Lu 4:42-44, Mt 4:23-25.

Mark 1:40-45	Luke 5:12-16	Matthew 8:1-4
40 And there came a leper to him, begging him, and kneeling down to him, and saying to him, If you are willing, you can make me clean.	[6]12 And it happened, when he was in a certain city, look a man full of leprosy: who seeing Jesus fell on his face, and begged him, saying, Lord, if you are willing, you can make me clean.	1 When he had come down from the mountain, great multitudes followed him. 2 And, look, there came a leper and worshipped him, saying, Lord, if you will, you can make me clean.
41 And Jesus, moved with compassion, reached out his hand, and touched him, and said to him, I am willing; be clean. 42 And as soon as he had spoken, immediately the leprosy departed from him, and he was cleansed.	13 And he reached out his hand, and touched him, saying, I am willing: be clean. And immediately the leprosy departed from him.	3 And Jesus reached out his hand, and touched him, saying, I am willing; be clean. And immediately his leprosy was cleansed.
43 And he sternly warned him, and immediately sent him away; 44 And said to him, See that you say nothing to any man: but go your way, show yourself to the priest, and offer for your cleansing those things which Moses commanded, for a testimony to them.	14 And he charged him to tell no man: but go, and show yourself to the priest, and offer for your cleansing, as the things Moses commanded, for a testimony to them.	4 And Jesus said to him, See that you tell no man; but go your way, show yourself to the priest, and offer the gift that Moses commanded, for a testimony to them.
45 But he went out, and began to publish it much, and to blaze abroad the matter, so much so that Jesus could no more openly enter into the city, but was without in desert places: and they came to him from every quarter.	15 But so much the more his fame went abroad: and great multitudes came together to hear, and to be healed by him of their infirmities.	
	16 And he withdrew himself into the wilderness, and prayed.	

---

[6] Healing Miracle 6 (of 37). Leper. Lu 5:12-16, Mr 1:40-45, Mt 8:1-4.

3.10 Heals a paralyzed man (Capernaum) Mark 2:1-12, Luke 5:17-26, Matthew 9:1-8

Mark 2:1-12	Luke 5:17-26	Matthew 9:1-8
1 And again he entered into Capernaum after some days; and it was noised that he was in the house.		1 And he entered into a ship, and crossed over, and came into his own city.
	[7]**17** And it happened on a certain day, as he was teaching, that there were Pharisees and doctors of the law sitting by, who had come out of every town of Galilee, and Judea, and Jerusalem: and the power of the Lord was present to heal them.	
2 And straightaway many were gathered together, so much so that there was no room to receive them, no, not even around the door: And he preached the word to them.		
3 And some came to him, bringing one paralyzed, carried by four.	18 And, look, men brought in a bed a man who was paralyzed: and they looked for a way to bring him in, and to lay him before Jesus.	2a And, look, they brought to him a man paralyzed, lying on a bed:
4 And when they could not come near to him because of the crowd, they uncovered the roof where he was: and when they had broken it up, they let down the bed on which the paralyzed man lay.	19 And when they could not find a way to bring him in because of the multitude, they went upon the housetop, and let him down through the tiling with his couch right in front of Jesus.	
5 When Jesus saw their faith, he said to he who was paralyzed, Son, your sins are forgiven you.	20 And when he saw their faith, he said to him, Man, your sins are forgiven you.	2b and Jesus seeing their faith said to the paralyzed man; Son, be of good cheer; your sins are forgiven you.

---

[7] Healing Miracle 7 (of 37). Paralyzed man. Lu 5:17-26, Mr 2:1-12, Mt 9:1-8.

6 But there were certain of the scribes sitting there, and reasoning in their hearts, 7 Why does this man speak blasphemies? Who can forgive sins but God only?	21 And the scribes and the Pharisees began to reason, saying, Who is this who speaks blasphemies? Who can forgive sins, but God alone?	3 And, look, certain of the scribes said within themselves, This man blasphemes.
8 And immediately when Jesus perceived in his spirit that they so reasoned within themselves, he said to them, Why do you reason you these things in your hearts?	22 But when Jesus perceived their thoughts, he answering said to them, What are you reasoning in your hearts?	4 And Jesus knowing their thoughts said, you Why do you think evil in your hearts?
9 Which is easier to say to the paralyzed man, Your sins are forgiven you; or to say, Arise, and take up your bed, and walk?	23 Which is easier, to say, Your sins are forgiven you; or to say, Rise up and walk?	5 For which is easier, to say, Your sins are forgiven you; or to say, Arise, and walk?
10 But that you may know that the Son of man has power on earth to forgive sins, (he said to the paralyzed man,) 11 I say to you, Arise, and take up your bed, and go your way to your house.	24 But that you may know that the Son of man has power upon earth to forgive sins,(he said to the paralyzed man,) I say to you, Arise, and take up your couch, and go to your house.	6 But that you may know that the Son of man has power on earth to forgive sins, (then he said to the paralyzed man,) Arise, take up your bed, and go to your house.
12 And immediately right before all of them, he arose, took up the bed, and walked away; so much so that they were all amazed, and glorified God, saying, We have never seen anything like this.	25 And immediately he rose up before them, and took up what he was lying on, and departed to his own house, glorifying God.	7 And he arose, and departed to his house.
	26 And they were all amazed, and they glorified God, and were filled with awe, saying, We have seen strange things today.	8 But when the multitudes saw it, they marvelled, and glorified God, which had given such power to men.

3.11 Calls Matthew (Capernaum) Mark 2:13-17, Luke 5:27-32, Matthew 9:9-13

Mark 2:13-17	Luke 5:27-32	Matthew 9:9-13
13 And he went again by the sea		

side; and all the multitude resorted to him, and he taught them.		
14 And as he passed by, he saw Levi the son of Alphaeus sitting at the tax custom office, and said to him, Follow me. And he arose and followed him.	27 And after these things he walked on, and saw a tax collector, named Levi, sitting at the custom office: and he said to him, Follow me.	9 And as Jesus passed on from there, he saw a man, named Matthew, sitting at the custom office: and he said to him, Follow me. And he arose, and followed him.
	28 And he left all, rose up, and followed him.	
15 And it happened, that, as Jesus sat eating in his house, many tax collectors and sinners also sat together with Jesus and his disciples: for there were many, and they followed him.	29 And Levi made him a great feast in his own house: and there was a great company of tax collectors and of others that sat down with them.	10 And it happened, as Jesus sat eating in the house, look, many tax collectors and sinners came and sat down with him and his disciples.
16 And when the scribes and Pharisees saw him eat with tax collectors and sinners, they said to his disciples, How is it that he eats and drinks with tax collectors and sinners?	30 But their scribes and Pharisees murmured against his disciples, saying, Why do you eat and drink with tax collectors and sinners?	11 And when the Pharisees saw it, they said to his disciples, Why does your Master eat with tax collectors and sinners?
17 When Jesus heard it, he said to them, Those who are whole have no need of the physician, but those who are sick: I came not to call the righteous, but sinners to repentance.	31 And Jesus answering said to them, Those who are whole do not need a physician; but those who are sick.	12 But when Jesus heard that, he said to them, Those who are whole do not need a physician, but those who are sick.
		13a But go and learn what this means, I will have mercy, and not sacrifice:
	32 I came not to call the righteous, but sinners to repentance.	13b for I have not come to call the righteous, but sinners to repentance.

3.12 Parables on fasting, garments and wineskins (Capernaum) Mark 2:18-22, Luke 5:33-39, Matthew 9:14-17

Mark 2:18-22	Luke 5:33-39	Matthew 9:14-17
18 And the disciples of John and of the Pharisees used to fast: and they came and said to him, Why do the disciples of John and of the Pharisees fast, but your disciples do not fast?	[8]33 And they said to him, Why do the disciples of John fast often, and make prayers, and likewise the disciples of the Pharisees; but yours eat and drink?	14 Then the disciples of John came to him, saying, Why do we and the Pharisees fast often, but your disciples do not fast?
19 And Jesus said to them, Can the children of the bridal chamber fast, while the bridegroom is with them? As long as they have the bridegroom with them, they cannot fast.	34 And he said to them, Can you make the children of the bridal chamber fast, while the bridegroom is with them?	15 And Jesus said to them, Can the children of the bridal chamber mourn, as long as the bridegroom is with them? But the days will come, when the bridegroom shall be taken from them, then they shall fast.
20 But the days will come, when the bridegroom shall be taken away from them, then they shall fast in those days.	35 But the days will come, when the bridegroom shall be taken away from them, then they shall fast in those days.	
21 No man also sews a piece of new cloth on an old garment: or else the new piece that fills it up takes away from the old, and the tear is made worse.	36 And he spoke also a parable to them; No man puts a piece of a new garment upon an old; otherwise, the new makes a tear, and the piece that was taken out of the new does not agree with the old.	16 No man puts a piece of new cloth to an old garment, for that which is put in to fill it up pulls the garment, and the tear is made worse.
22 And no man puts new wine into old bottles: else the new wine will burst the bottles, and the wine is spilled, and the bottles will be destroyed: but new wine must be put into new bottles.	37 And no man puts new wine into old bottles; else the new wine will burst the bottles, and be spilled, and the bottles are destroyed.	17 Neither do men put new wine into old bottles: else the bottles break, and the wine runs out, and the bottles perish: but they put new wine into new bottles, and both are preserved.
	38 But new wine must be put into new bottles; and both are preserved.	

---

[8] Parable 1. Fasting, garments and wineskins. Lu 5:33-39, Mr 2:18-22, Mt 9:14-17.

	39 No man also having drunk old wine straightaway desires new: for he says, The old is better.	

3.13 Heals a sick man (Jerusalem) John 5:1-16

John 5:1-16

[9]**1** After this there was a feast of the Jews; and Jesus went up to Jerusalem.

2 Now there was at Jerusalem by the sheep market a pool, which is called in the Hebrew tongue Bethesda, having five porches.

3 In these lay a great multitude of sick folk, of blind, lame, paralyzed, waiting for the moving of the water.

4 For an angel went down at a certain season into the pool, and troubled the water: whoever stepped in first after the troubling of the water was made whole of whatever disease he had.

5 And a certain man was there, who had been infirm for thirty eight years.

6 When Jesus saw him lying there, and knew that he had been there a long time in that condition, he said to him, Do you want to be made whole?

7 The sick man answered him, Sir, I have no man, when the water is troubled, to put me into the pool: but while I am coming, another steps in before me.

8 Jesus said to him, Rise, take up your bed, and walk.

9 And immediately the man was made whole, and took up his bed, and walked: and that day was the Sabbath.

10 The Jews therefore said to he who was cured, It is the Sabbath: it is not lawful for you to carry your bed.

11 He answered them, He who made me whole, the same said to me, Take up your bed, and walk.12 Then they asked him, Who is the man that said to you, Take up your bed, and walk?

13 And he who was healed did not know who it was: for Jesus had conveyed himself away, a multitude being in that place.

14 Afterward Jesus found him in the temple, and said to him, Look, you are made whole: sin no more, lest something worse happens to you.

15 The man departed, and told the Jews that it was Jesus, who had made him whole.

16 Therefore did the Jews persecute Jesus, and sought to kill him, because he had done these things on the Sabbath.

---

[9] Healing Miracle 8 (of 37). Man sick for thirty-eight years, Joh 5:1-9

3.14 Jesus and His Father: works, resurrection, life, judgment and honour (Jerusalem) John 5:17-47

John 5.17-47

17 But Jesus answered them, My Father worked before now, and I work.

18 Therefore the Jews sought even more to kill him, because he had not only broken the Sabbath, but said also that God was his Father, making himself equal with God.

19 Then Jesus answered and said to them, Very Truly, I say to you, The Son can do nothing of himself, but what he sees the Father do: for whatever he does, the Son also does in like manner.

20 For the Father loves the Son, and shows him everything that he does: and he will show him greater works than these, that you may marvel.

21 For as the Father raises the dead, and quickens them; even so the Son quickens whom he wills.

22 For the Father judges no man, but has committed all judgment to the Son:

23 That all men should honour the Son, even as they honour the Father. He who does not honour the Son does not honour the Father who sent him.

24 Very Truly, I say to you, He who hears my word, and believes on him who sent me, has everlasting life, and shall not be condemned; but has passed from death to life.

25 Very Truly, I say to you, The hour is coming, and has now come, when the dead shall hear the voice of the Son of God: and those who hear shall live.

26 For as the Father has life in himself; so he has given the Son life in himself;

27 And has given him authority to execute judgment also, because he is the Son of man.

28 Do not marvel at this: for the hour is coming, when all those in graves shall hear his voice,

29 And shall come out; those who have done good, to the resurrection of life; and those who have done evil, to the resurrection of damnation.

30 I can of myself do nothing: as I hear, I judge: and my judgment is just; because I do not seek my own will, but the will of the Father who sent me.

31 If I bear witness of myself, my witness is not true.

32 There is another that bears witness of me; and I know that his witness of me is true.

33 You sent to John, and he bore witness to the truth.

34 But I do not receive testimony from man: but these things I say, that you may be saved.

35 He was a burning and a shining light: and you were willing for a season to rejoice in his light.

36 But I have greater witness than that of John: for the works which the Father gave me to finish, the same works that I do, bear witness of me, that the Father has sent me.

37 And the Father himself, who sent me, has borne witness of me. You have not heard his voice at any time, nor seen his shape.

38 And you do not have his word abiding in you: for you have not believed whom he sent.

39 Search the scriptures; for in them you think you have eternal life: and they testify of me.

40 And you will not come to me, that you may have life.

41 I do not receive honour from men.

42 But I know you, that you do not have the love of God in you.

43 I have come in my Father's name, and you did not receive me: if another shall come in his own name, you will receive him.

44 How can you believe, who receive honour from one another, and do not seek the honour that comes from God only?

45 Do not think that I will accuse you to the Father: there is one who accuses you, even Moses, in whom you trust.

46 For had you believed Moses, you would have believed me: for he wrote of me.

47 But if you do not believe his writings, how shall you believe my words?

3.15 Heals a man with a withered hand on the Sabbath (Galilee) Mark 3:1-6, Luke 6:6-11, Matthew 12:9-14

Mark 3:1-6	Luke 6:6-11	Matthew 12:9-14
[10]1 And he again entered the synagogue; and there was a man there who had a withered hand.	6 And it happened also on another Sabbath, that he entered the synagogue and taught: and there was a man whose right hand was withered.	9 And when he left there, he went into their synagogue: 10a And, look, there was a man who had a withered hand.
2 And they watched him, whether he would heal him on the Sabbath; that they might accuse him.	7 And the scribes and Pharisees watched him, whether he would heal on the Sabbath; that they might find an accusation against him.	10b.c And they asked him, saying, Is it lawful to heal on the Sabbath? That they might accuse him.
3 And he said to the man who had the withered hand, Stand in front.	8 But he knew their thoughts, and said to the man who had the withered hand, Rise up, and stand in front of everyone. And he arose and stood in front.	
4 And he said to them, Is it lawful to do good on the Sabbath, or to do evil? To save life, or to kill? But they did not respond.	9 Then said Jesus to them, I will ask you one thing; Is it lawful on the Sabbath to do good, or to do evil? To save life, or to destroy it?	
		11 And he said to them, Who among you, having one sheep, if it falls into a pit on the Sabbath, will not lay hold of it, and lift it

---

[10] Healing Miracle 9 (of 37). Man with a withered hand. Mr 3:1-6, Lu 6:6-11, Mt 12:9-14.

		out?
		12 How much then is a man better than a sheep? Therefore it is lawful to do well on the Sabbath.
5 And when he had looked round about at them with anger, being grieved for the hardness of their hearts, he said to the man, Stretch out your hand. And he stretched it out: and his hand was restored whole as the other hand.	10 And looking round about at all of them, he said to the man, Stretch out your hand. And he did so: and his hand was restored whole as the other one.	13 Then he said to the man, Stretch out your hand. And he stretched it forth; and it was restored whole, like the other one.
6 And the Pharisees went out, and straightaway took counsel with the Herodians against him, how they might destroy him.	11 And they were filled with madness; and communed with one another what they might do to Jesus.	14 Then the Pharisees went out, and held a council against him, how they might destroy him.

3.16 Heals many (by the Sea of Galilee) Mark 3:7-12, Luke 6:17-19, Matthew 12:15-21

Mark 3:7-12	Luke 6:17-19	Matthew 12:15-16
[11]7 But Jesus withdrew himself with his disciples to the sea: and a great multitude from Galilee followed him, and from Judea, 8 And from Jerusalem, and from Idumaea, and from beyond Jordan; and those about Tyre and Sidon, a great multitude, when they had heard what great things he did, came to him.	17 And he came down with them, and stood in the plain, and the company of his disciples, and a great multitude of people out of all Judea and Jerusalem, and from the sea coast of Tyre and Sidon, which came to hear him, and to be healed of their diseases;	15a But when Jesus knew it, he withdrew himself from there:
	18 And those who were troubled with unclean spirits: and they were healed.	15b and great multitudes followed him, and he healed them all;
9 And he spoke to his disciples, that a small ship should wait on him because of the multitude, lest they should throng him.		

---

[11] Healing Miracle 10 (of 37). Multitudes healed. Mark 3:7-12, Lu 6:17-19, Mt 12:15-21.

10 For he had healed many; so much so that they pressed upon him for to touch him, as many as had plagues.	19 And the whole multitude sought to touch him: for virtue went out of him, and healed them all.	
11 And unclean spirits, when they saw him, fell down before him, and cried, saying, You are the Son of God.		
12 And he sternly warned them that they should not make him known.		16 And charged them that they should not make him known:

Matthew 12:17-21
17 That it might be fulfilled which was spoken by Isaiah the prophet, saying,
18 Look my servant, whom I have chosen; my beloved, in whom my soul is well pleased: I will put my spirit upon him, and he shall show judgment to the Gentiles.
19 He shall not strive, nor cry; neither shall any man hear his voice in the streets.
20 A bruised reed he shall not break, and smoking flax he shall not quench, till he sends forth judgment to victory.
21 And in his name shall the Gentiles trust.

3.17 Selects twelve apostles (Near Capernaum) Mark 3:13-19, Luke 6:12-16

Mark 3:13-19	Luke 6:12-16
	12 And it happened in those days, that he went out into a mountain to pray, and continued all night in prayer to God.
13 And he went up to a mountain, and called to him whom he would: and they came to him.	13 And when it was day, he called to him his disciples: and of them he chose twelve, whom he also named apostles;
14 And he ordained twelve, that they should be with him, and that he might send them out to preach,	
15 And to have power to heal sicknesses, and to cast out devils:	
[12]**16** And Simon he surnamed Peter;	14 Simon, (whom he also named Peter,) and

---

[12] The disciple's power and authority 1 (of 10). Mr 3:13-19, Lu 6:12-16.

	Andrew his brother, James and John, Philip and Bartholomew,
17 And James the son of Zebedee, and John the brother of James; and he surnamed them Boanerges, which is, The sons of thunder:	15 Matthew and Thomas, James the son of Alphaeus, and Simon called the Zealot,
18 And Andrew, and Philip, and Bartholomew, and Matthew, and Thomas, and James the son of Alphaeus, and Thaddaeus, and Simon the Canaanite,	16 And Judas the brother of James, and Judas Iscariot, who was the traitor.
19 And Judas Iscariot, who would also betray him: and they went into a house.	

3.18 The Beatitudes (Near Capernaum) Matthew 5:1-7:29, Luke 6:20-49

Matthew 5:1-7:29	Luke 6:20-49
1 And seeing the multitudes, he went up into a mountain: and when he had sat down, his disciples came to him:	
2 And he opened his mouth, and taught them, saying,	
3 Blessed are the poor in spirit: for theirs is the kingdom of heaven.	20 And he lifted up his eyes on his disciples, and said, Blessed are you poor: for yours is the kingdom of God.
4 Blessed are those who mourn: for they shall be comforted.	
5 Blessed are the meek: for they shall inherit the earth.	
6 Blessed are those who hunger and thirst after righteousness: for they shall be filled.	21a Blessed are you that hunger now: for you shall be filled.
	21b Blessed are you that weep now: for you shall laugh.
7 Blessed are the merciful: for they shall obtain mercy.	
8 Blessed are the pure in heart: for they shall see God.	
9 Blessed are the peacemakers: for they shall be called the children of God.	
10 Blessed are they which are persecuted for righteousness' sake: for theirs is the kingdom of	

heaven.	
11 You are blessed, when men revile you, and persecute you, and say all manner of evil against you falsely, for my sake.	22 You are blessed, when men hate you, and when they separate you from their company, and reproach you, and cast out your name as evil, for the Son of man's sake.
12 Rejoice, and be exceeding glad: for great is your reward in heaven: for that is how they persecuted the prophets who came before you.	23 Rejoice in that day, and leap for joy: for, look, your reward is great in heaven: for their fathers did the same to the prophets.
	24 But woe to you who are rich! For you have received your consolation.
	25 Woe to you who are full! For you shall hunger. Woe to you that laugh now! For you shall mourn and weep.
	26 Woe to you, when all men shall speak well of you! For so did their fathers to the false prophets.

Matthew 5:13-38

13 You are the salt of the earth: but if salt loses its flavour, how shall you make it salty again? It is henceforth good for nothing, but to be cast out, and to be walked on by men.

14 You are the light of the world. A city that is set on a hill cannot be hidden.

15 Neither do men light a candle, and put it under a barrel, but on a candlestick; and it gives light to all who are in the house.

16 Let your light so shine before men, that they may see your good works, and glorify your Father which is in heaven.

17 Do not think that I have come to destroy the law, or the prophets: I have not come to destroy, but to fulfil.

18 For truly I say to you, Till heaven and earth pass, one jot or one tittle shall not pass from the law, till all be fulfilled.

19 Therefore whoever shall break one of these least commandments, and shall teach men so, he shall be called the least in the kingdom of heaven: but whoever shall do and teach them, he shall be called great in the kingdom of heaven.

20 For I say to you, That except your righteousness exceeds the righteousness of the scribes and Pharisees, you shall not enter into the kingdom of heaven.

21 You have heard that it was said by those of old, You shall not kill; and whoever kills shall be in danger of the judgment:

22 But I say to you, That whoever is angry with his brother without a cause shall be in danger of the judgment: and whoever says to his brother, Raca, shall be in danger of the council: but whoever shall say, You fool, shall be in danger of hell fire.

23 Therefore if you bring your gift to the altar, and there remember that your brother has something against you;

24 Leave your gift before the altar, and go your way; first be reconciled to your brother, and then come and offer your gift.

25 Agree with your adversary quickly, while you are in the way with him; lest at any time your adversary deliver you to the judge, and the judge delivers you to the officer, and you are thrown into prison.

26 Truly I say to you, You shall not in any way come out of there, till you have paid the last red cent.

27 You have heard that it was said by those of old, You shall not commit adultery:

28 But I say to you, That whoever looks on a woman to lust after her has committed adultery with her already in his heart.

29 And if your right eye offends you, pluck it out, and throw it away: for it is beneficial for you that one of your members perish, than for your whole body to be cast into hell.

30 And if your right hand offends you, cut it off, and throw it away: for it is beneficial for you that one of your members perish, than for your whole body to be cast into hell.

31 It has been said, Whoever shall put away his wife, should give her a certificate of divorce:

32 But I say to you, That whoever shall put away his wife, except for the cause of fornication, causes her to commit adultery: and whoever marries a divorcee commits adultery.

33 Again, you have heard that it has been said by those of old, You shall not swear falsely, but shall perform your oaths to the Lord:

34 But I say to you, Do not swear at all; not by heaven; for it is God's throne:

35 Nor by the earth; for it is his footstool: nor by Jerusalem; for it is the city of the great King.

36 Nor should you swear by your head, because you cannot make one hair white or black.

37 But let your communication be, Yes, yes; No, no: for whatever is more than these comes of evil.

38 You have heard that it has been said, An eye for an eye, and a tooth for a tooth:

Matthew 5:39-48	Luke 6:27-36
39 But I say to you, That you do not resist evil: but whoever smites you on your right cheek, turn the other cheek to him also.	29 And to him who strikes you on one cheek offer the other cheek as well; and to he who takes away your cloak do not withhold your coat as well.
40 And if any man will sue you, take you to court, and take away your coat, let him have your cloak also.	
41 And whoever shall compel you to go a mile, go with him two.	
42 Give to him who asks you, and from him who would borrow from you do not turn away.	30 Give to every man who asks from you; and of him who takes away your goods do not ask for them again.
	31 And as you would that men should do to you,

	you do also to them.
43 You have heard that it has been said, you shall love your neighbour, and hate your enemy.	
44 But I say to you, Love your enemies, bless those who curse you, do good to those who hate you, and pray for those who use you despitefully, and persecute you;	27 But I say to you who hear, Love your enemies, do good to those who hate you, 28 Bless those who curse you, and pray for those who despitefully use you.
45 That you may be the children of your Father who is in heaven: for he makes his sun to rise on the evil and on the good, and sends rain on the just and on the unjust.	
46 For if you love those who love you, what reward do you have? Do not even the tax collectors do the same?	32 For if you love those who love you, what thanks do you have? For sinners also love those who love them.
47 And if you salute your brethren only, what do you do more than others? Do not even the tax collectors do so?	
	33 And if you do good to those who do good to you, what thanks do you have? For sinners also do even the same.
	34 And if you lend to them of whom you hope to receive, what thanks do you have? For sinners also lend to sinners, to receive as much again.
	35 But love your enemies, and do good, and lend, hoping for nothing again; and your reward shall be great, and you shall be the children of the Highest: for he is kind to the unthankful and to the evil.
	36 Be therefore merciful, as your Father also is merciful.
48 Be therefore perfect, even as your Father who is in heaven is perfect.	

Matthew 6:1-34

1 Take heed that you do not give your alms before men, to be seen of them: otherwise you have no reward of your Father who is in heaven.

2 Therefore when you give alms, do not sound a trumpet before you, as the hypocrites do in the synagogues and in the streets, that they may have glory of men. Truly I say to you, They have their reward.

3 But when you give alms, do not let your left hand know what your right hand does:

4 That your alms may be in secret: and your Father who sees in secret himself shall reward you openly.

5 And when you pray, you shall not be as the hypocrites are: for they love to pray standing in the synagogues and in the corners of the streets, that they may be seen of men. Truly I say to you, They have their reward.

6 But you, when you pray , enter into your closet, and when you have shut your door, pray to your Father who is in secret; and your Father who sees in secret shall reward you openly.

7 But when you pray, do not use vain repetitions, as the heathen do: for they think that they shall be heard for their much speaking.

8 Therefore, do not be like them: for your Father knows what things you need, before you ask him.

9 After this manner therefore pray: Our Father who is in heaven, Hallowed be your name.

10 Your kingdom come. Your will be done in earth, as it is in heaven.

11 Give us this day our daily bread.

12 And forgive us our debts, as we forgive our debtors.

13 And do not lead us into temptation, but deliver us from evil: For yours is the kingdom, and the power, and the glory, for ever. Amen.

14 For if you forgive men their trespasses, your heavenly Father will also forgive you:

15 But if you do not forgive men their trespasses, neither will your Father forgive your trespasses.

16 Moreover when you fast, do not be as the hypocrites, of a sad countenance: for they disfigure their faces, that they may appear to men to fast. Truly I say to you, They have their reward.

17 But you, when you fast, anoint your head, and wash your face;

18 That you do not appear to men to fast, but to your Father which is in secret: and your Father, who sees in secret, shall reward you openly.

19 Do not lay up for yourselves treasures upon earth, where moth and rust do corrupt, and where thieves break through and steal:

20 But lay up for yourselves treasures in heaven, where neither moth nor rust do corrupt, and where thieves do not break through nor steal:

21 For where your treasure is, there your heart will be also.

22 The light of the body is the eye: if therefore your eye is single, your whole body shall be full of light.

23 But if your eye is evil, your whole body shall be full of darkness. If therefore the light that is in you is darkness, how great is that darkness!

24 No man can serve two masters: for either he will hate the one, and love the other; or else he will hold to the one, and despise the other. You cannot serve God and mammon.

25 Therefore I say to you, Do not worry about your life, what you shall eat, or what you shall drink; nor yet for your body, what you shall put on. Is not life more than meat, and the body than clothing?

26 Look the birds of the air: for they do not sow, neither do they reap, nor gather into barns; yet your heavenly Father feeds them. Are you not much better than they?

27 Which of you by taking thought can add one cubit to his stature?

28 And why take thought for clothing? Consider the lilies of the field, how they grow; they do not toil, neither do they spin:

29 And yet I say to you, That even Solomon in all his glory was not arrayed like one of these.

30 Therefore, if God so clothes the grass of the field, which to day is, and to morrow is cast into the oven, shall he not much more clothe you, O you of little faith?

31 Therefore take no thought, saying, What shall we eat? Or, What shall we drink? Or, with what shall we be clothed?

32 (For after all these things do the Gentiles seek:) for your heavenly Father knows that you have need of all these things.

33 But seek first the kingdom of God, and his righteousness; and all these things shall be added to you.

34 Therefore do not worry about tomorrow: for tomorrow shall take thought for the things of itself. Sufficient to the day is the evil in it.

Matthew 7:1-5	Luke 6:37-42
1 Do not judge, so that you will not be judged.	37 Do not judge, and you shall not be judged: do not condemn, and you shall not be condemned: forgive, and you shall be forgiven:
2 For with what judgment you judge, you shall be judged: and with what measure you measure out, it shall be measured to you again.	38 Give, and it shall be given to you; good measure, pressed down, and shaken together, and running over, shall men give into your bosom. For with the same measure that you measure out it shall be measured to you again.
	[13]39 And he spoke a parable to them, Can the blind lead the blind? Shall they not both fall into the ditch?
	40 The disciple is not above his master: but every one that is perfect shall be as his master.
3 And why do you look at the mote that is in your brother's eye, but do not consider the beam that is in your own eye?	41 And why do you look at the mote that is in your brother's eye, but do not perceive the beam that is in your own eye?
4 Or how will you say to your brother, Let me pull out the mote out of your eye; and, behold, a beam is in your own eye? 5 You hypocrite, first cast out the beam out of	42 Also, how can you say to your brother, Brother, let me pull out the mote that is in your eye, when you yourself do not look at the beam that is in your own eye? You hypocrite, cast out

[13] Parable 2. Blind leading the blind. Lu 6:39-42, Mt 7:3-5.

your own eye; and then you shall see clearly to cast out the mote out of your brother's eye.	first the beam out of your own eye, and then you shall see clearly to pull out the mote that is in your brother's eye.

Matthew 7:6-15

6 Do not give what is holy to the dogs, neither cast your pearls before swine, lest they trample them under their feet, and turn again and rend you.

7 Ask, and it shall be given you; seek, and you shall find; knock, and it shall be opened to you:

8 For every one who asks receives; and he who seeks finds; and to him who knocks it shall be opened.

9 Or what man is there among you, whom if his son asks for bread, will he give him a stone?

10 Or if he asks for a fish, will he give him a serpent?

11 If you then, being evil, know how to give good gifts to your children, how much more shall your Father who is in heaven give good things to those who ask him?

12 Therefore whatever you want men to do to you, do even so to them: for this is the law and the prophets.

13 Enter in at the strait gate: for wide is the gate, and broad is the way, that leads to destruction, and there are many who go in there:

14 Because strait is the gate, and narrow is the way, which leads to life, and there are few who find it.

15 Beware of false prophets, who come to you in sheep's clothing, but inwardly they are ravening wolves.

Matthew 7:16-25	Luke 6:43-49
16 You shall know them by their fruits. Do men gather grapes of thorns, or figs of thistles?	44 For every tree is known by his own fruit. For of thorns men do not gather figs, nor of a bramble bush gather grapes.
17 Even so every good tree brings forth good fruit; but a corrupt tree brings forth evil fruit.	43 For a good tree does not bring forth corrupt fruit; neither does a corrupt tree bring forth good fruit.
18 A good tree cannot bring forth evil fruit, neither can a corrupt tree bring forth good fruit.	
	45 A good man out of the good treasure of his heart brings forth that which is good; and an evil man out of the evil treasure of his heart brings forth that which is evil: for of the abundance of the heart his mouth speaks.
19 Every tree that does not bring forth good fruit is hewn down, and cast into the fire.	
20 Therefore by their fruits you shall know them.	
	46 And why do you call me, Lord, Lord, and do

	not do the things which I say?
21 Not every one who says to me, Lord, Lord, shall enter into the kingdom of heaven; but he who does the will of my Father who is in heaven.	
22 Many will say to me in that day, Lord, Lord, have we not prophesied in your name? And in your name have cast out devils? And in your name done many wonderful works?	
23 And then will I profess to them, I never knew you: depart from me, you who work iniquity.	
[14]24 Therefore whoever hears these sayings of mine, and does them, I will liken him to a wise man, who built his house upon a rock:	47 Whoever comes to me, and hears my sayings, and does them, I will show you who he is like: 48a He is like a man who built a house, and dug deep, and laid the foundation on a rock:
25 And the rain descended, and the floods came, and the winds blew, and beat upon that house; and it did not fall: for it was founded upon a rock.	48b and when the flood arose, the stream beat vehemently upon that house, and could not shake it: for it was founded upon a rock.
26 And every one that hears these sayings of mine, and does not do them, shall be likened to a foolish man, who built his house upon the sand:	49a But he who hears and does not do, is like a man who without a foundation built a house upon the earth;
27 And the rain descended, and the floods came, and the winds blew, and beat upon that house; and it fell: and great was the fall of it.	49b against which the stream beat vehemently, and immediately it fell; and the ruin of that house was great.
28 And it happened, when Jesus had ended these sayings, the people were astonished at his doctrine:	
29 For he taught them as one having authority, and not as the scribes.	

3.19 Jesus heals a centurion's servant (Capernaum) Luke 7:1-10, Matthew 8:5-13

Luke 7:1-10	Matthew 8:5-13
1 Now when he had ended all his sayings in the audience of the people, he entered Capernaum.	[15]5 And when Jesus had entered Capernaum, a centurion came to him, begging him,
2 And a certain centurion's servant, who was dear to him, was sick, and ready to die.	6 And saying, Lord, my servant lies at home paralyzed, grievously tormented.

---

[14] Parable 3. Wise and foolish builders. Mt 7:24-27, Lu 6:47-49.

[15] Healing Miracle 11 (of 37). Centurion's servant. Lu 7:1-10, Mt 8:5-13.

3 And when he heard of Jesus, he sent the elders of the Jews to him, begging him to come and heal his servant.	
4 And when they came to Jesus, they begged him urgently, saying, That he was worthy for whom he should do this:	
5 For he loves our nation, and he has built us a synagogue.	
6 Then Jesus went with them. And when he was now not far from the house, the centurion sent friends to him, saying, Lord, do not trouble yourself: for I am not worthy that you should come under my roof:	7 And Jesus said to him, I will come and heal him.
7 Therefore neither did I think myself worthy to come to you: but say a word, and my servant shall be healed.	8 The centurion answered and said, Lord, I am not worthy that you should come under my roof: but speak the word only, and my servant shall be healed.
8 For I also am a man set under authority, having under me soldiers, and I say to one, Go, and he goes; and to another, Come, and he comes; and to my servant, Do this, and he does it.	9 For I am a man under authority, having soldiers under me: and I say to this man, Go, and he goes; and to another, Come, and he comes; and to my servant, Do this, and he does it.
9 When Jesus heard these things, he marvelled at him, and turned about, and said to the people that followed him, I say to you, I have not found so great faith, no, not in Israel.	10 When Jesus heard it, he marvelled, and said to those who followed, Truly I say to you, I have not found so great faith, no, not in Israel.
	11 And I say to you, That many shall come from the east and west, and shall sit down with Abraham, and Isaac, and Jacob, in the kingdom of heaven.
	12 But the children of the kingdom shall be cast out into outer darkness: there shall be weeping and gnashing of teeth.
10 And those he had sent, returning to the house, found the servant who had been sick whole.	13 And Jesus said to the centurion, Go your way; and as you have believed, so be it done to you. And his servant was healed that very hour.

4: Second tour of Galilee

4.01 Jesus raises a widow's dead son (Nain) Luke 7:11-17

Luke 7:11-17

[16]**11** And it happened the day after, that he went into a city called Nain; and many of his disciples went with him, as did many people.

12 Now when he came near to the gate of the city, look, there was a dead man carried out, the only son of his mother, and she was a widow: and many people of the city were with her.

13 And when the Lord saw her, he had compassion on her, and said to her, Weep not.

14 And he came and touched the bier: and those that bore him stood still. And he said, Young man, I say to you, Arise.

15 And he who was dead sat up, and began to speak. And he delivered him to his mother.

16 And a fear came on all: and they glorified God, saying, That a great prophet is risen up among us; and, That God has visited his people.

17 And this report of him went forth throughout all Judea, and throughout all the region round about.

4.02 Allays John's doubts and speaks about John (Galilee) Luke 7:18-35, Matthew 11:2-19

Luke 7:18-35	Matthew 11:2-19
18 And the disciples of John told him all these things.	
19 And John calling to him two of his disciples sent them to Jesus, saying, Are you he who should come? Or should we look for another?	2 Now when John had heard in the prison about the works of Christ, he sent two of his disciples,
20 When the men came to him, they said, John Baptist has sent us to you, saying, Are you he who should come? Or should we look for another?	3 And said to him, Are you he who should come, or do we look for another?
[17]21 And in that same hour he cured many of their infirmities and plagues, and of evil spirits; and to many that were blind he gave sight.	
22a Then Jesus answering said to them, Go your way, and tell John what things you have seen and heard;	4 Jesus answered and said to them, Go and tell John again those things which you do hear and see:

[16] Healing Miracle 12 (of 37). Widow's dead son. Lu7:11-17

[17] Healing Miracle 13 (of 37). Multitudes healed. Lu 7:18-35, Mt 11:2-19

22b how the blind see, the lame walk, the lepers are cleansed, the deaf hear, the dead are raised, to the poor the gospel is preached.	5 The blind receive their sight, and the lame walk, the lepers are cleansed, and the deaf hear, the dead are raised up, and the poor have the gospel preached to them.
23 And blessed is he, who shall not be offended in me.	6 And blessed is he, who shall not be offended in me.
24 And when the messengers of John had departed, he began to speak to the people concerning John, What did you go out into the wilderness for to see? A reed shaken with the wind?	7 And as they departed, Jesus began to say to the multitudes concerning John, What did you go out into the wilderness to see? A reed shaken with the wind?
25 But what did you go out to see? A man clothed in soft raiment? Look, those who are gorgeously appareled, and live delicately, are in kings' courts.	8 But what went you out for to see? A man clothed in soft raiment? Look, those who wear soft clothing are in kings' houses.
26 But what did you go out to see? A prophet? Yes, I say to you, and much more than a prophet.	9 But what did you go out to see? A prophet? Yes, I say to you, and more than a prophet.
27 This is he, of whom it is written, Look, I send my messenger before your face, who shall prepare your way before you.	10 For this is he, of whom it is written, Look, I send my messenger before your face, which shall prepare your way before you.
28 For I say to you, Among those that are born of women there is not a greater prophet than John the Baptist: but he who is least in the kingdom of God is greater than he.	11 Truly I say to you, Among those who are born of women there has not risen a greater than John the Baptist: notwithstanding he who is least in the kingdom of heaven is greater than he.
	12 And from the days of John the Baptist until now the kingdom of heaven suffers violence, and the violent take it by force.
	13 For all the prophets and the law prophesied until John.
	14 And if you will receive it, this is Elias, which was for to come.
	15 He who has ears to hear, let him hear.
29 And all the people that heard him, and the tax collectors, justified God, being baptized with the baptism of John.	
30 But the Pharisees and lawyers rejected the counsel of God against themselves, not being baptized of him.	
31 And the Lord said, To what then shall I liken the men of this generation? And what are they	16a But to what shall I liken this generation?

like?	
32 They are like children sitting in the marketplace, and calling to one another, and saying, We have piped to you, and you have not danced; we have mourned to you, and you have not wept.	16b, c It is like children sitting in the markets, and calling to their fellows, 17 And saying, We have piped to you, and you have not danced; we have mourned to you, and you have not lamented.
33 For John the Baptist came neither eating bread nor drinking wine; and you say, He has a devil.	18 For John came neither eating nor drinking, and they say, He has a devil.
34 The Son of man has come eating and drinking; and you say, Look a gluttonous man, and a winebibber, a friend of tax collectors and sinners!	19a-c The Son of man came eating and drinking, and they say, Look a gluttonous man, and a winebibber, a friend of tax collectors and sinners.
35 But wisdom is justified of all her children.	19d But wisdom is justified of her children.

4.03 Woes on unrepentant cities Matthew 11:20-30

Matthew 11:20-30

20 Then he began to upbraid the cities where most of his mighty works were done, because they did not repent:

21 Woe to you, Chorazin! Woe to you, Bethsaida! For if the mighty works, which were done in you, had been done in Tyre and Sidon, they would have repented long ago in sackcloth and ashes.

22 But I say to you, It shall be more tolerable for Tyre and Sidon in the day of judgment, than for you.

23 And you, Capernaum, which is exalted to heaven, shall be brought down to hell: for if the mighty works, which have been done in you, had been done in Sodom, it would have remained until this day.

24 But I say to you, That it shall be more tolerable for the land of Sodom in the day of judgment, than for you.

25 At that time Jesus answered and said, I thank you, O Father, Lord of heaven and earth, because you have hidden these things from the wise and prudent, and have revealed them to babes.

26 Even so, Father: for so it seemed good in your sight.

27 All things are delivered to me by my Father: and no man knows the Son, but the Father; neither knows any man the Father, except the Son, and he to whom the Son reveals him.

28 Come to me, all you who labour and are heavy laden, and I will give you rest.

29 Take my yoke upon you, and learn of me; for I am meek and lowly in heart: and you shall find rest for your souls.

30 For my yoke is easy, and my burden is light.

4.04 A woman washes then anoints Jesus' feet (Simon's house, Capernaum) Luke 7:36-50

Luke 7:36-50

[18]**36** And one of the Pharisees invited him to eat with him. And he went into the Pharisee's house, and sat down to eat.

37 And, look, a woman in the city, who was a sinner, when she knew that Jesus sat to eat in the Pharisee's house, brought an alabaster box of ointment,

38 And stood at his feet behind him weeping, and began to wash his feet with tears, and did wipe them with the hairs of her head, and kissed his feet, and anointed them with the ointment.

39 Now when the Pharisee who had invited him saw it, he spoke within himself, saying, This man, if he were a prophet, would have known who and what manner of woman this is that is touching him: for she is a sinner.

40 And Jesus answering said to him, Simon, I have somewhat to say to you. And he said, Master, say on.

41 There was a certain creditor who had two debtors: the one owed five hundred pence, and the other fifty.

42 And when they had nothing to pay, he frankly forgave them both. Tell me therefore, which of them will love him more?

43 Simon answered and said, I suppose the one to whom he forgave more. And he said to him, You have judged rightly.

44 And he turned to the woman, and said to Simon, Do you see this woman? I entered into your house, you gave me no water for my feet: but she has washed my feet with tears, and wiped them with the hairs of her head.

45 You gave me no kiss: but this woman since the time I came in has not ceased to kiss my feet.

46 You did not anoint my head with oil: but this woman has anointed my feet with ointment.

47 Therefore I say to you, Her sins, which are many, are forgiven; for she loved much: but to whom little is forgiven, the same loves little.

48 And he said to her, Your sins are forgiven.

49 And those who sat to eat with him began to say within themselves, Who is this who forgives sins also?

[19]**50** And he said to the woman, Your faith has saved you; go in peace.

---

[18] Parable 4. Two debtors. Lu 7:36-50.

[19] Your faith has saved you (according to your faith) 1 (of 8). Lu 7:50.

4.05 Second Tour Continues (Galilee) Luke 8:1-3

Luke 8:1-3

1 And it happened afterward, that he went throughout every city and village, preaching and showing the glad tidings of the kingdom of God: and the twelve were with him,

2 As were certain women, which had been healed of evil spirits and infirmities, Mary called Magdalene, out of whom went seven devils,

3 And Joanna the wife of Chuza Herod's steward, and Susanna, and many others, which ministered to him of their substance.

4.06 Heals a devil-possessed, blind and dumb man (Capernaum) Mark 3:20-30, Luke 11:14-23, Matthew 12:22-37

Mark 3:20-30	Luke 11:14-23	Matthew 12:22-33
20 And the multitude came together again, so that they could not so much as eat bread.		
21 And when his friends heard of it, they went out to lay hold on him: for they said, He is beside himself.		
	14 And he was casting out a devil, and it was dumb. And it happened, when the devil was gone out, the dumb spoke; and the people wondered.	[20]22 Then was brought to him one possessed with a devil, blind, and dumb: and he healed him, so much so that the blind and dumb both spoke and saw.
		23 And all the people were amazed, and said, Is not this the son of David?
22 And the scribes who came down from Jerusalem said, He has Beelzebub, and by the prince of the devils he casts out devils.	15 But some of them said, He casts out devils through Beelzebub the chief of the devils.	[21]24 But when the Pharisees heard it, they said, This fellow does not cast out devils, but by Beelzebub the prince of the devils.
	16 And others, tempting him, sought a sign from heaven from	

---

[20] Healing Miracle 14 (of 37). Dumb, devil-possessed man. Mr 3:20-30, Lu 11:14-23, Mt 12:22-37.

[21] Parable 5. Subduing a strong man. Lu 11:14-23, Mr 3:22-30, Mt 12:22-37.

	him.	
23 And he called them to him, and said to them in parables, How can Satan cast out Satan?	17 But he, knowing their thoughts, said to them, Every kingdom divided against itself is brought to desolation; and a house divided against a house falls.	25 And Jesus knew their thoughts, and said to them, Every kingdom divided against itself is brought to desolation; and every city or house divided against itself shall not stand:
24 And if a kingdom is divided against itself, that kingdom cannot stand. 25 And if a house is divided against itself, that house cannot stand. 26 And if Satan rise up against himself, and be divided, he cannot stand, but has an end.	18 If Satan also be divided against himself, how shall his kingdom stand? Because you say that I cast out devils through Beelzebub.	26 And if Satan cast out Satan, he is divided against himself; how shall then his kingdom stand?
	19 And if I by Beelzebub cast out devils, by whom do your sons cast them out? Therefore they shall be your judges.	27 And if I by Beelzebub cast out devils, by whom do your children cast them out? Therefore they shall be your judges.
	20 But if I with the finger of God cast out devils, no doubt the kingdom of God has come upon you.	28 But if I cast out devils by the Spirit of God, then the kingdom of God has come to you.
27 No man can enter into a strong man's house, and spoil his goods, except he will first bind the strong man; and then he will spoil his house.	21 When a strong man armed keeps his palace, his goods are in peace:	29 Or else how can one enter into a strong man's house, and spoil his goods, except he first bind the strong man? And then he will spoil his house.
	22 But when a stronger than he shall come upon him, and overcome him, he takes from him all his armour wherein he trusted, and divides his spoils.	
	23 He who is not with me is against me: and he who does not gather with me scatters.	30 He who is not with me is against me; and he who does not gather with me scatters abroad.
28 Truly I say to you, All sins shall be forgiven to the sons of men, and whatever blasphemies they commit:		31 Therefore I say to you, All manner of sin and blasphemy shall be forgiven to men: but the blasphemy against the Holy Spirit shall not be forgiven men.

30 Because they said, He has an unclean spirit.		
		33 Either make the tree good, and his fruit good; or else make the tree corrupt, and his fruit corrupt: for the tree is known by his fruit.

Matthew 12:34-37
34 O generation of vipers, how can you, being evil, speak good things? For out of the abundance of the heart the mouth speaks.
35 A good man out of the good treasure of the heart brings forth good things: and an evil man out of the evil treasure brings forth evil things.
36 But I say to you, That every idle word that men shall speak, they shall give account for it in the day of judgment.
37 For by your words you shall be justified, and by your words you shall be condemned.

4.07 Some scribes and Pharisees ask for a sign (Capernaum) Luke 11:16, 29-36, Matthew 12:38-42

Luke 11:16, 29-32	Matthew 12:38-42
16 And others, tempting him, sought a sign from heaven of him.	38 Then certain of the scribes and of the Pharisees answered, saying, Master, we would see a sign from you.
29 And when the people were gathered thick together, he began to say, This is an evil generation: they seek a sign; and there shall no sign be given it, but the sign of Jonah the prophet.	39 But he answered and said to them, An evil and adulterous generation seeks after a sign; and there shall no sign be given to it, but the sign of the prophet Jonah:
30 For as Jonah was a sign to the Ninevites, so also shall the Son of man be to this generation.	40 For as Jonah was three days and three nights in the whale's belly; so shall the Son of man be three days and three nights in the heart of the earth.
31 The queen of the south shall rise up in the judgment with the men of this generation, and condemn them: for she came from the utmost parts of the earth to hear the wisdom of Solomon; and, look, a greater than Solomon is here.	41 The men of Nineveh shall rise in judgment with this generation, and shall condemn it: because they repented at the preaching of Jonah; and, look, a greater than Jonah is here.
32 The men of Nineveh shall rise up in the judgment with this generation, and shall condemn	42 The queen of the south shall rise up in the judgment with this generation, and shall condemn

it: for they repented at the preaching of Jonah; and, look, a greater than Jonah is here.	it: for she came from the uttermost parts of the earth to hear the wisdom of Solomon; and, look, a greater than Solomon is here.

Luke 11:33-36
33 No man, after lighting a candle, puts it in a secret place, nor under a bushel, but on a candlestick, that those who come in may see the light.
34 The light of the body is the eye: therefore when your eye is single, your whole body also is full of light; but when your eye is evil, your body also is full of darkness.
35 Take heed therefore that the light which is in you is not darkness.
36 If your whole body therefore is full of light, having no part dark, the whole shall be full of light, as when the bright shining of a candle gives you light.

4.08 The unclean spirit Luke 11:24-28, Matthew 12:43-45

Luke 11:24-28	Matthew 12:43-45
24 When the unclean spirit has gone out of a man, he walks through dry places, seeking rest; and finding none, he says, I will return to my house from where I came out.	43 When the unclean spirit has gone out of a man, he walks through dry places, seeking rest, and finds none.
25 And when he comes, he finds it swept and garnished.	44 Then he says, I will return to my house from where I came out; and when he comes, he finds it empty, swept, and garnished.
26 Then he goes, and takes to him seven other spirits more wicked than himself; and they enter in, and dwell there: and the last state of that man is worse than the first.	45 Then he goes, and takes with him seven other spirits more wicked than himself, and they enter in and dwell there: and the last state of that man is worse than the first. Even so shall it be also to this wicked generation.
27 And it happened, as he spoke these things, a certain woman of the company lifted up her voice, and said to him, Blessed is the womb that bore you, and the breasts which you sucked.	
28 But he said, Yes rather, blessed are those who hear the word of God, and keep it.	

4.09 Brothers, sisters and mother seek audience (Capernaum) Mark 3:31-35, Luke 8:19-21, Matthew 12:46-50

Mark 3:31-35	Luke 8:19-21	Matthew 12:46-50
31 Then there came his brothers	19 Then his mother, his	46 While he yet talked to the

and sisters and his mother, and, standing outside, sent to him, calling him.	brothers, and sisters came to him, and could not come close to him because of the crowd.	people, look, his mother and his brothers and sisters stood outside, desiring to speak with him.
32 And the multitude sat about him, and they said to him, Look, your mother and your brothers and sisters outside seek you.	20 And certain people told him, Your mother and your brothers and sisters stand outside, desiring to see you.	47 Then one said to him, Look, your mother and your brothers and sisters stand outside, desiring to speak with you.
33 And he answered them, saying, Who is my mother, or my brethren?	21 And he answered and said to them, My mother and my brothers and sisters are these which hear the word of God, and do it.	48 But he answered and said to he who told him, Who is my mother? And who are my brothers and sisters?
34 And he looked round about at them which sat about him, and said, Look my mother and my brethren!		49 And he stretched forth his hand toward his disciples, and said, Look my mother and my brothers and sisters!
35 For whoever shall do the will of God, the same is my brother, and my sister, and mother.		50 For whoever shall do the will of my Father who is in heaven, the same is my brother, and sister, and mother.

4.10 Parable of the soils (Bay of parables, Sea of Galilee) Mark 4:1-20, Luke 8:4-15, Matthew 13:1-23

Mark 4:1-12	Luke 8:4-10	Matthew 13:1-13
1 And he began again to teach by the sea side: and a great multitude gathered to him, so that he entered into a ship, and sat in the sea; and the whole multitude was by the sea on the land.	4a, b And when many people had gathered together, and had come to him out of every city,	1 The same day Jesus went out of the house, and sat by the sea side. 2 And great multitudes were gathered together to him, so that he went into a ship, and sat; and the whole multitude stood on the shore.
2 And he taught them many things by parables, and said his doctrine to them,	4c he spoke by a parable:	3a And he spoke many things to them in parables, saying,

3 Listen; Look, there went out a sower to sow:	5a A sower went out to sow his seed:	[22]3b Look, a sower went forth to sow;
4 And it happened, as he sowed, some fell by the way side, and the fowls of the air came and devoured it.	5b-d and as he sowed, some fell by the way side; and it was trodden down, and the fowls of the air devoured it.	4 And when he sowed, some seeds fell by the way side, and the fowls came and devoured them:
5 And some fell on stony ground, where it did not have much earth; and immediately it sprang up, because it had no depth of earth:	6 And some fell upon a rock; and as soon as it sprung up, it withered away, because it lacked moisture.	5 Some fell upon stony places, where they did not have much earth: and forthwith they sprung up, because they had no depth of earth:
6 But when the sun was up, it was scorched; and because it had no root, it withered away.		6 And when the sun was up, they were scorched; and because they had no root, they withered away.
7 And some fell among thorns, and the thorns grew up, and choked it, and it yielded no fruit.	7 And some fell among thorns; and the thorns sprang up with it, and choked it.	7 And some fell among thorns; and the thorns sprang up, and choked them:
8 And others fell on good ground, and did yield fruit that sprang up and increased; and brought forth, some thirty, and some sixty, and some a hundred.	8 And others fell on good ground, and sprang up, and bore fruit a hundredfold. And when he had said these things, he cried, He who has ears to hear, let him hear.	8 But others fell into good ground, and brought forth fruit, some a hundredfold, some sixtyfold, some thirtyfold.
9 And he said to them, He who has ears to hear, let him hear.		9 Who has ears to hear, let him hear.
10 And when he was alone, those who were around him with the twelve asked him about the parable.	9 And his disciples asked him, saying, What might this parable mean?	10 And the disciples came, and said to him, Why do you speak to them in parables?
11 And he said to them, To you it is given to know the mystery of the kingdom of God: but to those who are without, all these things are done in parables:	10 And he said, to you it is given to know the mysteries of the kingdom of God: but to others in parables; that seeing they might not see, and hearing they might not understand.	11 He answered and said to them, Because it is given to you to know the mysteries of the kingdom of heaven, but to them it is not given.

---

[22] Parable 6. The soils. Lu 8:5-8, 11-15, Mt 13:1-9, 18-23, Mr 4:1-9, 14-20.

		12 For whoever has, to him shall be given, and he shall have more abundance: but whoever has not, from him shall be taken away even what he has.
12 That seeing they may see, and not perceive; and hearing they may hear, and not understand; lest at any time they should be converted, and their sins should be forgiven them.		13 Therefore I speak to them in parables: because seeing they see not; and hearing they hear not, neither do they understand.

Matthew 13:14-17		
14 And in them is fulfilled the prophecy of Isaiah, which says, By hearing you shall hear, and shall not understand; and seeing you shall see, and shall not perceive:		
15 For this people's heart is waxed gross, and their ears are dull of hearing, and their eyes they have closed; lest at any time they should see with their eyes, and hear with their ears, and should understand with their heart, and should be converted, and I should heal them.		
16 But blessed are your eyes, for they see: and your ears, for they hear.		
17 For truly I say to you, That many prophets and righteous men have desired to see those things which you see, and have not seen them; and to hear those things which you hear, and have not heard them.		

Mark 4:13-20	Luke 8:11-15	Matthew 13:18-23
13 And he said to them, Do you not know this parable? How then will you know all parables?		
	11a Now the parable is this:	18 Therefore hear the parable of the sower.
14 The sower sows the word.		
	11b The seed is the word of God.	
15 And these are those by the way side, where the word is sown; but when they have heard, Satan comes immediately, and takes away the word that was sown in their	12 Those by the way side are those who hear; then the devil comes, and takes away the word out of their hearts, for fear that they should believe and be saved.	19 When any one hears the word of the kingdom, and does not understand it, then the wicked one comes, and snatches away that which was sown in his heart. This is he who received

hearts.		seed by the way side.
16 And these are those which in like manner are sown on stony ground; who, when they have heard the word, immediately receive it with gladness;	13 Those on the rock are those, who, when they hear, receive the word with joy; and these have no root, which for a while believe, and in time of temptation fall away.	20 But he who received the seed into stony places, the same is he who hears the word, and immediately receives it with joy;
17 And have no root in themselves, and so endure but for a time: afterward, when affliction or persecution arises for the word's sake, immediately they are offended.		21 Yet he has not root in himself, but endures for a while: for when tribulation or persecution arises because of the word, by and by he is offended.
18 And these are those which are sown among thorns; such as hear the word, 19 And the cares of this world, and the deceitfulness of riches, and the lusts of other things entering in, choke the word, and it becomes unfruitful.	14 And those which fell among thorns are those, who, when they have heard, go forth, and are choked with cares and riches and pleasures of this life, and bring no fruit to perfection.	22 He also who received seed among the thorns is he who hears the word; and the care of this world, and the deceitfulness of riches, choke the word, and he becomes unfruitful.
20 And these are they which are sown on good ground; such as hear the word, and receive it, and bring forth fruit, some thirtyfold, some sixty, and some a hundred.	15 But those on the good ground are those, who in an honest and good heart, having heard the word, keep it, and bring forth fruit with patience.	23 But he who received seed into the good ground is he who hears the word, and understands it; who also bears fruit, and brings forth, some a hundredfold, some sixty, some thirty.

4.11 Parable of the candle (Bay of parables, Sea of Galilee) Mark 4:21-25, Luke 8:16-18

Mark 4:21-25	Luke 8:16-18
[23]21 And he said to them, Is a candle brought to be put under a candle stand, or under a bed? And not to be set on a candlestick?	16 No man, when he has lit a candle, covers it with a vessel, or puts it under a bed; but sets it on a candlestick, that those who enter in may see the light.
22 For there is nothing hidden, which shall not be revealed; neither was anything kept secret, but	17 For nothing is secret, that shall not be revealed; neither is anything hidden, that shall

---

[23] Parable 7. The candle. Mr 4:21-25, Lu 8:16-18.

that it should broadcast.	not be known and broadcast.
23 If any man has ears to hear, let him hear.	
24 And he said to them, Take heed what you hear: with what measure you give out, it shall be measured to you: and to you who hear more shall be given. 25 For he who has, to him shall be given: and he who does not have, from him shall be taken even that which he has.	18 Take heed therefore how you hear: for whoever has, to him shall be given; and whoever does not have, from him shall be taken even that which he seems to have.

4.12 Parable of the seed (Bay of parables, Sea of Galilee) Mark 4:26-29

Mark 4:26-29

[24]**26** And he said, So is the kingdom of God, as if a man should cast seed into the ground;

27 And should sleep, and rise night and day, and the seed should spring and grow; he does not know how.

28 For the earth brings forth fruit of herself; first the blade, then the ear, after that the full corn in the ear.

29 But when the fruit is brought forth, immediately he puts in the sickle, because the harvest has come.

4.13 Parable of the mustard seed (Bay of parables, Sea of Galilee) Mark 4:30-34, Matthew 13:31-32, Luke 13:18-19

Mark 4:30-34	Luke 13:18-19	Matthew 13:31-32
[25]**30** And he said, To what shall we liken the kingdom of God? Or with what shall we compare it?	18 Then said he, What is the kingdom of God like? And what does it resemble?	
31 It is like a grain of mustard seed, which, when it is sown in the earth, is less than all the seeds that are in the earth:	19a It is like a grain of mustard seed, which a man took, and cast into his garden;	31 Another parable he put to them, saying, The kingdom of heaven is like a grain of mustard seed, which a man took, and sowed in his field: 32a Which indeed is the least of all seeds:

---

[24] Parable 8. The growing seed. Mr 4:26-29

[25] Parable 9. The mustard seed. Mr 4:30-34, Mt 13:31-32, Lu 13:18,19

32 But when it is sown, it grows up, and becomes greater than all herbs, and shoots out great branches; so that the fowls of the air may lodge under its shadow	19b and it grew, and became a great tree; and the fowls of the air lodged in its branches.	32b-d but when it is grown, it is the greatest among herbs, and becomes a tree, so that the birds of the air come and lodge in its branches.
33 And with many such parables he spoke the word to them, as they were able to hear it.		
34 But without a parable he did not speak to them: and when they were alone, he expounded all things to his disciples.		

4.14 Parables of the wheat and tares, and leaven (Bay of parables, Sea of Galilee) Matthew 13:24-30, 33-43, Luke 13:20, 21

Matthew 13:24-30, 33-43

[26]**24** Another parable he presented to them, saying, The kingdom of heaven is like a man who sowed good seed in his field:

25 But while men slept, his enemy came and sowed tares among the wheat, and went his way.

26 But when the blade had sprung up, and brought forth fruit, then the tares also appeared.

27 So the servants of the owner came and said to him, Sir, did you not sow good seed in your field? Where then did these tares come from?

28 He said to them, An enemy has done this. The servants said to him, Do you want us to go and gather them up?

29 But he said, No; lest while you gather up the tares, you also root up the wheat with them.

30 Let both grow together until the harvest: and in the time of harvest I will say to the reapers, First gather together the tares, and bind them in bundles to burn them: but gather the wheat into my barn.

[27]**Matthew 13:33a** Another parable he spoke to them; The kingdom of heaven	**Luke 13:20** And again he said, With what shall I liken the kingdom of God?
Matthew 13:33b, c is like leaven, which a woman took, and hid in three measures of meal, till the whole was leavened.	**Luke 13.21** It is like leaven, which a woman took and hid in three measures of meal, till the whole was leavened.

---

[26] Parable 10. The tares. Mt 13:24-30, 36-43.

[27] Parable 11. The leaven. Mt 13:33, Lu 13:20-21.

34 All these things Jesus spoke to the multitude in parables; and he did not speak to them without a parable:

35 That it might be fulfilled which was spoken by the prophet, saying, I will open my mouth in parables; I will utter things which have been kept secret from the foundation of the world.

36 Then Jesus sent the multitude away, and went into the house: and his disciples came to him, saying, Tell us the parable of the tares of the field.

37 He answered and said to them, He who sows the good seed is the Son of man;

38 The field is the world; the good seed are the children of the kingdom; but the tares are the children of the wicked one;

39 The enemy that sowed them is the devil; the harvest is the end of the world; and the reapers are the angels.

40 Therefore as the tares are gathered and burned in the fire; so shall it be in the end of this world.

41 The Son of man shall send forth his angels, and they shall gather out of his kingdom all things that offend, and those who do iniquity;

42 And shall cast them into a furnace of fire: there shall be wailing and gnashing of teeth.

43 Then shall the righteous shine forth as the sun in the kingdom of their Father. Who has ears to hear, let him hear.

4.15 Parables of the treasure, pearl, fishing net, homeowner (Bay of parables, Sea of Galilee) Matthew 13:44-52

Matthew 13:44-52

[28]**44** Again, the kingdom of heaven is like treasure hidden in a field; which when a man has found, he hides, and for the joy of finding it goes and sells all that he has, and buys that field.

[29]**45** Again, the kingdom of heaven is like a merchant, seeking goodly pearls:

46 Who, when he had found one pearl of great price, went and sold all that he had, and bought it.

[30]**47** Again, the kingdom of heaven is like a net, that was cast into the sea, and gathered of every kind:

48 Which, when it was full, they drew to shore, and sat down, and gathered the good into vessels, but cast the bad away.

49 So shall it be at the end of the world: the angels shall come forth, and sever the wicked from among the just,

50 And shall cast them into the furnace of fire: there shall be wailing and gnashing of teeth.

[31]**51** Jesus said to them, Have you understood all these things? They say to him, Yes, Lord.

52 Then he said to them, Therefore every scribe which is instructed in the things of the kingdom of

---

[28] Parable 12. The hidden treasure. Mt 13:44.

[29] Parable 13. The Pearl of great price. Mt 13:45-46.

[30] Parable 14. The net. Mt 13:47-50.

[31] Parable 15. The scribe and homeowner. Mt 13:51-52.

heaven is like a man that is a homeowner, who brings forth out of his treasure things new and old.

4.16 Jesus calms the sea (Sea of Galilee) Mark 4:35-41, Luke 8:22-25, Matthew 8:23-27

Mark 4:35-41	Luke 8:22-25	Matthew 8:23-27
35 And the same day, when it was evening, he said to them, Let us pass over to the other side.	22 Now it happened on a certain day, that he went into a ship with his disciples: and he said to them, Let us go over to the other side of the lake. And they launched forth.	23 And when he had entered into a ship, his disciples followed him.
36 And when they had sent the multitude away, they took him as the way he was in the ship. And there were also with him other little ships.		
37 And there arose a great wind storm, and the waves beat on the ship, so that it was now full.	23 But as they sailed he fell asleep: and there came down a storm of wind on the lake; and they were filled with water, and were in jeopardy.	24 And, look, there arose a great tempest in the sea, so much so that the ship was covered with the waves: but he was asleep.
38 And he was in the hinder part of the ship, asleep on a pillow: and they woke him up, and said to him, Master, do you not care that we perish?	24a And they came to him, and woke him, saying, Master, master, we perish.	25 And his disciples came to him, and woke him, saying, Lord, save us: we perish.
39 And he arose, and rebuked the wind, and said to the sea, Peace, be still. And the wind ceased, and there was a great calm.	24b Then he arose, and rebuked the wind and the raging of the water, and they ceased, and there was calm.	26b Then he arose, and rebuked the winds and the sea; and there was a great calm.
40 And he said to them, Why are you so fearful? How is it that you have no faith?	25a And he said to them, Where is your faith?	26a And he said to them, Why are you fearful, O you of little faith?
41 And they feared exceedingly, and said one to another, What manner of man is this, that even the wind and the sea obey him?	25b-d And they being afraid wondered, saying one to another, What manner of man is this! For he commands even the winds and water, and they obey	27 But the men marvelled, saying, What manner of man is this, that even the winds and the sea obey him!

	him.	

4.17 Heals Gadarene with an unclean spirit (East shore of Galilee) Mark 5:1-20, Luke 8:26-39, Matthew 8:28-34

Mark 5:1-2	Luke 8:26-27	Matthew 8:28-34
[32]1 And they came over to the other side of the sea, into the country of the Gadarenes.		
2 And when he had come out of the ship, immediately there met him out of the tombs a man with an unclean spirit,	26 And they arrived at the country of the Gadarenes, which is over against Galilee. 27 And when he came to land, there met him out of the city a certain man, who had had devils for a long time, and wore no clothes, neither lived in any house, but in the tombs.	28 And when he was come to the other side into the country of the Gergesenes, there met him two possessed with devils, coming out of the tombs, exceeding fierce, so that no man might pass by that way.

Mark 5:3-6
3 Who had his dwelling among the tombs; and no man could bind him, no, not with chains:
4 Because he had often been bound with fetters and chains, and the chains had been pulled apart by him, and the fetters broken in pieces: neither could any man tame him.
5 And always, night and day, he was in the mountains, and in the tombs, crying, and cutting himself with stones.
6 But when he saw Jesus afar off, he ran and worshipped him,

Mark 5:7-15	Luke 8:28-35	Matthew 8:29-34
7 And cried with a loud voice, and said, What have I to do with you, Jesus, you Son of the most high God? I adjure you by God, that you torment me not.	28 When he saw Jesus, he cried out, and fell down before him, and with a loud voice said, What have I to do with you, Jesus, you Son of God most high? I beg you, do not torment me.	29 And, look, they cried out, saying, What have we to do with you, Jesus, you Son of God? Have you come here to torment us before the time?
8 For he said to him, Come out of the man, you unclean spirit.	29 (For he had commanded the unclean spirit to come out of the	

---

[32] Healing miracle 15 (of 37). Gadarene with an unclean spirit. Mr 5:1-20, Lu 8:26-39, Mt 8:28-34.

	man. For often it had caught him: and he was kept bound with chains and in fetters; and he broke the bands, and was driven by the devil into the wilderness.)	
9 And he asked him, What is your name? And he answered, saying, My name is Legion: for we are many.	30 And Jesus asked him, saying, What is your name? And he said, Legion: because many devils had entered into him.	
10 And he begged him a lot that he would not send them away out of the country.	31 And they begged him that he would not command them to go out into the deep.	
11 Now there was there near to the mountains a great herd of swine feeding. 12 And all the devils begged him, saying, Send us into the swine, that we may enter into them.	32 And there was a herd of many swine feeding on the mountain there: and they begged him that he would permit them to enter into them. And he permitted them.	30 And there was a good way off from them a herd of many swine feeding. 31 So the devils begged him, saying, If you cast us out, permit us to go away into the herd of swine.
13 And immediately Jesus gave them leave. And the unclean spirits went out, and entered into the swine: and the herd ran violently down a steep place into the sea, (they were about two thousand;) and were drowned in the sea.	33 Then the devils went out of the man, and entered into swine: and the herd ran violently down a steep place into the lake, and were drowned.	32 And he said to them, Go. And when they were come out, they went into the herd of swine: and, look, the whole herd of swine ran violently down a steep place into the sea, and perished in the waters.
14 And those who fed the swine fled, and told it in the city, and in the country. And they went out to see what had been done.	34 When those who fed them saw what was done, they fled, and went and told it in the city and in the country.	33 And those who kept them fled, and went their way into the city, and told everything, and what had happened to those possessed of the devils.
15 And they came to Jesus, and saw he who had been possessed with the devil, and had the legion, sitting, and clothed, and in his right mind: and they were afraid.	35 Then they went out to see what was done; and came to Jesus, and found the man, out of whom the devils had departed, sitting at the feet of Jesus, clothed, and in his right mind:	34 And, look, the whole city came out to meet Jesus: and when they saw him, they begged him that he would depart out of their coasts.

	and they were afraid.	

Mark 5:16-20	Luke 8:36-39
16 And those who saw it told them what had happened to he who was possessed with the devil, and also concerning the swine.	36 Those who also saw it told them how he who was possessed of the devils was healed.
17 And they began to pray him to depart out of their coasts.	37 Then the whole multitude of the country of the Gadarenes round about begged him to depart from them; for they were greatly afraid: and he went up into the ship, and returned to where he came from.
18 And when he had come into the ship, he who had been possessed with the devil prayed him that he might be with him.	38 Now the man out of whom the devils had departed begged him that he might be with him: but Jesus sent him away, saying,
19 However Jesus did not permit him, but said to him, Go home to your friends, and tell them what great things the Lord has done for you, and has had compassion on you.	39 Return to your house, and show what great things God has done for you. And he went his way, and proclaimed throughout the whole city what great things Jesus had done for him.
20 And he departed, and began to proclaim in Decapolis what great things Jesus had done for him: and everyone marvelled.	

4.18 Heals woman with flow of blood and raises Jairus' dead daughter (Galilee) Mark 5:21-43, Luke 8:40-56, Matthew 9:18-26

Mark 5:21-43	Luke 8:40-56	Matthew 9:18-26
21 And when Jesus had passed over again by ship to the other side, many people gathered to him: and he was near to the sea.	40 And it happened, that, when Jesus had returned, the people gladly received him: for they were all waiting for him.	
22 And, look, there came one of the rulers of the synagogue, Jairus by name; and when he saw him, he fell at his feet,	41 And, look, there came a man named Jairus, and he was a ruler of the synagogue: and he fell down at Jesus' feet, and begged him that he would come into his house:	18 While he spoke these things to them, look, there came a certain ruler, and worshipped him, saying, My daughter is even now dead: but come and lay your hand upon her, and she shall live.
23 And begged him greatly, saying, My little daughter lies at	42 For he had only one daughter, about twelve years of	19 And Jesus rose, and followed him, and so did his disciples.

the point of death: I beg you, come and lay your hands on her, that she may be healed; and she shall live.	age, and she lay dying. But as he went the people crowded him.	
24 And Jesus went with him; and many people followed him, and thronged him.		
[33]25 And a certain woman, which had a flow of blood for twelve years,	43 And a woman having a flow of blood twelve years, who had spent all her living upon physicians, neither could be healed by any,	20a And, look, a woman, who was diseased with a flow of blood twelve years,
26 And had suffered many things of many physicians, and had spent all that she had, and was no better, but rather grew worse,		
27 When she had heard of Jesus, came in the crowd that pressed behind him, and touched his garment.	44a Came behind him, and touched the border of his garment:	20b came behind him, and touched the hem of his garment:
28 For she said, If I may touch but his clothes, I shall be whole.		21 For she said within herself, If I may but touch his garment, I shall be whole.
29 And straightaway the fountain of her blood was dried up; and she felt in her body that she was healed of the disease.	44 b and immediately her flow of blood stopped.	
30 And Jesus, immediately knowing in himself that power had gone out of him, turned around in the crowd, and said, Who touched my clothes?	45 And Jesus said, Who touched me? When all denied, Peter and those who were with him said, Master, the multitude crowd you and press you, and you are asking, Who touched me?	
31 And his disciples said to him, You see the multitude thronging you, and you are	46 And Jesus said, Somebody has touched me: for I perceive that power is gone out of me.	

---

[33] Healing miracle 16 (of 37). Woman with a flow of blood. Mr 5:25-34, Lu 8:43-48, Mt 9:20-22.

asking, Who touched me?		
32 And he looked around to see her who had done this thing.		22a-b But Jesus turned about, and when he saw her,
33 But the woman fearing and trembling, knowing what had happened in her, came and fell down before him, and told him all the truth.	47 And when the woman saw that she could not hide, she came trembling, and falling down before him, she declared to him before all the people her reason for touching him, and how she was healed immediately.	
[34]34 And he said to her, Daughter, your faith has made you whole; go in peace, and be whole of your disease.	48 And he said to her, Daughter, be of good comfort: your faith has made you whole; go in peace.	22c-e he said, Daughter, be of good comfort; your faith has made you whole. And the woman was made whole from that hour.
[35]35 While he was still speaking, there came from the ruler of the synagogue's house some who said, Your daughter is dead: why trouble the Master any further?	49 While he was still speaking, there came one from the ruler of the synagogue's house, saying to him, Your daughter is dead; do not trouble the Master.	
36 As soon as Jesus heard the word that was spoken, he said to the ruler of the synagogue, Do not be afraid, only believe.	50 But when Jesus heard it, he answered him, saying, Do not be afraid: only believe, and she shall be made whole.	
37 And he did not permit any one to follow him, except Peter, and James, and John the brother of James.	51 And when he came into the house, he did not permit any man to go in, save Peter, and James, and John, and the father and the mother of the maiden.	
38 And he came to the house of the ruler of the synagogue, and saw the tumult, and those who wept and wailed greatly.	52 And all wept, and bewailed her: but he said, Do not weep; she is not dead, but is sleeping.	23 And when Jesus came into the ruler's house, and saw the minstrels and the people making a noise,

---

[34] Your faith has made you well (according to your faith) 2 (of 8). Mr 5:34, Lu 8:48, Mt 9:22

[35] Healing miracle 17 (of 37). Jairus' dead daughter. Mr 5:21-24, 35-43, Lu 8:40-42, 49-56, Mt 9:18-19, 23-26.

39 And when he had come in, he said to them, Why do you make this ado, and weep? The young girl is not dead, but is sleeping.		24a.b He said to them, Give place: for the maid is not dead, but is sleeping.
40 And they laughed him to scorn. But when he had put them all out, he took the father and the mother of the young girl, and those who were with him, and went in to where the young girl was lying.	53 And they laughed him to scorn, knowing that she was dead. 54a And he put them all out,	24c And they laughed him to scorn. 25a But when the people were put forth,
41 And he took the young girl by the hand, and said to her, Talitha cumi; which is, being interpreted, Young girl, I say to you, arise.	54b, c and took her by the hand, and called, saying, Maid, arise.	25b he went in, and took her by the hand,
42 And straightaway the damsel arose, and walked; for she was twelve years old. And they were astonished with a great astonishment.	55 And her spirit came again, and she arose straightaway: and he commanded to give her meat.	25c and the maid arose.
43 And he charged them strictly that no man should know it; and commanded that something should be given her to eat.	56 And her parents were astonished: but he charged them that they should tell no man what was done.	
		26 And the fame of this event went abroad into all that land.

4.19 Heals two blind men Matthew 9:27-31

Matthew 9:27-31

[36]**27** And when Jesus departed from there, two blind men followed him, crying, and saying, Son of David, have mercy on us.

28 And when he had come into the house, the blind men came to him: and Jesus said to them, Do you believe that I am able to do this? They said to him, Yes, Lord.

[37]**29** Then he touched their eyes, saying, According to your faith be it to you.

30 And their eyes were opened; and Jesus strictly charged them, saying, See that no man knows it.

---

[36] Healing miracle 18 (of 37). Two blind men. Mt 9:27-31.

[37] According to your faith… 3 (of 8). Mt 9:29.

31 But when they were departed, they spread abroad his fame in all that country.

4.20 Heals mute devil-possessed man Matthew 9:32-34

Matthew 9:32-34

[38]32 As they went out, look, they brought to him a dumb man possessed with a devil.

33 And when the devil was cast out, the dumb spoke: and the multitudes marvelled, saying, This has never been seen in Israel.

34 But the Pharisees said, He casts out devils through the prince of the devils.

4.21 Second rejection in Nazareth (Nazareth) Mark 6:1-6, Matthew 13:53-58

Mark 6:1-6	Matthew 13:53-58
1 And he went out from there, and came into his own country; and his disciples followed him.	53 And it happened, that when Jesus had finished these parables, he departed from there.
2 And when the Sabbath had come, he began to teach in the synagogue: and many hearing him were astonished, saying, Where did this man get these things? And what wisdom is this which is given to him, that even such mighty works are done by his hands?	54 And when he was come into his own country, he taught them in their synagogue, so much so that they were astonished, and said, Where did this man get this wisdom, and these mighty works?
3 Is this not the carpenter, the son of Mary, the brother of James, and Joses, and of Juda, and Simon? And are not his sisters here with us? And they were offended at him.	55 Is this not the carpenter's son? Is not his mother called Mary? And his brethren, James, and Joses, and Simon, and Judas? 56 And his sisters, are they not all with us? Where then did this man get all these things?
4 But Jesus said to them, A prophet is not without honour, but in his own country, and among his own kin, and in his own house.	57 And they were offended in him. But Jesus said to them, A prophet is not without honour, except in his own country, and in his own house.
[39]5 And he could do no mighty work there, except that he laid his hands upon a few sick folk, and healed them.	58 And he did not do many mighty works there because of their unbelief.
6 And he marvelled because of their unbelief. And he went round about the villages, teaching.	

---

[38] Healing miracle 19 (of 37). Dumb, devil-possessed man. Mt 9:32-34.

[39] Healing miracle 20 (of 37). Few sick people in Nazareth. Mr 6:1-6, Mt 13:53-58.

5: Third tour of Galilee

5.01 Preaching, teaching and healing Matthew 9:35-38

Matthew 9:35-38

[40]**35** And Jesus went about all the cities and villages, teaching in their synagogues, and preaching the gospel of the kingdom, and healing every sickness and every disease among the people.

36 But when he saw the multitudes, he was moved with compassion on them, because they fainted, and were scattered abroad, as sheep having no shepherd.

37 Then he said to his disciples, The harvest truly is plenteous, but the labourers are few;

38 Therefore, pray to the Lord of the harvest, that he will send forth labourers into his harvest.

5.02 Jesus sends out the twelve Mark 6:7-11, Luke 9:1-5, Matthew 10:1-16

Mark 6:7	Luke 9:1	Matthew 10:1
7 And he called to him the twelve, and began to send them out two and two; and gave them power over unclean spirits;	1 Then he called his twelve disciples together, and gave them power and authority over all devils, and to cure diseases.	[41]1 And when he had called to him his twelve disciples, he gave them power against unclean spirits, to cast them out, and to heal all manner of sickness and all manner of disease.

Matthew 10:2-6
2 Now the names of the twelve apostles are these; The first, Simon, who is called Peter, and Andrew his brother; James the son of Zebedee, and John his brother;
3 Philip, and Bartholomew; Thomas, and Matthew the tax collector; James the son of Alphaeus, and Lebbaeus, whose surname was Thaddaeus;
4 Simon the Canaanite, and Judas Iscariot, who also betrayed him.
5 These twelve Jesus sent forth, and commanded them, saying, Do not go into the way of the Gentiles, and do not enter into any city of the Samaritans:
6 But go rather to the lost sheep of the house of Israel.

Mark 6:8-11	Luke 9:2-5	Matthew 10:7-16
	2 And he sent them to preach the kingdom of God, and to heal the sick.	7 And as you go, preach, saying, The kingdom of heaven is at hand.
		8 Heal the sick, cleanse the

---

[40] Healing miracle 21 (of 37). Multitudes in the cities and villages. Mt 9:35-38.

[41] The disciple's power and authority 2 (of 10). Mt 10:1-16, Mr 6:7-11, Lu 9:1-5.

		lepers, raise the dead, cast out devils: freely you have received, freely give.
8 And commanded them that they should take nothing for their journey, except a staff; no wallet, no bread, no money in their purse:	3 And he said to them, Take nothing for your journey, neither staffs, nor wallet, no bread, no money; do not have two coats each.	9 Do not provide gold, silver, or brass in your purses,
9 Put on sandals; and do not put on two coats.		10 Nor wallet for your journey, neither two coats, neither shoes, nor yet staves: for the workman is worthy of his meat.
10 And he said to them, In wherever you enter into a house, there stay till you depart from that place.	4 And whatever house you enter into, there abide, and from there depart.	11 And into whatever city or town you shall enter, inquire who in it is worthy; and there stay till you go from there.
		12 And when you come into a house, salute it.
		13 And if the house is worthy, let your peace come upon it: but if it is not worthy, let your peace return to you.
11a And whoever shall not receive you, nor hear you, when you depart from there, shake off the dust under your feet for a testimony against them.	5 And whoever will not receive you, when you go out of that city, shake off the very dust from your feet for a testimony against them.	14 And whoever shall not receive you, nor hear your words, when you depart out of that house or city, shake off the dust of your feet.
11b Truly I say to you, It shall be more tolerable for Sodom and Gomorrah in the day of judgment, than for that city.		15 Truly I say to you, It shall be more tolerable for the land of Sodom and Gomorrah in the day of judgment, than for that city.
		16 Look, I send you forth as sheep in the midst of wolves: therefore be wise as serpents, and harmless as doves.

5.03 Further instructions to the twelve Matthew 10:17-42

Matthew 10:17-42

17 But beware of men: for they will deliver you up to the councils, and they will scourge you in their synagogues;

18 And you shall be brought before governors and kings for my sake, for a testimony against them and the Gentiles.

19 But when they deliver you up, do not worry about what to say or how to say it: for what you shall speak shall be given you in that same hour..

20 For it is not you who speaks, but the Spirit of your Father who speaks in you.

21 And brother shall deliver up brother to death, and fathers their children: and children shall rise up against their parents, and cause them to be put to death.

22 And you shall be hated of all men for my name's sake: but he who endures to the end shall be saved.

23 But when they persecute you in this city, flee into another: for truly I say to you, You shall not have gone over the cities of Israel, till the Son of man comes.

24 The disciple is not above his master, nor the servant above his lord.

25 It is enough for the disciple to be as his master, and the servant as his lord. If they have called the master of the house Beelzebub, how much more shall they call those of his household?

26 Therefore do not fear them: for there is nothing covered, that shall not be revealed; and hidden, that shall not be known.

27 What I tell you in darkness, speak in light: and what you hear in the ear, preach upon housetops.

28 And do not fear those who kill the body, but are not able to kill the soul: but rather fear him who is able to destroy both soul and body in hell.

29 Are not two sparrows sold for a farthing? And one of them shall not fall on the ground without your Father.

30 But the very hairs of your head are all numbered.

31 Therefore do not fear, You are of more value than many sparrows.

32 Whoever therefore shall confess me before men, him will I confess also before my Father who is in heaven.

33 But whoever shall deny me before men, him will I also deny before my Father who is in heaven.

34 Do not think that I am come to send peace on earth: I came not to send peace, but a sword.

35 For I am come to set a man at variance against his father, and the daughter against her mother, and the daughter in law against her mother in law.

36 And a man's foes shall be those of his own household.

37 He who loves father or mother more than me is not worthy of me: and he who loves son or daughter more than me is not worthy of me.

38 And he who does not take his cross, and follow after me, is not worthy of me.

39 He who finds his life shall lose it: and he who loses his life for my sake shall find it.

40 He who receives you receives me, and he who receives me receives him who sent me.

41 He who receives a prophet in the name of a prophet shall receive a prophet's reward; and he who

receives a righteous man in the name of a righteous man shall receive a righteous man's reward.
42 And whoever shall give only a drink of a cup of cold water to one of these little ones in the name of a disciple, truly I say to you, he shall by no means lose his reward.

5.04 Activity of Jesus and the twelve Mark 6:12-13, Luke 9:6, Matthew 11:1

Mark 6:12-13	Luke 9:6	Matthew 11:1
		1 And it happened, when Jesus had finished commanding his twelve disciples, he departed from there to teach and to preach in their cities.
[42]12 And they went out, and preached that men should repent.	6 And they departed, and went through the towns, preaching the gospel, and healing everywhere.	
13 And they cast out many devils, and anointed with oil many that were sick, and healed them.		

5.05 Herod beheads John (Galilee) Mark 6:21-29, Matthew 14:6-12

Mark 6:21-29	Matthew 14:6-12
21 And when an opportune day came, that Herod on his birthday made a supper for his lords, high captains, and chiefs of Galilee;	
22 And when the daughter of the said Herodias came in, and danced, and pleased Herod and those who sat with him, the king said to the girl, Ask me for whatever you want, and I will give it to you.	6 But when Herod's birthday was being observed, the daughter of Herodias danced before them, and pleased Herod.
23 And he swore to her, Whatever you shall ask of me, I will give it to you, up to half of my kingdom.	7 Whereupon he promised with an oath to give her whatever she would ask.
24 And she went forth, and said to her mother, What shall I ask? And she said, The head of John	8a And she, being before instructed of her mother, said,

---

[42] The disciple's power and authority 3 (of 10). Mr 6:12-13, Lu 9:6

the Baptist.	
25 And she came in straightaway with haste to the king, and asked, saying, I want you to give me soon on a platter the head of John the Baptist.	8b Give me here John Baptist's head on a platter.
26 And the king was exceedingly sorry; yet for his oath's sake, and for the sake of those who sat with him, he would not reject her.	9 And the king was sorry: nevertheless for the oath's sake, and those who sat with him at meat, he commanded it to be given to her.
27 And immediately the king sent an executioner, and commanded his head to be brought: and he went and beheaded him in prison,	10 And he sent, and beheaded John in the prison.
28 And brought his head on a platter, and gave it to the girl: and the girl gave it to her mother.	11 And his head was brought on a platter, and given to the girl: and she brought it to her mother.
29 And when his disciples heard of it, they came and took up his corpse, and laid it in a tomb.	12 And his disciples came, and took up the body, and buried it, and went and told Jesus.

5.06 Herod thinks Jesus is John resurrected (Galilee) Mark 6:14-16, Luke 9:7-9, Matthew 14:1-2

Mark 6:14-16	Luke 9:7-9	Matthew 14:1-2
14 And king Herod heard of him; (for his name was spread abroad:) and he said, That John the Baptist was risen from the dead, and therefore mighty works do show forth themselves in him.	7 Now Herod the tetrarch heard of all that was done by him: and he was perplexed, because some said, that John had risen from the dead;	1 At that time Herod the tetrarch heard of the fame of Jesus,
15 Others said, That it is Elijah. And others said, That it is a prophet, or as one of the prophets.	8 And of some, that Elijah had appeared; and of others, that one of the old prophets was risen again.	2 And said to his servants, This is John the Baptist; he is risen from the dead; and therefore mighty works do show forth themselves in him.
16 But when Herod heard of it, he said, It is John, whom I beheaded: he is risen from the dead.	9 And Herod said, John have I beheaded: but who is this, of whom I hear such things? And he desired to see him.	

5.07 Return of the twelve, withdrawal and healing the sick (Magadan), Mark 6:30-34, Luke 9:10-11, Matthew 14:13-14, John 6:1-2

Mark 6:30-34	Luke 9:10-11	Matthew 14:13-14	John 6:1-2
[43]30 And the apostles gathered themselves together to Jesus, and told him all things, both what they had done, and what they had taught.	10 And the apostles, when they had returned, told him all that they had done. And he took them, and went aside privately into a desert place belonging to the city called Bethsaida.	13 When Jesus heard of it, he departed from there by ship into a desert place apart: and when the people had heard of it, they followed him on foot out of the cities.	1 After these things Jesus went over the sea of Galilee, which is the sea of Tiberias.
31 And he said to them, Come apart into a desert place, and rest a while: for there were many coming and going, and they had no leisure not even to eat.			
32 And they departed into a desert place by ship privately.			
33 And the people saw them departing, and many knew him, and ran there on foot out of all cities, and got there before them, and came together to him.			
34 And when Jesus, came out, he saw many people, and was moved with compassion toward them, because they were as sheep not having a shepherd: and	11a And the people, when they knew it, followed him:	14 And Jesus went forth, and saw a great multitude, and was moved with compassion toward them, and he healed their sick.	2 And a great multitude followed him, because they saw his miracles which he did on those who were diseased.

[43] Healing miracle 22 (of 37). Multitudes healed. Mr 6:30-34, Lu 9:10-11, Mt 14:13-14, Joh 6:1-2

he began to teach them many things.			
	11b and he received them, and spoke to them of the kingdom of God, and healed those that had need of healing.		

5.08 Jesus feeds five thousand (Magadan) Mark 6:35-44, Luke 9:12-17, Matthew 14:15-21, John 6:3-14

Mark 6:35-44	Luke 9:12-17	Matthew 14:15-21	John 6:3-14
			3 And Jesus went up into a mountain, and there he sat with his disciples.
			4 And the Passover, a feast of the Jews, was near.
35 And when it was now late in the day, his disciples came to him, and said, This is a desert place, and now the time is far passed: 36 Send them away, that they may go into the country round about, and into the villages, and buy themselves bread: for they have nothing to eat.	12 And when the day began to wear away, then the twelve came, and said to him, Send the multitude away, that they may go into the towns and country round about, and lodge, and get food: for we are here in a desert place.	15 And when it was evening, his disciples came to him, saying, This is a desert place, and it is now late; send the multitude away, that they may go into the villages, and buy themselves food.	5 When Jesus then lifted up his eyes, and saw a great company coming to him, he said to Philip, Where shall we buy bread, that these may eat? 6 And this he said to test him: for he himself knew what he would do.
37 He answered and said to them, You give them something to eat. And they said to him, Shall we go and buy two hundred pennies		16 But Jesus said to them, They need not depart; You give them something to eat.	7 Philip answered him, Two hundred pennies worth of bread is not sufficient for them, that every one of them may take a little.

90

worth of bread, and give them to eat?			
38 He said to them, How many loaves do you have? Go and see. And when they knew, they say, Five, and two fishes.	13 But he said to them, You give them something to eat. And they said, We have no more but five loaves and two fishes; except we should go and buy food for all this people.	17 And they said to him, We have here but five loaves, and two fishes. 18 He said, Bring them here to me.	8 One of his disciples, Andrew, Simon Peter's brother, said to him, 9 There is a lad here, who has five barley loaves, and two small fishes: but what are they among so many?
39 And he commanded them to make everyone sit down in groups upon the green grass.	14 For they were about five thousand men. And he said to his disciples, Make them sit down by fifties in a company.	19 And he commanded the multitude to sit down on the grass, and took the five loaves, and the two fishes, and looking up to heaven, he blessed, and broke, and gave the loaves to his disciples, and the disciples to the multitude.	10 And Jesus said, Make the men sit down. Now there was much grass in the place. So the men sat down, in number about five thousand.
40 And they sat down in ranks, by hundreds, and by fifties.	15 And they did so, and made them all sit down.		
41 And when he had taken the five loaves and the two fishes, he looked up to heaven, and blessed, and broke the loaves, and gave them to his disciples to set before them; and he divided the two fishes among all of them.	16 Then he took the five loaves and the two fishes, and looking up to heaven, he blessed and broke them, and gave to the disciples to set before the multitude.		11 And Jesus took the loaves; and when he had given thanks, he distributed to the disciples, and the disciples to those who were sitting down; and likewise of the fishes, as much as they wanted.
42 And they all did eat, and were filled.	17 And they did eat, and were all filled: and of the fragments that remained, twelve baskets were taken up.	20 And they all did eat, and were filled: and they took up of the fragments that remained twelve	12 When they were filled, he said to his disciples, Gather up the fragments that remain, so that nothing is lost.

		baskets full.	
43 And they took up twelve baskets full of the fragments, and of the fishes.			13 Therefore they gathered them together, and filled twelve baskets with the fragments of the five barley loaves, which remained over and above what had been eaten.
44 And those who did eat of the loaves were about five thousand men.		21 And those who had eaten were about five thousand men, beside women and children.	
			14 Then those men, when they had seen the miracle that Jesus did, said, This of a truth is that prophet that should come into the world.

5.09 Walks on the water (Sea of Galilee) Mark 6:45-52, Matthew 14:22-33, John 6:15-21

Mark 6:45-52	Matthew 14:22-33	John 6:15-21
		15 When Jesus therefore perceived that they would come and take him by force, to make him a king, he departed again into a mountain alone by himself.
		16 And when it was now evening, his disciples went down to the sea,
45 And straightaway he constrained his disciples to get into the ship, and to go to the other side, to Bethsaida, while he sent the people away.	22 And straightaway Jesus constrained his disciples to get into a ship, and to go before him to the other side, while he sent the multitudes away.	17 And entered into a ship, and went over the sea toward Capernaum. And it was now dark, and Jesus had not come to them.

46 And when he had sent them away, he departed into a mountain to pray.	23 And when he had sent the multitudes away, he went up into a mountain apart to pray: and when evening came, he was there alone.	
47 And when evening came, the ship was in the middle of the sea, and he alone was on the land.	24 But the ship was now in the middle of the sea, tossed with waves: for the wind was contrary.	18 And the sea rose because of a great wind that blew.
48 And he saw them toiling in rowing; for the wind was contrary to them: and about the fourth watch of the night he came to them, walking upon the sea, and would have passed by them.	25 And in the fourth watch of the night Jesus went to them, walking on the sea.	
49 But when they saw him walking upon the sea, they supposed he was a spirit, and cried out:	26 And when the disciples saw him walking on the sea, they were troubled, saying, It is a spirit; and they cried out for fear.	19 So when they had rowed about twenty five or thirty furlongs [five thousand to six thousand metres], they saw Jesus walking on the sea, and drawing near to the ship: and they were afraid.
50 For they all saw him, and were troubled. And immediately he talked with them, and said to them, Be of good cheer: it is I; do not be afraid.	27 But straightaway Jesus spoke to them, saying, Be of good cheer; it is I; do not be afraid.	20 But he said to them, It is I; do not be afraid.
	28 And Peter answered him and said, Lord, if it is you, tell me to come to you on the water.	
	29 And he said, Come. And when Peter had come down out of the ship, he walked on the water, to go to Jesus.	
	30 But when he saw the wind boisterous, he was afraid; and beginning to sink, he cried out, saying, Lord, save me.	

	31 And immediately Jesus stretched forth his hand, and caught him, and said to him, O you of little faith, why did you doubt?	
51 And he went up to them into the ship; and the wind ceased: and they were greatly amazed in themselves beyond measure, and wondered.	32 And when they had come into the ship, the wind ceased.	21 Then they willingly received him into the ship: and immediately the ship was at the land to which they were going.
52 For they did not consider the miracle of the loaves: for their heart was hardened.		
	33 Then those who were in the ship came and worshipped him, saying, Of a truth you are the Son of God.	

5.10 Heals the sick in Gennesaret (Gennesaret) Mark 6:53-56, Matthew 14:34-36

Mark 6:53-56	Matthew 14:34-36
[44]53 And when they had passed over, they came into the land of Gennesaret, and drew to the shore.	34 And when they were gone over, they came into the land of Gennesaret.
54 And when they had come out of the ship, straightaway they knew him,	35 And when the men of that place had knowledge of him, they sent out into all that country round about, and brought to him all that were diseased;
55 And ran through that whole region round about, and began to carry about in beds those that were sick, where they heard he was.	
56 And wherever he entered, into villages, or cities, or country, they laid the sick in the streets, and begged him that they might touch if it were but the border of his garment: and as many as touched him were made whole.	36 And begged him that they might only touch the hem of his garment: and as many as touched him were made perfectly whole.

---

[44] Healing miracle 23 (of 37). Sick of Gennesaret. Mr 6:53-56, Mt 14:34-36.

5.11 The bread of life (Capernaum) John 6:22-71; 7:1

John 6:22-71

2:20 *en on audio*

22 The day following, when the people who stood on the other side of the sea saw that there was no other boat there, except the one into which his disciples had entered, and that Jesus did not go with his disciples into the boat, but that his disciples had gone away alone;

23 (However, other boats came from Tiberias near the place where they did eat bread, after the Lord had given thanks:)

24 When the people therefore saw that Jesus was not there, nor were his disciples, they also took ships, and came to Capernaum, seeking Jesus.

25 And when they had found him on the other side of the sea, they said to him, Rabbi, when did you come here?

26 Jesus answered them and said, Very Truly, I say to you, You seek me, not because you saw the miracles, but because you did eat of the loaves, and were filled.

27 Do not labour for the meat that perishes, but for that meat which endures to everlasting life, which the Son of man shall give to you: for him has God the Father sealed.

28 Then said they to him, What shall we do, that we might work the works of God?

29 Jesus answered and said to them, This is the work of God, that you believe on him whom he has sent.

30 They therefore said to him, What sign do you show then, that we may see, and believe you? What work do you do?

31 Our fathers did eat manna in the desert; as it is written, He gave them bread from heaven to eat.

32 Then Jesus said to them, Very Truly, I say to you, Moses did not give you that bread from heaven; but my Father gives you the true bread from heaven.

33 For the bread of God is he who comes down from heaven, and gives life to the world.

34 Then they said to him, Lord, forever give us this bread.

35 And Jesus said to them, I am the bread of life: he who comes to me shall never hunger; and he who believes on me shall never thirst.

36 But I said to you, That you also have seen me, and do not believe.

37 All who the Father give me shall come to me; and he who comes to me I will in no wise cast out.

38 For I came down from heaven, not to do my own will, but the will of him who sent me.

39 And this is the will of the Father who has sent me, that of all he has given me I should lose nothing, but should raise it up again at the last day.

40 And this is the will of him who sent me, that everyone who sees the Son, and believes on him, may have everlasting life: and I will raise him up at the last day.

41 The Jews then murmured at him, because he said, I am the bread which came down from heaven.

42 And they said, Is not this Jesus, the son of Joseph, whose father and mother we know? How is it then that he says, I came down from heaven?

43 Jesus therefore answered and said to them, Do not murmur among yourselves.

44 No man can come to me, except the Father who has sent me draws him: and I will raise him up at the

last day.

45 It is written in the prophets, And they shall be all taught of God. Every man therefore that has heard, and has learned of the Father, comes to me.

46 Not that any man has seen the Father, except he who is of God, he has seen the Father.

47 Very Truly, I say to you, He who believes on me has everlasting life.

48 I am that bread of life.

49 Your fathers did eat manna in the wilderness, and are dead.

50 This is the bread who comes down from heaven, that a man may eat of it, and not die.

51 I am the living bread who came down from heaven: if any man eats of this bread, he shall live forever: and the bread that I will give is my flesh, which I will give for the life of the world.

52 The Jews therefore strove among themselves, saying, How can this man give us his flesh to eat?

53 Then Jesus said to them, Very Truly, I say to you, Except you eat the flesh of the Son of man, and drink his blood, you have no life in you.

54 Whoever eats my flesh, and drinks my blood, has eternal life; and I will raise him up at the last day.

55 For my flesh is meat indeed, and my blood is drink indeed.

56 He who eats my flesh, and drinks my blood, dwells in me, and I in him.

57 As the living Father has sent me, and I live by the Father: so he who eats me, even he shall live by me.

58 This is that bread who came down from heaven: not as your fathers did eat manna, and are dead: he who eats of this bread shall live forever.

59 These things he said in the synagogue, as he taught in Capernaum.

60 Therefore many of his disciples, when they had heard this, said, This is a hard saying; who can receive it?

61 When Jesus knew in himself that his disciples murmured at it, he said to them, Does this offend you?

62 And what if you shall see the Son of man ascend up where he was before?

63 It is the spirit that quickens; the flesh profits nothing: the words that I speak to you, they are spirit, and they are life.

64 But there are some of you that do not believe. For Jesus knew from the beginning who they were that did not believe, and who should betray him.

65 And he said, Therefore I said to you, that no man can come to me, except it were given to him of my Father.

66 From that time many of his disciples went back, and no more walked with him.

67 Then said Jesus to the twelve, Will you also go away?

68 Then Simon Peter answered him, Lord, to whom shall we go? You have the words of eternal life.

69 And we believe and are sure that you are that Christ, the Son of the living God.

70 Jesus answered them, Have not I chosen you twelve, and one of you is a devil?

71 He spoke of Judas Iscariot the son of Simon: for it was he who should betray him, being one of the twelve.

John 7:1

1 After these things Jesus walked in Galilee: for he would not walk in Jewry, because the Jews sought to kill him.

5.12 Jesus attacks Pharisaic traditions (Capernaum) Mark 7:1-23, Matthew 15:1-20

Mark 7:1-2	Matthew 15:1-2
1 Then the Pharisees and some of the scribes who came from Jerusalem came together to him.	1 Then scribes and Pharisees who were of Jerusalem, came to Jesus , saying,
2 And when they saw some of his disciples eat bread with defiled, that is to say, with unwashed, hands, they found fault.	2 Why do your disciples transgress the tradition of the elders? For they do not wash their hands when they eat bread.

Mark 7:3-8
3 For the Pharisees, and all the Jews, except they wash their hands often, do not eat, holding the tradition of the elders.
4 And when they come from the market, except they wash, they do not eat. And there are many other things, which they have received and hold, such as the washing of cups, and pots, brass vessels, and of tables.
5 Then the Pharisees and scribes asked him, Why do your disciples not walk according to the tradition of the elders, but eat bread with unwashed hands?
6 He answered and said to them, Well has Isaiah prophesied of you hypocrites, as it is written, This people honour me with their lips, but their heart is far from me.
7 However in vain do they worship me, teaching for doctrines the commandments of men.
8 For laying aside the commandment of God, you hold the tradition of men, as the washing of pots and cups: and many other such like things you do.

Mark 7:9-23	Matthew 15:3-20
9 And he said to them, Full well you reject the commandment of God, that you may keep your own tradition.	3 But he answered and said to them, Why do you also transgress the commandment of God by your tradition?
10 For Moses said, Honour your father and your mother; and, Whoever curses father or mother, let him be put to death:	4 For God commanded, saying, Honour your father and mother: and, He who curses father or mother, let him die the death.
11 But you say, If a man shall say to his father or mother, It is Corban, that is to say, a gift, by whatever you might be profited by me; he shall be free.	5 But you say, Whoever shall say to his father or his mother, It is a gift, by whatever you might be profited by me; 6a And does not honour his father or his mother, he shall be free.

12 And you allow him not to do anything anymore for his father or his mother;	6b Thus you have made the commandment of God of none effect by your tradition.
13 Making the word of God of no effect through your tradition, which you have delivered: and many such like things you do.	
	7 You hypocrites, well did Isaiah prophesy of you, saying,
	8 These people draw near to me with their mouth, and honour me with their lips; but their hearts are far from me.
	9 But in vain they do worship me, teaching for doctrines the commandments of men.
14 And when he had called all the people to him, he said to them, Listen to me every one of you, and understand:	10 And he called the multitude, and said to them, Hear, and understand:
15 There is nothing from without a man, that entering into him can defile him: but the things which come out of him, those are the things that defile the man.	11 It is not that which goes into the mouth defiles a man; but that which comes out of the mouth, this defiles a man.
16 If any man has ears to hear, let him hear.	
	12 Then his disciples came, and said to him, Do you know you that the Pharisees were offended, after they heard this saying?
	13 But he answered and said, Every plant, which my heavenly Father has not planted, shall be rooted up.
	14 Let them alone: they are blind leaders of the blind. And if the blind lead the blind, both shall fall into the ditch.
17 And when he had entered into the house away from the people, his disciples asked him about the parable.	15 Then Peter answered and said to him, Declare to us this parable.
18 And he said to them, Are you also without understanding? Do you not perceive, that anything from without entering into the man, cannot defile him;	16 And Jesus said, Are you also yet without understanding?
19 Because it does not enter into his heart, but into the stomach, and goes out into the waste, thus purifying all that was eaten?	17 Do you not yet understand, that whatever enters the mouth goes into the stomach, and is passed out into the waste?

20 And he said, That which comes out of the man, is what defiles the man.	18 But those things which proceed out of the mouth come forth from the heart; and they defile the man.
21 For from within, out of the heart of men, proceeds evil thoughts, adulteries, fornications, murders,	19 For out of the heart proceed evil thoughts, murders, adulteries, fornications, thefts, false witness, blasphemies:
22 Thefts, covetousness, wickedness, deceit, lasciviousness, an evil eye, blasphemy, pride, foolishness:	20 These are the things which defile a man: but to eat with unwashed hands does not defile a man.
23 All these evil things come from within, and defile the man.	

5.13 Plucks grain on the Sabbath (En route to Phoenicia) Mark 2:23-28, Luke 6:1-5, Matthew 12:1-8

Mark 2:23-28	Luke 6:1-5	Matthew 12:1-8
23 And it happened, that he went through the corn fields on the Sabbath; as they went, his disciples began to pluck the ears of corn.	1 And it happened on the second Sabbath after the first, that he went through the corn fields; and his disciples plucked the ears of corn, and did eat, rubbing them in their hands.	1 At that time Jesus went on the Sabbath through the corn; and his disciples were hungry, and began to pluck the ears of corn, and to eat.
24 And the Pharisees said to him, Look, why are they doing what is not lawful to be done on the Sabbath?	2 And certain of the Pharisees said to them, Why do you do that which is not lawful to do on the Sabbath?	2 But when the Pharisees saw it, they said to him, Look, your disciples do that which is not lawful to do upon the Sabbath.
25 And he said to them, Have you never read what David did, when he had a need, and was hungry, he, and those who were with him?	3 And Jesus answering them said, Have you not read so much as this, what David did, when he himself was hungry, and those who were with him;	3 But he said to them, Have you not read what David did, when he was hungry, and those who were with him;
26 How he went into the house of God in the days of Abiathar the high priest, and ate the showbread, which is not lawful for any to eat, except the priests, and he also gave to those who were with him?	4 How he went into the house of God, and took and ate the showbread, and gave also to those who were with him; which it is not lawful to eat but for the priests alone?	4 How he entered into the house of God, and did eat the showbread, which was not lawful for him to eat, neither for them which were with him, but only for the priests?
27 And he said to them, The		

Sabbath was made for man, and not man for the Sabbath:		
		5 Or have you not read in the law, how on the Sabbath the priests in the temple profane the Sabbath, and are blameless?
		6 But I say to you, That in this place is one greater than the temple.
		7 But if you had known what this means, I will have mercy, and not sacrifice, you would not have condemned the guiltless.
28 Therefore the Son of man is Lord also of the Sabbath.	5 And he said to them, That the Son of man is Lord also of the Sabbath.	8 For the Son of man is Lord even of the Sabbath.

5.14 Heals daughter of Syrophoenician (Phoenicia) Mark 7:24-30, Matthew 15:21-28

Mark 7:24-30	Matthew 15:21-28
24 And from there he got up, and went into the borders of Tyre and Sidon, and entered into a house, and did not want anyone to know it: but he could not be hidden.	[45]21 Then Jesus went away from there, and departed into the coasts of Tyre and Sidon.
25 For a certain woman, whose young daughter had an unclean spirit, heard of him, and came and fell at his feet:	22 And, look, a woman of Canaan came out of the same coasts, and cried to him, saying, Have mercy on me, O Lord, Son of David; my daughter is grievously troubled with a devil.
	23 But he answered her not a word. And his disciples came and begged him, saying, Send her away; for she cries after us.
26 The woman was a Greek, from the Syrophoenician nation; and she begged him that he would cast out the devil out of her daughter.	
	24 But he answered and said, I am not sent but to the lost sheep of the house of Israel.
	25 Then she came and worshipped him, saying,

---

[45] Healing miracle 24 (of 37). Daughter of Syrophoenician woman. Mr 7:24-30, Mt 15:21-28.

	Lord, help me.
27 But Jesus said to her, Let the children first be filled: for it is not right to take the children's bread, and to cast it to the dogs.	26 But he answered and said, It is not right to take the children's bread, and to cast it to dogs.
28 And she answered and said to him, Yes, Lord: yet the dogs under the table eat of the children's crumbs.	27 And she said, Truth, Lord: yet the dogs eat of the crumbs which fall from their masters' table.
29 And he said to her, For this saying go your way; the devil is gone out of your daughter.	[46]**28** Then Jesus answered and said to her, O woman, great is your faith: be it to you even as you will. And her daughter was made whole from that very hour.
30 And when she had come to her house, she found the devil gone out, and her daughter laid upon the bed.	

5.15 Heals many (Decapolis) Mark 7:31, Matthew 15:29-31

Mark 7:31	Matthew 15:29-31
31 And again, departing from the coasts of Tyre and Sidon, he came to the sea of Galilee, through the midst of the coasts of Decapolis.	[47]**29** And Jesus departed from thence, and came near to the sea of Galilee; and went up into a mountain, and sat down there.
	30 And great multitudes came to him, having with them those that were lame, blind, dumb, maimed, and many others, and cast them down at Jesus' feet; and he healed them:
	31 So much so that the multitude wondered, when they saw the dumb speak, the maimed made whole, the lame walk, and the blind see: and they glorified the God of Israel.

5.16 Heals deaf man with speech impediment (Decapolis) Mark 7:32-37

Mark 7:32-37

[48]**32** And they brought to him one that was deaf, and had an impediment in his speech; and they begged him to put his hand on him.

---

[46] According to your faith 4 (of 8). Mt 15:28.

[47] Healing miracle 25 (of 37). Multitudes in Decapolis. Mr 7:31, Mt 15:29-31.

[48] Healing miracle 26 (of 37). Deaf man with speech impediment. Mr. 7:31-37.

33 And he took him aside from the multitude, and put his fingers into his ears, and he spit, and touched his tongue;

34 And looking up to heaven, he sighed, and said to him, Ephphatha, that is, Be opened.

35 And straightaway his ears were opened, and the string of his tongue was loosed, and he spoke plainly.

36 And he commanded them that they should tell no man: but the more he commanded them, the more they widely proclaimed it;

37 And were greatly astonished, saying, He has done all things well: he makes both the deaf to hear, and the dumb to speak.

5.17 Feeds four thousand (Decapolis) Mark 8:1-10, Matthew 15:32-39

Mark 8:1-10	Matthew 15:32-39
1 In those days the multitude being very great, and having nothing to eat, Jesus called his disciples to him, and said to them,	32a Then Jesus called his disciples to him, and said,
2 I have compassion on the multitude, because they have now been with me three days, and have nothing to eat:	32b I have compassion on the multitude, because they continue with me now three days, and have nothing to eat:
3 And if I send them away fasting to their own houses, they will faint by the way: for several of them came from far away.	32c and I will not send them away fasting, lest they faint in the way.
4 And his disciples answered him, From where can a man satisfy these men with bread here in the wilderness?	33 And his disciples said to him, Where should we have so much bread in the wilderness, as to fill so great a multitude?
5 And he asked them, How many loaves do you have? And they said, Seven.	34 And Jesus said to them, How many loaves do you have? And they said, Seven, and a few little fishes.
6 And he commanded the people to sit down on the ground: and he took the seven loaves, and gave thanks, and broke them, and gave to his disciples to set before them; and they did set them before the people.	35 And he commanded the multitude to sit down on the ground.
7 And they had a few small fishes: and he blessed, and commanded to set them also before them.	36 And he took the seven loaves and the fishes, and gave thanks, and broke them, and gave to his disciples, and the disciples to the multitude.
8 So they did eat, and were filled: and they took up of the food that Jesus had broken seven baskets leftover.	37 And they did all eat, and were filled: and they took up of the food that Jesus had broken, leftovers seven baskets full.

9 And those who had eaten were about four thousand: and he sent them away.	38 And those who ate were four thousand men, beside women and children.
10 And straightaway he entered into a ship with his disciples, and came into the parts of Dalmanutha.	39 And he sent away the multitude, and took a ship, and came into the coasts of Magdala.

5.18 Pharisees increase their attack (Magdala) Mark 8:11-12, Matthew 16:1-4

Mark 8:11-12	Matthew 16:1-4
11 And the Pharisees came forward, and began to question with him, seeking of him a sign from heaven, tempting him.	1 The Pharisees also with the Sadducees came, and tempting him, desired him that he would show them a sign from heaven.
	2 He answered and said to them, When it is evening, you say, It will be fair weather: for the sky is red.
	3 And in the morning, It will be foul weather today: for the sky is red and cloudy. O you hypocrites, you can discern the face of the sky; but can you not discern the signs of the times?
12 And he sighed deeply in his spirit, and said, Why does this generation seek after a sign? Truly I say to you, There no sign shall be given to this generation.	4 A wicked and adulterous generation seeks after a sign; and no sign shall be given to it, but the sign of the prophet Jonas. And he left them, and departed.

5.19 Rejects brothers' advice (Galilee) John 7:2-9

John 7:2-9

2 Now the Jews' feast of tabernacles was at hand.

3 His brethren therefore said to him, Depart from here, and go into Judea, that your disciples also may see the works that you do.

4 For there is no man that does anything in secret, and he himself seeks to be known openly. If you do these things, show yourself to the world.

5 For neither did his brethren believe in him.

6 Then Jesus said to them, My time has not yet come: but your time is always ready.

7 The world cannot hate you; but it hates me, because I testify of it, that its works are evil.

8 You go up to this feast: I will not yet go up to this feast; for my time has not yet fully come.

9 When he had said these words to them, he remained still in Galilee.

5.20 Goes to the Feast of Tabernacles (Jerusalem) John 7:10-8:1

John 7:10-8:1

10 But when his family had gone up, then he also went up to the feast, not openly, but as it were in secret.

11 Then the Jews looked for him at the feast, and said, Where is he?

12 And there was a lot of murmuring among the people concerning him: because some said, He is a good man: others said, No; he is not, he deceives the people.

13 Nevertheless no man spoke openly of him for fear of the Jews.

14 Now about the midst of the feast Jesus went up into the temple, and taught.

15 And the Jews marvelled, saying, How is this man so knowledgeable, having never learned?

16 Jesus answered them, and said, My doctrine is not mine, but that of the one who sent me.

17 If any man will do his will, he shall know of the doctrine, whether it is of God, or whether I speak of myself.

18 He who speaks of himself seeks his own glory: but he who seeks the glory of the one who sent him, the same is true, and there is no unrighteousness in him.

19 Did not Moses give you the law, and yet none of you keep the law? Why do you go about to kill me?

20 The people answered and said, You have a devil: who goes about to kill you?

21 Jesus answered and said to them, I have done one work, and you all marvel.

22 Moses therefore gave you circumcision; (not because it is of Moses, but of the fathers;) and on the Sabbath you circumcise a man.

23 If a man on the Sabbath receives circumcision, that the law of Moses should not be broken; are you angry at me, because I have made a man every bit whole on the Sabbath?

24 Do not judge according to appearance, but judge righteously.

25 Then some of them of Jerusalem said, Is this not, whom they seek to kill?

26 But, look, he speaks boldly, and they say nothing to him. Do the rulers know indeed that this is the very Christ?

27 But we know where this man is from: but when Christ comes, no man will know where he is from.

28 Then Jesus cried in the temple as he taught, saying, You both know me, and you know where I am from: and I have not come of myself, but he who sent me is true, whom you do not know.

29 But I know him: for I am from him, and he has sent me.

30 Then they sought to take him: but no man laid hands on him, because his hour had not yet come.

31 And many of the people believed on him, and said, When Christ comes, will he do more miracles than these which this man has done?

32 The Pharisees heard that the people murmured such things about him; and the Pharisees and the chief priests sent officers to seize him.

33 Then Jesus said to them, Yet a little while I am with you, and then I go to him who sent me.

34 You shall seek me, and shall not find me: and where I am, there you cannot come.

35 Then said the Jews among themselves, Where will he go, that we shall not find him? will he go to the dispersed among the Gentiles, and teach the Gentiles?

36 What type of saying is this that he said, You shall seek me, and shall not find me: and where I am, there you cannot come?

37 In the last day, that great day of the feast, Jesus stood and cried, saying, If any man thirsts, let him come to me, and drink.

38 He who believes on me, as the scripture has said, out of his belly shall flow rivers of living water.

39 (But this he spoke of the Spirit, which those who believe on him should receive: for the Holy Spirit was not yet given; because Jesus was not yet glorified.)

40 Many of the people therefore, when they heard this saying, said, Of a truth this is the Prophet.

41 Others said, This is the Christ. But some said, Shall Christ come out of Galilee?

42 Has not the scripture said, That Christ comes of the seed of David, and out of the town of Bethlehem, where David was?

43 So there was a division among the people because of him.

44 And some of them would have seized him; but no man laid hands on him.

45 Then the officers came to the chief priests and Pharisees; and they said to them, Why have you not brought him?

46 The officers answered, No one has ever spoken like this man.

47 Then the Pharisees answered them, Are you also deceived?

48 Have any of the rulers or of the Pharisees believed on him?

49 But this people who do not know the law are cursed.

50 Nicodemus said to them, (he who came to Jesus by night, being one of them,)

51 Does our law judge any man, before it hears him, and knowing what he did?

52 They answered and said to him, Are you also of Galilee? Search, and look: for out of Galilee arises no prophet.

53 And every man went to his own house.

John 8:1 Jesus went to the Mount of Olives.

5.21 Forgives adulteress (Jerusalem) John 8:2 - 11

John 8:2-11

2 And early in the morning he came again into the temple, and all the people came to him; and he sat down, and taught them.

3 And the scribes and Pharisees brought to him a woman taken in adultery; and when they had set her in the midst,

4 They said to him, Master, this woman was taken in adultery, in the very act.

5 Now Moses in the law commanded us, that such should be stoned: but what do you say?

6 This they said, tempting him, that they might have reason to accuse him. But Jesus stooped down, and with his finger wrote on the ground, as though he had not heard them.

7 So when they continued asking him, he lifted up himself, and said to them, He who is without sin

among you, let him first cast a stone at her.

8 And again he stooped down, and wrote on the ground.

9 And those which heard it, being convicted by their own conscience, went out one by one, beginning at the eldest, even to the last: and Jesus was left alone, and the woman standing in the midst.

10 When Jesus had lifted up himself, and saw none but the woman, he said to her, Woman, where are those your accusers? Has no man condemned you?

11 She said, No man, Lord. And Jesus said to her, Neither do I condemn you: go, and sin no more.

6: Third tour continues (Judea and Galilee)

6.01 The light of the world (Jerusalem) John 8:12-20

John 8:12-20

12 Then Jesus spoke again to them, saying, I am the light of the world: he who follows me shall not walk in darkness, but shall have the light of life.

13 The Pharisees therefore said to him, You bear record of yourself; your record is not true.

14 Jesus answered and said to them, Though I bear record of myself, yet my record is true: for I know where I came from, and where I am going; but you cannot tell where I came from, and where I am going.

15 You judge after the flesh; I judge no man.

16 And yet if I judge, my judgment is true: for I am not alone, but I and the Father that sent me.

17 It is also written in your law, that the testimony of two men is true.

18 I am one who bears witness of myself, and the Father who sent me bears witness of me.

19 Then they said to him, Where is your Father? Jesus answered, You neither know me, nor my Father: if you had known me, you should have known my Father also.

20 Jesus spoke these words in the treasury, as he taught in the temple: and no man laid hands on him; for his hour had not yet come.

6.02 Before Abraham was, I am (Jerusalem - Temple) John 8:21-59

John 8:21-59

21 Then Jesus said to them again, I go my way, and you shall seek me, and shall die in your sins: where I go, you cannot come.

22 Then the Jews said, Will he kill himself? Because he said, Where I go, you cannot come.

23 And he said to them, You are from beneath; I am from above: you are of this world; I am not of this world.

24 I therefore said to you, that you shall die in your sins: for if you do not believe that I am he, you shall die in your sins.

25 Then they said to him, Who are you? And Jesus said to them, Even the same person that I said to you from the beginning.

26 I have many things to say and to judge of you: but he who sent me is true; and I speak to the world those things which I have heard of him.

27 They did not understand that he spoke to them of the Father.

28 Then said Jesus to them, When you have lifted up the Son of man, then you shall know that I am he, and that I do nothing of myself; but as my Father has taught me, I speak these things.

29 And he who sent me is with me: the Father has not left me alone; for I always do those things that please him.

30 As he spoke these words, many believed on him. *Authority*

31 Then Jesus said to those Jews who believed on him, If you continue in my word, then you are my disciples indeed;

32 And you shall know the truth, and the truth shall make you free.

33 They answered him, We are Abraham's seed, and were never in bondage to any man: why do you say, You shall be made free?

34 Jesus answered them, Very Truly, I say to you, Whoever commits sin is the servant of sin.

35 And the servant does not abide in the house for ever: but the Son ever abides.

36 If the Son therefore shall make you free, you shall be free indeed.

37 I know that you are Abraham's seed; but you seek to kill me, because my word has no place in you.

38 I speak that which I have seen with my Father: and you do that which you have seen with your father.

39 They answered and said to him, Abraham is our father. Jesus said to them, If you were Abraham's children, you would do the works of Abraham.

40 But now you seek to kill me, a man who has told you the truth, which I have heard of God: Abraham did not do this.

41 You do the deeds of your father. Then they said to him, We were not born of fornication; we have one Father, even God. *Many virgin birth*

42 Jesus said to them, If God were your Father, you would love me: for I proceeded and came from God; neither did I come of myself, but he sent me.

43 Why do you not understand my speech? Even because you cannot hear my word.

44 You are of your father the devil, and the lusts of your father you will do. He was a murderer from the beginning, and did not abide in the truth, because there is no truth in him. When he speaks a lie, he speaks of his own: for he is a liar, and the father of it.

45 And because I tell you the truth, you do not believe.

46 Which of you convicts me of sin? And if I say the truth, why do you not believe me?

47 He who is of God hears God's words: therefore you do not hear them, because you are not of God.

48 Then the Jews answered, and said to him, Did we not say rightly you are a Samaritan, and have a devil?

49 Jesus answered, I do not have a devil; but I honour my Father, and you do dishonour me.

50 And I do not seek my own glory: there is one that seeks and judges.

51 Very Truly, I say to you, If a man keeps my saying, he shall never see death.

52 Then said the Jews to him, Now we know that you have a devil. Abraham is dead, and the prophets; and you say, If a man keeps my saying, he shall never taste of death.

53 Are you greater than our father Abraham, who is dead? And the prophets are dead: who do you make yourself out to be?

54 Jesus answered, If I honour myself, my honour is nothing: it is my Father who honours me; of whom you say, that he is your God:

55 Yet you have not known him; but I know him: and if I should say, I do not know him, I shall be a liar like you: but I know him, and keep his saying.

56 Your father Abraham rejoiced to see my day: and he saw it, and was glad.

57 Then said the Jews to him, you are not yet fifty years old, and have you seen Abraham?

58 Jesus said to them, Very Truly, I say to you, Before Abraham was, I am.

59 Then took they up stones to throw at him: but Jesus hid himself, and went out of the temple, going through their midst, and so passed by.

6.03 Heals a man born blind (Jerusalem) John 9:1-41

John 9:1-41

[49]**1** And as Jesus passed by, he saw a man who was blind from his birth.

2 And his disciples asked him, saying, Master, who did sin, this man, or his parents, that he was born blind?

3 Jesus answered, Neither has this man sinned, nor his parents: but that the works of God should be made manifest in him.

4 I must do the works of him who sent me, while it is day: the night is coming, when no man can work.

5 As long as I am in the world, I am the light of the world.

6 When he had said this, he spat on the ground, and made clay of the spittle, and he anointed the eyes of the blind man with the clay,

7 And said to him, Go, wash in the pool of Siloam, (which is by interpretation, Sent.) He went his way therefore, and washed, and came seeing.

8 Therefore the neighbours, and those who before had seen that he was blind, said, Is this not he who sat and begged?

9 Some said, This is he: others said, He is like him: but he said, I am he.

10 Therefore they said to him, How were your eyes opened?

11 He answered and said, A man that is called Jesus made clay, and anointed mine eyes, and said to me, Go to the pool of Siloam, and wash: and I went and washed, and I received sight.

12 Then said they to him, Where is he? He said, I do not know.

13 They brought to the Pharisees him who was previously blind.

14 And it was the Sabbath when Jesus made the clay, and opened his eyes.

15 Then again the Pharisees also asked him how he had received his sight. He said to them, He put clay

---

[49] Healing Miracle 27 (of 37). Man born blind. Joh 9:1-41.

on my eyes, and I washed, and do see.

16 Therefore some of the Pharisees said, This man is not of God, because he does not keep the Sabbath. Others said, How can a man who is a sinner do such miracles? And there was a division among them.

17 They said to the blind man again, What do you say of him who has opened your eyes? He said, He is a prophet.

18 But the Jews did not believe that he had been blind, and received his sight, until they called the parents of him who had received his sight.

19 And they asked them, saying, Is this your son, who you say was born blind? How then does he now see?

20 His parents answered them and said, We know that this is our son, and that he was born blind:

21 But by what means he now sees, we do not know; or who has opened his eyes, we do not know: he is of age; ask him: he shall speak for himself.

22 His parents spoke these words, because they feared the Jews: for the Jews had agreed already, that if any man did confess that he was Christ, he should be put out of the synagogue.

23 Therefore his parents said, He is of age; ask him.

24 Then again they called the man that was blind, and said to him, Give God the praise: we know that this man is a sinner.

25 He answered and said, Whether he is a sinner or not, I do not know: one thing I know, that, whereas I was blind, now I see.

26 Then said they to him again, What did he to you? How did he open your eyes?

27 He answered them, I have told you already, and you did not hear: why would you hear it again? Will you also be his disciples?

28 Then they reviled him, and said, You are his disciple; but we are Moses' disciples.

29 We know that God spoke to Moses: as for this fellow, we know not where he came from.

30 The man answered and said to them, Why herein is a marvellous thing, that you do not know not where he has come from, and yet he has opened my eyes.

31 Now we know that God does not hear sinners: but if any man is a worshipper of God, and does his will, he hears him.

32 Since the world began it has not been heard that any man opened the eyes of one who was born blind.

33 If this man were not of God, he could do nothing.

34 They answered and said to him, You were altogether born in sins, and do you teach us? And they cast him out.

35 Jesus heard that they had cast him out; and when he had found him, he said to him, Do you believe on the Son of God?

36 He answered and said, Who is he, Lord, that I might believe on him?

37 And Jesus said to him, You have both seen him, and it is he who talks with you.

38 And he said, Lord, I believe. And he worshipped him.

39 And Jesus said, For judgment I have come into this world, that they who do not see might see; and

that they who see might be made blind.

40 And some of the Pharisees who were with him heard these words, and said to him, Are we blind also?

41 Jesus said to them, If you were blind, you should have no sin: but now you say, We see; therefore your sin remains.

6.04 Parable of the Good Shepherd (Jerusalem) John 10:1-21

John 10:1-21

[50]**1** Very Truly, I say to you, He who does not enter by the door into the sheepfold, but climbs up some other way, the same is a thief and a robber.

2 But he who enters in by the door is the shepherd of the sheep.

3 To him the porter opens; and the sheep hear his voice: and he calls his own sheep by name, and leads them out.

4 And when he puts forth his own sheep, he goes before them, and the sheep follow him: for they know his voice.

5 And a stranger they will not follow, but will flee from him: for they do not know the voice of strangers.

6 Jesus spoke this parable to them: but they did not understand what he said to them.

7 Then Jesus said to them again, Very Truly, I say to you, I am the door of the sheep.

8 All who ever came before me are thieves and robbers: but the sheep did not hear them.

9 I am the door: by me if any man enters in, he shall be saved, and shall go in and out, and find pasture.

10 The thief does not come except to steal, and to kill, and to destroy: I have come that they might have life, and that they might have it more abundantly.

11 I am the good shepherd: the good shepherd gives his life for the sheep.

12 But he who is a hireling, and not the shepherd, whose own the sheep are not, sees the wolf coming, and leaves the sheep, and flees: and the wolf catches them, and scatters the sheep.

13 The hireling flees, because he is a hireling, and does not care for the sheep.

14 I am the good shepherd, and know my sheep, and am known of mine.

15 As the Father knows me, even so I know the Father: and I lay down my life for the sheep.

16 And other sheep I have, which are not of this fold: they also I must bring, and they shall hear my voice; and there shall be one fold, and one shepherd.

17 This is why my Father loves me, because I lay down my life, that I might take it again.

18 No man takes it from me, but I lay it down of myself. I have power to lay it down, and I have power to take it again. This commandment I have received of my Father.

19 There was a division therefore again among the Jews for these sayings.

20 And many of them said, He has a devil, and is mad; why do you hear him?

_____

[50] Parable 16. The good shepherd. Joh 10:1-16.

21 Others said, These are not the words of he who has a devil. Can a devil open the eyes of the blind?

6.05 Beware of the leaven on the Pharisees and of Herod Mark 8:13-21, Matthew 16:5-12

Mark 8:13-26	Matthew 16:5-12
13 And he left them, and entering into the ship again departed to the other side.	5 And when his disciples had come to the other side, they had forgotten to take bread.
14 Now the disciples had forgotten to take bread, neither had they in the ship with them more than one loaf.	
15 And he charged them, saying, Take heed, beware of the leaven of the Pharisees, and of the leaven of Herod.	6 Then Jesus said to them, Take heed and beware of the leaven of the Pharisees and of the Sadducees.
16 And they reasoned among themselves, saying, It is because we have no bread.	7 And they reasoned among themselves, saying, It is because we have taken no bread.
17 And when Jesus knew it, he said to them, Why do you reason because you have no bread? Do you not perceive nor understand? Is your heart yet hardened?	8 Which when Jesus perceived, he said to them, O you of little faith, why do you reason among yourselves, because you have brought no bread?
18 Having eyes, do you not see? And having ears, do you not hear? And do you not remember?	
19 When I broke the five loaves among five thousand, how many baskets full of fragments did you take up? They said to him, Twelve.	9 Do you not yet understand, neither remember the five loaves of the five thousand, and how many baskets you took up?
20 And when the seven among four thousand, how many baskets full of fragments did you take up? And they said, Seven.	10 Nor the seven loaves of the four thousand, and how many baskets did you take up?
21 And he said to them, How is it that you do not understand?	11 How is it that you do not understand that I did not speak to you concerning bread, but that you should beware of the leaven of the Pharisees and of the Sadducees?
	12 Then they understood how he told them not to beware of the leaven of bread, but of the doctrine of the Pharisees and of the Sadducees.

6.06 Heals a blind man (Bethsaida) Mark 8:22-26

[51]22 And he came to Bethsaida; and they brought a blind man to him, and begged him to touch him.

23 And he took the blind man by the hand, and led him out of the town; and when he had spit on his eyes, and put his hands upon him, he asked him if he saw anything.

24 And he looked up, and said, I see men as trees, walking.

25 After that he put his hands again upon his eyes, and made him look up: and he was restored, and saw every man clearly.

26 And he sent him away to his house, saying, Neither go into the town, nor tell it to any in the town.

6.07 Peter confesses that Jesus is the Christ (near Caesarea Philippi) Mark 8:27-30, Luke 9:18-21, Matthew 16:13-20

Mark 8:27-29	Luke 9:18-20	Matthew 16:13-16
27 And Jesus went out, and his disciples, into the towns of Caesarea Philippi: and by the way he asked his disciples, saying to them, Who do men say that I am?	18 And it happened, as he was alone praying, his disciples were with him: and he asked them, saying, Who say the people that I am?	13 When Jesus came into the coasts of Caesarea Philippi, he asked his disciples, saying, Who do men say that I the Son of man am?
28 And they answered, John the Baptist: but some say, Elijah; and others, One of the prophets.	19 They answering said, John the Baptist; but some say, Elijah; and others say, that one of the old prophets has risen again.	14 And they said, Some say that you are John the Baptist: some, Elijah; and others, Jeremiah, or one of the prophets.
29a And he said to them, But whom do you say that I am?	20a He said to them, But who do you say that I am?	15 He said to them, But who do you say that I am?
29b And Peter answered and said to him, You are the Christ.	20b Peter answering said, The Christ of God.	16 And Simon Peter answered and said, You are the Christ, the Son of the living God.

Matthew 16:17-20
17 And Jesus answered and said to him, Blessed are you, Simon Bar Jona: for flesh and blood has not revealed it to you, but my Father who is in heaven.
18 And I say also to you, That you are Peter, and upon this rock I will build my church; and the gates of hell shall not prevail against it.
19 And I will give to you the keys of the kingdom of heaven: and whatever you shall bind on earth shall be bound in heaven: and whatever you shall loose on earth shall be loosed in heaven.

---

[51] Healing miracle 28 (of 37). Blind man. Mr 8:22-26.

Mark 8:30	Luke 9:21	Matthew 16:20
30 And he charged them that they should tell no man about him.	21 And he strictly charged them, and commanded them to tell no man that thing;	20 Then he charged his disciples that they should tell no man that he was Jesus the Christ.

6.08 Jesus foretells His death (Caesarea Philippi) Mark 8:31-9:1, Luke 9:22-27, Matthew 16:21-28

Mark 8:31-9:1	Luke 9:22-25	Matthew 16:21-26
31 And he began to teach them, that the Son of man must suffer many things, and be rejected of the elders, and of the chief priests, and scribes, and be killed, and after three days rise again.	22 Saying, The Son of man must suffer many things, and be rejected of the elders and chief priests and scribes, and be slain, and be raised the third day.	21 From that time forth began Jesus to show to his disciples, how he must go to Jerusalem, and suffer many things of the elders and chief priests and scribes, and be killed, and be raised again the third day.
32 And he spoke that saying openly. And Peter took him, and began to rebuke him.		22 Then Peter took him, and began to rebuke him, saying, Far be it from you, Lord: this shall not happen to you.
33 But when he had turned about and looked on his disciples, he rebuked Peter, saying, You get behind me, Satan: for you do not mind the things that be of God, but the things that are of men.		23 But he turned, and said to Peter, You get behind me, Satan: you are an offence to me: for you do not mind the things that are of God, but those that are of men.
34 And when he had called the people to him with his disciples also, he said to them, Whoever will come after me, let him deny himself, and take up his cross, and follow me.	23 And he said to them all, If any man will come after me, let him deny himself, and take up his cross daily, and follow me.	24 Then Jesus said to his disciples, If any man will come after me, let him deny himself, and take up his cross, and follow me.
35 For whoever will save his life shall lose it; but whoever shall lose his life for my sake and the gospel's, the same shall save it.	24 For whoever will save his life shall lose it: but whoever will lose his life for my sake, the same shall save it.	25 For whoever will save his life shall lose it: and whoever will lose his life for my sake shall find it.

36 For what shall it profit a man, if he shall gain the whole world, and lose his own soul? 37 Or what shall a man give in exchange for his soul?	25 For what is a man advantaged, if he gains the whole world, and loses himself, or is cast away?	26 For what is a man profited, if he shall gain the whole world, and lose his own soul? Or what shall a man give in exchange for his soul?
38 Whoever therefore shall be ashamed of me and of my words in this adulterous and sinful generation; of him also shall the Son of man be ashamed, when he comes in the glory of his Father with the holy angels.	26 For whoever shall be ashamed of me and of my words, of him shall the Son of man be ashamed, when he shall come in his own glory, and in his Father's, and of the holy angels.	27 For the Son of man shall come in the glory of his Father with his angels; and then he shall reward every man according to his works.
1 And he said to them, Truly I say to you, That there are some of those who stand here, which shall not taste of death, till they have seen the kingdom of God come with power.	27 But I tell you of a truth, there are some standing here, who shall not taste of death, till they see the kingdom of God.	28 Truly I say to you, There are some standing here, who shall not taste of death, till they see the Son of man coming in his kingdom.

6.09 The transfiguration (Mount Hermon) Mark 9:2-13, Luke 9:28-36, Matthew 17:1-13

Mark 9:2-7	Luke 9:28-36	Matthew 17:1-9
2 And after six days Jesus took with him Peter, and James, and John, and led them up to a high mountain apart by themselves: and he was transfigured before them.	28 And it happened about eight days after these sayings, he took Peter and John and James, and went up to a mountain to pray.	1 And after six days Jesus took Peter, James, and John his brother, and brought them up into a high mountain apart,
3 And his clothing became shining, exceeding white as snow; so as no launderer on earth can whiten them.	29 And as he prayed, his countenance was altered, and his raiment was white and glistering.	2 And was transfigured before them: and his face did shine as the sun, and his raiment was white as the light.
4 And there appeared to them Elijah with Moses: and they were talking with Jesus.	30 And, look, there talked with him two men, which were Moses and Elijah:	3 And, look, there appeared to them Moses and Elijah talking with him.
	31 Who appeared in glory, and spoke of his decease which he should accomplish at Jerusalem.	

114

	32 But Peter and those that were with him were heavy with sleep: and when they had woken up, they saw his glory, and the two men that stood with him.	*man of action*
5 And Peter answered and said to Jesus, Master, it is good for us to be here: and let us make three tabernacles; one for you, and one for Moses, and one for Elijah. 6 For he did not know what to say; for they were very afraid.	33 And it happened, as they departed from him, Peter said to Jesus, Master, it is good for us to be here: and let us make three tabernacles; one for you, and one for Moses, and one for Elijah: not knowing what he said.	4 Then Peter answered, and said to Jesus, Lord, it is good for us to be here: if you will, let us make here three tabernacles; one for you, and one for Moses, and one for Elias.
7 And there was a cloud that overshadowed them: and a voice came out of the cloud, saying, This is my beloved Son: hear him.	34 While he was still speaking, there came a cloud, and overshadowed them: and they feared as they entered into the cloud.	5 While he yet spoke, look, a bright cloud overshadowed them: and look a voice out of the cloud, which said, This is my beloved Son, in whom I am well pleased; you hear him.
	35 And there came a voice out of the cloud, saying, This is my beloved Son: hear him.	
		6 And when the disciples heard it, they fell on their face, and were very afraid.
		7 And Jesus came and touched them, and said, Arise, and do not be afraid.
8 And suddenly, when they had looked around, they saw no man any more, except Jesus with them.	36a And when the voice had receded, Jesus was found alone.	8 And when they had lifted up their eyes, they saw no man, except Jesus only.
9 And as they came down from the mountain, he charged them that they should tell no man what they had seen, till the Son of man had risen from the dead.	36b And they kept it close, and told no man in those days any of those things which they had seen.	9 And as they came down from the mountain, Jesus charged them, saying, Tell the vision to no man, until the Son of man has risen again from the dead.

Mark 9:10-13	Matthew 17:10-13
10 And they kept that saying to themselves, questioning with one another what the rising from the dead meant.	
11 And they asked him, saying, Why did the scribes say that Elijah must first come?	10 And his disciples asked him, saying, Why then did the scribes say that Elijah must first come?
12 And he answered and told them, Elijah truly comes first, and restores all things; and how it is written of the Son of man, that he must suffer many things, and be brought to nothing.	11 And Jesus answered and said to them, Elijah truly shall first come, and restore all things.
13 But I say to you, That Elijah has indeed come, and they have done to him whatever they wanted, as it was written of him.	12 But I say to you, That Elijah has come already, and they did not know him, but have done to him whatever they wanted. Likewise shall the Son of man suffer at their hands.
	13 Then the disciples understood that he spoke to them of John the Baptist.

6.10 Heals dumb boy possessed by an unclean spirit (foot of Mount Hermon) Mark 9:14-29, Luke 9:37-42, Matthew 17:14-21

Mark 9:14-29	Luke 9:37-42	Matthew 17:14-21
[52]14 And when he came to his disciples, he saw a great multitude about them, and the scribes questioning them.		
15 And straightaway all the people, when they saw him, were greatly amazed, and running to him greeted him.	37 And it happened, that on the next day, when they had come down from the hill, many people met him.	
16 And he asked the scribes, What are you asking them?		
17 And one of the multitude answered and said, Master, I have brought you my son, who has a dumb spirit;	38 And, look, a man of the company cried out, saying, Master, I beg you, look upon my son: for he is my only child.	14 And when they were come to the multitude, there came to him a certain man, kneeling down to him, and saying,

---

[52] Healing miracle 29 (of 37). Dumb and deaf boy with unclean spirit. Mr 9:14-29, Lu 9:37-42, Mt 17:14-21.

18a. b And wherever he takes him, he tears him: and he foams, and gnashes with his teeth, and pines away:	39 And, look, a spirit takes him, and he suddenly cries out; and it tears him that he foams again, and bruising him hardly departs from him.	15 Lord, have mercy on my son: for he is lunatic, and greatly vexed: for oftentimes he falls into the fire, and often into the water.
18c, d and I spoke to your disciples that they should cast him out; and they could not.	40 And I begged your disciples to cast him out; and they could not.	16 And I brought him to your disciples, and they could not cure him.
[53]**19** He answered him, and said, O faithless generation, how long shall I be with you? How long shall I put up with you? Bring him to me.	41 And Jesus answering said, O faithless and perverse generation, how long shall I be with you, and put up with you? Bring your son here.	17 Then Jesus answered and said, O faithless and perverse generation, how long shall I be with you? How long shall I put up with you? Bring him here to me.
20 And they brought him to him: and when he saw him, straightaway the spirit tore him; and he fell on the ground, and wallowed foaming.	42a And as he was still coming, the devil threw him down, and tore him.	
21 And he asked his father, How long has this been happening to him? And he said, Since childhood.		
22 And often it has cast him into the fire, and into the waters, to destroy him: but if you can do anything, have compassion on us, and help us.		
[54]**23** Jesus said to him, If you can believe, all things are possible to him who believes.		
24 And straightaway the father of the child cried out, and said with tears, Lord, I believe; help mine unbelief.		

[53] The disciple's power and authority (faithless and perverse generation) 4 (of 10). Mr 9:14-19, Lu 9:27-41, Mt 17:14-17

[54] If you can believe … (according to your faith) 5 (of 8). Mr 9:23-24

25 When Jesus saw that the people came running together, he rebuked the foul spirit, saying to him, You dumb and deaf spirit, I charge you, come out of him, and do not enter him anymore.	42b And Jesus rebuked the unclean spirit,	18a And Jesus rebuked the devil;
26 And the spirit cried, and tore him greatly, and came out of him: and he was as one dead; so much so that many said, He is dead.		18 b and he departed out of him:
27 But Jesus took him by the hand, and lifted him up; and he arose.	42c and healed the child, and delivered him again to his father.	18c and the child was cured from that very hour.
[55]28 And when he had come into the house, his disciples asked him privately, Why could we not cast him out?		19 Then the disciples came to Jesus apart, and said, Why could we not cast him out?
		20 And Jesus said to them, Because of your unbelief: for truly I say to you, If you have faith as a grain of mustard seed, you shall say to this mountain, Move from here to there; and it shall move; and nothing shall be impossible to you.
29 And he said to them, This kind can come forth by nothing, but by prayer and fasting.		21 Howbeit this kind does not go out except by prayer and fasting.

6.11 Jesus tells of His death and resurrection (Galilee) Mark 9:30-32, Luke 9:43-45, Matthew 17:22, 23

Mark 9:30-32	Luke 9:43-45	Matthew 17:22-23
30 And they departed from there, and passed through Galilee; and he did not want any	43 And they were all amazed at the mighty power of God. But while everyone wondered at all	22a And while they abode in Galilee, Jesus said to them,

---

[55] The disciple's power and authority 5 (of 10). Mr 9:28, Mt 17:20, 21

man to know it.	things which Jesus did, he said to his disciples,	
31 For he taught his disciples, and said to them, The Son of man will be delivered into the hands of men, and they shall kill him; and after he has been killed, he shall rise the third day.	44 Let these sayings sink down into your ears: for the Son of man shall be delivered into the hands of men.	22b The Son of man shall be betrayed into the hands of men: 23 And they shall kill him, and the third day he shall be raised again. And they were exceedingly sorry.
32 But they did not understand that saying, and were afraid to ask him.	45 But they did not understand, and it was hidden from them, that they did not perceive: and they feared to ask him about that saying.	

6.12 Pays tribute money (Capernaum) Matthew 17:24-27

Matthew 17:24-27

24 And when they had come to Capernaum, those who receive tribute money came to Peter, and said, Does not your master pay tribute?

25 He said, Yes. And when he had come into the house, Jesus met him, saying, What do you think, Simon? Of whom do the kings of the earth take custom or tribute? Of their own children, or of strangers?

26 Peter said to him, Of strangers. Jesus said to him, Then are the children free.

27 Notwithstanding, lest we should offend them, you go to the sea, and cast a hook, and take up the fish that first comes up; and when you have opened his mouth, you shall find a piece of money: take it, and give to them for you and me.

6.13 Who is the greatest? (Capernaum) Mark 9:33-50, Luke 9:46-50, Matthew 18:1-11

Mark 9:33-39	Luke 9:46-50	Matthew 18:1-5
33 And he came to Capernaum: and being in the house he asked them, What was it that you disputed among yourselves along the way?		
34 But they kept quiet: for by the way they had disputed among themselves, who should	46 Then there arose a reasoning among them, which of them should be greatest.	1 At the same time the disciples came to Jesus, saying, Who is the greatest in the kingdom of

be the greatest.		heaven?
35 And he sat down, and called the twelve, and said to them, If any man desire to be first, the same shall be last of all, and servant of all.		
36 And he took a child, and set him in the midst of them: and when he had taken him in his arms, he said to them,	47 And Jesus, perceiving the thought of their heart, took a child, and set him by him,	2 And Jesus called a little child to him, and set him in their midst,
		3 And said, Truly I say to you, Except you are converted, and become as little children, you shall not enter into the kingdom of heaven.
		4 Whoever therefore shall humble himself as this little child, the same is greatest in the kingdom of heaven.
37 Whoever shall receive one of such children in my name, receives me: and whoever shall receive me, receives not me, but he who sent me.	48 And said to them, Whoever shall receive this child in my name receives me: and whoever shall receive me receives him who sent me: for he who is least among you all, the same shall be great.	5 And whoso shall receive one such little child in my name receives me.
38 And John answered him, saying, Master, we saw one casting out devils in your name, and he does not follow us: and we forbade him, because he does not follow us.	49 And John answered and said, Master, we saw one casting out devils in your name; and we forbade him, because he does not follow us.	
39 But Jesus said, Do not forbid him: for there is no man who shall do a miracle in my name, that can lightly speak evil of me.	50 And Jesus said to him, Forbid him not: for he who is not against us is for us.	

Mark 9:40-50	Matthew 18:6-11
40 For he who is not against us is for us.	

41 For whoever shall give you a cup of water to drink in my name, because you belong to Christ, truly I say to you, he shall not lose his reward.	
42 And whoever shall offend one of these little ones who believe in me, it would be better for him that a millstone were hung about his neck, and he were cast into the sea.	6 But whoever shall offend one of these little ones who believes in me, it would be better for him that a millstone were hung around his neck, and that he were drowned in the depth of the sea.
	7 Woe to the world because of offences! For it is unavoidable that offences come; but woe to that man by whom the offence comes!
43 And if your hand offends you, cut it off: it is better for you to enter into life maimed, than having two hands to go into hell, into the fire that never shall be quenched:	8 Wherefore if your hand or your foot offends you, cut them off, and cast them from you: it is better for you to enter into life halt or maimed, rather than having two hands or two feet to be cast into everlasting fire.
44 Where their worm does not die, and the fire is not quenched.	
45 And if your foot offends you, cut it off: it is better for you to enter halting into life, than having two feet to be cast into hell, into the fire that shall never be quenched:	
46 Where their worm does not die, and the fire is not quenched.	
47 And if your eye offends you, pluck it out: it is better for you to enter into the kingdom of God with one eye, than having two eyes to be cast into hell fire:	9 And if your eye offends you, pluck it out, and cast it from you: it is better for you to enter into life with one eye, rather than having two eyes to be cast into hell fire.
48 Where their worm does not die, and the fire is not quenched.	
	10 Take heed that you do not despise one of these little ones; for I say to you, That in heaven their angels do always look at the face of my Father who is in heaven.
	11 For the Son of man has come to save that which was lost.
49 For every one shall be salted with fire, and every sacrifice shall be salted with salt.	
50 Salt is good: but if the salt has lost his saltiness,	

with what will you season it? Have salt in yourselves, and have peace one with another.	

6.14 The lost sheep (Capernaum) Matthew 18:12-35

Matthew 18:12-35

12 What do you think? If a man has a hundred sheep, and one of them goes astray, does he not leave the ninety and nine, and go into the mountains, and seek the one that has gone astray?

13 And if it happens that he finds it, truly I say to you, he rejoices more over that sheep, than of the ninety and nine which did not go astray.

14 Even so it is not the will of your Father who is in heaven, that one of these little ones should perish.

15 Moreover if your brother shall trespass against you, go and tell him his fault between you and him alone: if he shall hear you, you have gained your brother.

16 But if he will not hear you, then take with you one or two more, that in the mouth of two or three witnesses every word may be established.

17 And if he shall neglect to hear them, tell it to the church: but if he neglects to hear the church, let him be to you as a heathen and a tax collector.

18 Truly I say to you, Whatever you shall bind on earth shall be bound in heaven: and whatever you shall loose on earth shall be loosed in heaven.

19 Again I say to you, That if two of you shall agree on earth as touching anything that they shall ask, it shall be done for them by my Father who is in heaven.

20 For where two or three are gathered together in my name, there am I in the midst of them.

21 Then Peter came to him, and said, Lord, how often shall my brother sin against me, and I forgive him? Till seven times?

22 Jesus said to him, I do not say to you, Until seven times: but, Until seventy times seven.

[56]**23** Therefore the kingdom of heaven is likened to a certain king, who would take account of his servants.

24 And when he had begun reckoning, one was brought to him, who owed him ten thousand talents.

25 But forasmuch as he did not have it to pay, his lord commanded him to be sold, and his wife, and children, and all that he had, and the payment be made.

26 The servant therefore fell down, and worshipped him, saying, Lord, have patience with me, and I will pay you all.

27 Then the lord of that servant was moved with compassion, and loosed him, and forgave him the debt.

28 But the same servant went out, and found one of his fellow servants, who owed him a hundred pence: and he laid hands on him, and took him by the throat, saying, Pay me what you owe.

29 And his fellow servant fell down at his feet, and begged him, saying, Have patience with me, and I

---

[56] Parable 17. The wicked (unmerciful) servant. Mt 18:23-35.

will pay you all.

30 And he would not: but went and cast him into prison, till he should pay the debt.

31 So when his fellow servants saw what was done, they were very sorry, and came and told their lord all that was done.

32 Then his lord, after he had called him, said to him, O you wicked servant, I forgave you all that debt, because you begged me to:

33 Should you not also have had compassion on your fellow servant, even as I had pity on you?

34 And his lord was angry, and delivered him to the tormentors, till he should pay all that was due to him.

35 So likewise shall my heavenly Father do also to you, if you from your hearts do not forgive his brother's trespasses.

7: Journeys through Galilee and Samaria toward Jerusalem

7.01 Leaves Galilee and is rejected in Samaria Mark 10:1, Luke 9:51-56, Matthew 19:1

Luke 9:51-56

51 And it happened, when the time had come that he should be received up, he steadfastly set his face to go to Jerusalem,

52 And sent messengers ahead of him: and they went, and entered into a village of the Samaritans, to get things ready for him.

53 And they did not receive him, because his face was as though he would go to Jerusalem.

54 And when his disciples James and John saw this, they said, Lord, do you want us to command fire to come down from heaven, and consume them, even as Elijah did?

55 But he turned, and rebuked them, and said, You do not know what manner of spirit you are of.

56 For the Son of man has not come to destroy men's lives, but to save them. And they went to another village.

7.02 Heals ten lepers (Samaria) Luke 17:11-19

Luke 17:11- 19

[57]11 And it happened, as he went to Jerusalem, that he passed through the midst of Samaria and Galilee.

12 And as he entered into a certain village, there met him ten men who were lepers, who stood far off:

13 And they lifted up their voices, and said, Jesus, Master, have mercy on us.

14 And when he saw them, he said to them, Go, show yourselves to the priests. And it happened, that,

---

[57] Healing miracle 30 (of 37). Ten lepers. Lu 17:12-19.

as they went, they were cleansed.

15 And one of them, when he saw that he was healed, turned back, and with a loud voice glorified God,

16 And fell down on his face at his feet, giving him thanks: and he was a Samaritan.

17 And Jesus answering said, Were there not ten cleansed? But where are the nine?

18 There are none found that returned to give glory to God, except this stranger.

[58]**19** And he said to him, Arise, go your way: your faith has made you whole.

7.03 Cost of discipleship Luke 9:57-62, Matthew 8:18-22

Luke 9:57-62	Matthew 8:18-22
	18 Now when Jesus saw great multitudes about him, he gave commandment to depart to the other side.
57 And it happened, that, as they went on their way, a certain man said to him, Lord, I will follow you wherever you go.	19 And a certain scribe came, and said to him, Master, I will follow you wherever you go.
58 And Jesus said to him, Foxes have holes, and birds of the air have nests; but the Son of man has nowhere to lay his head.	20 And Jesus said to him, The foxes have holes, and the birds of the air have nests; but the Son of man has nowhere to lay his head.
59 And he said to another, Follow me. But he said, Lord, permit me first to go and bury my father.	21 And another of his disciples said to him, Lord, permit me first to go and bury my father.
60 Jesus said to him, Let the dead bury their dead: but go you and preach the kingdom of God.	22 But Jesus said to him, Follow me; and let the dead bury their dead.
61 And another also said, Lord, I will follow you; but let me first go bid farewell, to those at home, at my house.	
62 And Jesus said to him, No man, having put his hand to the plough, and looking back, is fit for the kingdom of God.	

7.04 The service of the seventy (Samaria) Luke 10:1-24

Luke 10:1-24

[59]**1** After these things the Lord appointed another seventy also, and sent them two by two ahead of him into every city and place, where he himself would come.

2 Therefore he said to them, The harvest truly is great, but the labourers are few: therefore pray the

---

[58] Your faith has made you well (according to your faith) 6 (of 8). Lu 17:19.

[59] The disciple's power and authority 6 (of 10). Lu 10:1-24 (verses 9, 17).

Lord of the harvest, that he would send forth labourers into his harvest.

3 Go your ways: look, I send you forth as lambs among wolves.

4 Do not carry purse, or bag, or shoes: and do not salute any man by the way.

5 And into whatever house you enter, first say, Peace be to this house.

6 And if the son of peace is there, your peace shall rest upon it: if not, it shall return to you.

7 And remain in the same house, eating and drinking whatever they give: for the labourer is worthy of his hire. Do not go from house to house.

8 And into whatever city you enter, and they receive you, eat whatever is set before you:

9 And heal the sick that are there, and say to them, The kingdom of God has come near to you.

10 But into whatever city you enter, and they do not receive you, go your ways out into the streets of the same, and say,

11 Even the very dust of your city, which cleaves on us, we do wipe off against you: notwithstanding you be sure of this, that the kingdom of God is come near to you.

12 But I say to you, that it shall be more tolerable in that day for Sodom, than for that city.

13 Woe to you, Chorazin! Woe to you, Bethsaida! For if the mighty works had been done in Tyre and Sidon, which have been done in you, they would have a great while ago repented, sitting in sackcloth and ashes.

14 But it shall be more tolerable for Tyre and Sidon at the judgment, than for you.

15 And you, Capernaum, who is exalted to heaven, shall be thrust down to hell.

16 He who hears you hears me; and he who despises you despises me; and he who despises me despises him who sent me.

17 And the seventy returned again with joy, saying, Lord, even the devils are subject to us through your name.

18 And he said to them, I beheld Satan as lightning fall from heaven.

19 Look, I give to you power to tread on serpents and scorpions, and over all the power of the enemy: and nothing shall by any means hurt you.

20 Notwithstanding do not rejoice in this, that the spirits are subject to you; but rather rejoice, because your names are written in heaven.

21 In that hour Jesus rejoiced in spirit, and said, I thank you, O Father, Lord of heaven and earth, that you have hidden these things from the wise and prudent, and have revealed them to babes: even so, Father; for so it seemed good in your sight.

22 All things are delivered to me by my Father: and no man knows who the Son is, but the Father; and who the Father is, but the Son, and he to whom the Son will reveal him.

23 And he turned to his disciples, and said privately, Blessed are the eyes which see the things that you see:

24 For I tell you, that many prophets and kings have desired to see those things which you see, and have not seen them; and to hear those things which you hear, and have not heard them.

7.05 Parable of the Samaritan (Samaria) Luke 10:25-37

Luke 10:25-37

[60]**25** And, look, a certain lawyer stood up, and tempted him, saying, Master, what shall I do to inherit eternal life?

26 He said to him, What is written in the law? How do you read it?

27 And he answering said, You shall love the Lord your God with all your heart, and with all your soul, and with all your strength, and with all your mind; and your neighbour as yourself.

28 And he said to him, You have answered right: do this, and you shall live.

29 But he, willing to justify himself, said to Jesus, And who is my neighbour?

30 And Jesus answering said, A certain man went down from Jerusalem to Jericho, and fell among thieves, who stripped him of his raiment, and wounded him, and departed, leaving him half dead.

31 And by chance a certain priest came down that way: and when he saw him, he passed by on the other side.

32 And likewise a Levite, when he was at the place, came and looked on him, and passed by on the other side.

33 But a certain Samaritan, as he journeyed, came where he was: and when he saw him, he had compassion on him,

34 And went to him, and bound up his wounds, pouring in oil and wine, and set him on his own beast, and brought him to an inn, and took care of him.

35 And on the morrow when he departed, he took out two pence, and gave them to the host, and said to him, Take care of him; and whatever more you spend, when I come again, I will repay you.

36 Which now of these three, do you think, was neighbour to him who fell among the thieves?

37 And he said, He who showed mercy on him. Then said Jesus to him, Go, and do likewise.

7.06 Feast of the Dedication (Jerusalem) John 10:22-39

John 10:22-39

22 And it was at Jerusalem the feast of the dedication, and it was winter.

23 And Jesus walked in the temple in Solomon's porch.

24 Then the Jews came round about him, and said to him, How long do you make us to doubt? If you are the Christ, tell us plainly.

25 Jesus answered them, I told you, and you did not believe: the works that I do in my Father's name, they bear witness of me.

26 But you do not believe, because you are not of my sheep, as I said to you.

27 My sheep hear my voice, and I know them, and they follow me:

28 And I give to them eternal life; and they shall never perish, neither shall any man pluck them out of my hand.

---

[60] Parable 18. The Samaritan. Lu 10:25-37.

29 My Father, who gave them to me, is greater than all; and no man is able to pluck them out of my Father's hand.

30 I and my Father are one.

31 Then the Jews took up stones again to stone him.

32 Jesus answered them, Many good works have I shown you from my Father; for which of those works do you stone me?

33 The Jews answered him, saying, For a good work we do not stone you; but for blasphemy; and because you, being a man, make yourself God.

34 Jesus answered them, Is it not written in your law, I said, You are gods?

35 If he called them gods, to whom the word of God came, and the scripture cannot be broken;

36 Do you say of him, whom the Father has sanctified, and sent into the world, you blaspheme; because I said, I am the Son of God?

37 If I do not do the works of my Father, do not believe me.

38 But if I do, though you do not believe me, believe the works: that you may know, and believe, that the Father is in me, and I in him.

39 Therefore they again sought to take him: but he escaped out of their hand,

7.07 Withdraws to Judea beyond Jordan Mark 10:1b, Matthew 19:1b, John 10:40-42

Mark 10:1	Matthew 19:1	John 10:40-42
1 And he arose from there, and came into the coasts of Judea by the farther side of Jordan: and the people resorted to him again; and, as was his habit, he taught them again.	1 And it happened, that when Jesus had finished these sayings, he departed from Galilee, and came into the coasts of Judea beyond Jordan;	40 And went away again beyond Jordan into the place where John at first baptized; and he stayed there.
		41 And many came to him, and said, John did no miracle: but everything that John said of this man was true.
		42 And many believed on him there.

7.08 At Martha and Mary's house (Bethany beyond the Jordan) Luke 10:38-42

Luke 10:38-42

38 Now it happened, as they went, that he entered into a certain village: and a certain woman named Martha received him into her house.

39 And she had a sister called Mary, who also sat at Jesus' feet, and heard his words.

40 But Martha was weighed down with much serving, and came to him, and said, Lord, do you not care that my sister has left me to serve alone? Command her therefore to help me.

41 And Jesus answered and said to her, Martha, Martha, you are careful and troubled about many things:

42 But one thing is needful: and Mary has chosen that good part, which shall not be taken away from her.

7.09 Teach us to pray; Parable of the importunate friend (Judea beyond the Jordan) Luke 11:1-13

Luke 11:1-13

1 And it happened, that, as he was praying in a certain place, when he ceased, one of his disciples said to him, Lord, teach us to pray, as John also taught his disciples.

2 And he said to them, When you pray, say, Our Father who is in heaven, Hallowed be your name. Your kingdom come. Your will be done, as in heaven, so in earth.

3 Give us day by day our daily bread.

4 And forgive us our sins; for we also forgive every one that is indebted to us. And do not lead us into temptation; but deliver us from evil.

[61]5 And he said to them, Which of you shall have a friend, and shall go to him at midnight, and say to him, Friend, lend me three loaves;

6 For a friend of mine on his journey has come to me, and I have nothing to set before him?

7 And he from within shall answer and say, Do not trouble me: the door is now shut, and my children are with me in bed; I cannot rise and give you.

8 I say to you, Though he will not rise and give him, because he is his friend, yet because of his importunity he will rise and give him as many as he needs.

9 And I say to you, Ask, and it shall be given you; seek, and you shall find; knock, and it shall be opened to you.

10 For every one that asks receives; and he who seeks finds; and to him who knocks it shall be opened.

11 If a son shall ask bread of any of you that is a father, will he give him a stone? Or if he asks for a fish, will he instead of a fish give him a serpent?

12 Or if he shall ask for an egg, will he offer him a scorpion?

13 If you then, being evil, know how to give good gifts to your children: how much more shall your heavenly Father give the Holy Spirit to those who ask him?

---

[61] Parable 19. The persistent friend. Lu 11:5-8

7.10 Pronounces woe to Pharisees and lawyers Luke 11:37-54

Luke 11:37-54

37 And as he spoke, a certain Pharisee begged him to dine with him: and he went in, and sat down to eat.

38 And when the Pharisee saw it, he marvelled that he had not first washed before dinner.

39 And the Lord said to him, Now do you Pharisees make clean the outside of the cup and the platter; but your inward part is full of greed and wickedness.

40 You fools, did not he who made what is without make what is within also?

41 But rather give alms of whatever you have; and, look, all things are clean to you.

42 But woe to you, Pharisees! For you tithe mint and rue and all manner of herbs, and pass over judgment and the love of God: these you ought to have done, and not leave the other undone.

43 Woe to you, Pharisees! For you love the uppermost seats in the synagogues, and greetings in the markets.

44 Woe to you, scribes and Pharisees, hypocrites! For you are as graves which do not appear (to be graves), and the men that walk over them are not aware of them.

45 Then one of the lawyers answered, and said to him, Master, in saying this you reproach us also.

46 And he said, Woe to you also, you lawyers! For you load men with burdens grievous to be borne, and you yourselves do not touch the burdens with one of your fingers.

47 Woe to you! For you build the graves of the prophets, and your fathers killed them.

48 Truly you bear witness that you agree with the deeds of your fathers: for they indeed killed them, and you build their graves.

49 Therefore also said the wisdom of God, I will send them prophets and apostles, and some of them they shall slay and persecute:

50 That the blood of all the prophets, shed from the foundation of the world, may be required of this generation;

51 From the blood of Abel to the blood of Zacharias, who perished between the altar and the temple: Truly I say to you, It shall be required of this generation.

52 Woe to you, lawyers! For you have taken away the key of knowledge: you did not enter in yourselves, and those who were entering you hindered.

53 And as he said these things to them, the scribes and the Pharisees began to urge him vehemently, and to provoke him to speak of many things:

54 Lying in wait for him, and seeking to catch something out of his mouth, that they might accuse him.

7.11 Beware the leaven of the Pharisees Luke 12:1-59

Luke 12:1-12

1 In the mean time, when there were gathered together an innumerable multitude of people, so much so that they tread on each another, he began to say to his disciples first of all, Beware of the leaven of the

Pharisees, which is hypocrisy.

2 For there is nothing covered, that shall not be revealed; neither hidden, that shall not be known.

3 Therefore whatever you have spoken in darkness shall be heard in the light; and that which you have spoken in the ear in closets shall be proclaimed upon the housetops.

4 And I say to you my friends, Do not be afraid of those who kill the body, and after that have no more that they can do.

5 But I will forewarn you whom you shall fear: Fear him, who after he has killed has power to cast into hell; yes, I say to you, Fear him.

6 Are not five sparrows sold for two farthings, and not one of them is forgotten before God?

7 But even the very hairs of your head are all numbered. Do not fear therefore: you are of more value than many sparrows.

8 Also I say to you, Whoever shall confess me before men, him shall the Son of man also confess before the angels of God:

9 But he who denies me before men shall be denied before the angels of God.

10 And whoever shall speak a word against the Son of man, it shall be forgiven him: but to him who blasphemes against the Holy Spirit it shall not be forgiven.

11 And when they bring you to the synagogues, and to magistrates, and powers, take no thought how or what you shall answer, or what you shall say:

12 For the Holy Spirit shall teach you in the same hour what you ought to say.

7.12 Beware of covetousness Luke 12:13-34

13 And one of the company said to him, Master, speak to my brother, that he divide the inheritance with me.

14 And he said to him, Man, who made me a judge or a divider over you?

15 And he said to them, Take heed, and beware of covetousness: for a man's life does not consist in the abundance of the things which he possesses.

[62]16 And he spoke a parable to them, saying, The ground of a certain rich man produced plentifully:

17 And he thought within himself, saying, What shall I do, because I have no room where to store my fruits?

18 And he said, This I will do: I will pull down my barns, and build greater; and there will I store all my fruits and my goods.

19 And I will say to my soul, Soul, you have much goods laid up for many years; take your ease, eat, drink, and be merry.

20 But God said to him, You fool, this night your soul shall be required of you: then whose shall those things be, which you have provided?

21 So is he who lays up treasure for himself, and is not rich toward God.

22 And he said to his disciples, Therefore I say to you, Take no thought for your life, what you shall

---

[62] Parable 20. The rich fool. Lu 12:16-21.

eat; neither for the body, what you shall put on.

23 The life is more than meat, and the body is more than clothing.

24 Consider the ravens: for they neither sow nor reap; which neither have storehouse nor barn; and God feeds them: how much more are you better than the birds?

25 And which of you with taking thought can add one cubit to his stature?

26 If you then are not able to do that thing which is least, why do you take thought for the rest?

27 Consider the lilies how they grow: they do not toil, they do not spin; and yet I say to you, that Solomon in all his glory was not arrayed like one of these.

28 If then God so clothes the grass, which is to day in the field, and tomorrow is cast into the oven; how much more will he clothe you, O you of little faith?

29 And do not seek what you shall eat, or what you shall drink, neither be of doubtful mind.

30 For all these things do the nations of the world seek after: and your Father knows that you have need of these things.

31 But rather seek the kingdom of God; and all these things shall be added to you.

32 Do not fear, little flock; for it is your Father's good pleasure to give you the kingdom.

33 Sell what you have, and give alms; provide yourselves bags which do not grow old, a treasure in the heavens that does not fail, where no thief approaches, neither moth corrupts.

34 For where your treasure is, there will your heart be also.

7.13 Parable of the servants waiting for their lord Luke 12:35-48

[63]**35** Let your loins be girded about, and your lights burning;

36 And you yourselves like men who wait for their lord, when he returns from the wedding; that when he comes and knocks, they may open to him immediately.

37 Blessed are those servants, whom the lord when he comes shall find watching: truly I say to you, that he shall gird himself, and make them sit down to eat, and will come forward and serve them.

38 And if he shall come in the second watch, or come in the third watch, and finds them so, blessed are those servants.

39 And know this, that if the owner of the house had known what hour the thief would come, he would have watched, and not have allowed his house to be broken into.

40 Therefore you be ready also: for the Son of man comes at an hour when you do not think (that he will).

41 Then Peter said to him, Lord, do you speak this parable to us, or even to all?

42 And the Lord said, Who then is that faithful and wise steward, whom his lord shall make ruler over his household, to give them their portion of food in due season?

43 Blessed is that servant, whom his lord when he comes shall find so doing.

44 Of a truth I say to you, that he will make him ruler over all that he has.

---

[63] Parable 21. The servants waiting for their lord. Lu 12:35-48.

45 But and if that servant says in his heart, My lord delays his coming; and shall begin to beat the male servants and maidens, and to eat and drink, and be drunk;

46 The lord of that servant will come in a day when he is not looking for him, and at an hour when he is not aware, and will cut him in pieces, and will appoint him his portion with the unbelievers.

47 And that servant, which knew his lord's will, and did not prepare himself, neither did according to his will, shall be beaten with many stripes.

48 But he who did not know, and did commit things worthy of stripes, shall be beaten with few stripes. For to whomever much is given, of him shall much bee required: and to whom men have committed much, of him they will ask the more.

7.14 Fire on the earth Luke 12:49-53

49 I have come to send fire on the earth; and how I will that it is already kindled?

50 But I have a baptism to be baptized with; and how I am constrained till it is accomplished!

51 Do you suppose that I have come to give peace on earth? I tell you, No; but rather division:

52 For from henceforth there shall be five in one house divided, three against two, and two against three.

53 The father shall be divided against the son, and the son against the father; the mother against the daughter, and the daughter against the mother; the mother in law against her daughter in law, and the daughter in law against her mother in law.

7.15 Discerning the face of the sky and earth Luke 12:54-59

Luke 12:54-59

54 And he said also to the people, When you see a cloud rise out of the west, straightaway you say, A shower is coming; and so it is.

55 And when you see the south wind blow, you say, There will be heat; and it comes to pass.

56 You hypocrites, you can discern the face of the sky and of the earth; but how is it that you do not discern this time?

57 Yea, and why even of yourselves do you not judge what is right?

58 When you go with your adversary to the magistrate, as you are in the way, give diligence that you may be delivered from him; lest he haul you to the judge, and the judge deliver you to the officer, and the officer cast you into prison.

59 I tell you, you shall not depart from there, till you have paid the very last cent.

7.16 Repent or perish Luke 13:1-5

Luke 13:1-5

1 There were present at that season some that told him of the Galileans, whose blood Pilate had mingled with their sacrifices.

2 And Jesus answering said to them, Do you suppose that these Galileans were sinners above all the

Galileans, because they suffered such things?

3 I tell you, No: but, except you repent, you shall all likewise perish.

4 Or those eighteen, upon whom the tower in Siloam fell, and slew them, do you think that they were sinners above all men dwelling in Jerusalem?

5 I tell you, No: but, except you repent, you shall all likewise perish.

7.17 The fruitless fig tree Luke 13:6-9

Luke 13:6-9

[64]**6** He spoke also this parable; A certain man had a fig tree planted in his vineyard; and he came and sought fruit on it, and found none.

7 Then he said to the dresser of his vineyard, Look, these three years I have come seeking fruit on this fig tree, and found none: cut it down; why does it take up space in the ground?

8 And he answering said to him, Lord, leave it alone this year also, till I shall dig about it, and fertilize it:

9 And if it bears fruit, well: and if not, then after that you shall cut it down.

7.18 Heals woman who was bent over Luke 13:10-17

Luke 13:10-17

[65]**10** And he was teaching in one of the synagogues on the Sabbath.

11 And, look, there was a woman who had a spirit of infirmity eighteen years, and was bent over, and could not lift up herself.

12 And when Jesus saw her, he called her to him, and said to her, Woman, you are loosed from your infirmity.

13 And he laid his hands on her: and immediately she was made straight, and glorified God.

14 And the ruler of the synagogue answered with indignation, because Jesus had healed on the Sabbath, and said to the people, There are six days in which men ought to work: in them therefore come and be healed, and not on the Sabbath.

15 The Lord then answered him, and said, You hypocrite, does not each one of you on the Sabbath loose his ox or his ass from the stall, and lead him away to watering?

16 And ought not this woman, being a daughter of Abraham, whom Satan has bound, look, these eighteen years, be loosed from this bond on the Sabbath?

17 And when he had said these things, all his adversaries were ashamed: and all the people rejoiced for all the glorious things that were done by him.

---

[64] Parable 22. The fruitless fig tree. Lu 13:6-9.

[65] Healing miracle 32 (of 37). Woman bent over. Lu 13:10-17

7.19 Parables of the mustard seed and leaven (Judea beyond the Jordan) Luke 13:18-21

Luke 13:18-21

18 Then said he, What is the kingdom of God like? And what does it resemble?

19 It is like a grain of mustard seed, which a man took, and cast in his garden; and it grew, and became a great tree; and the fowls of the air lodged in its branches.

20 And again he said, To what shall I liken the kingdom of God?

21 It is like leaven, which a woman took and hid in three measures of meal, till the whole was leavened.

7.20 Enter by the strait gate (Judea beyond the Jordan) Luke 13:22-30

Luke 13:22-30

22 And he went through the cities and villages, teaching, and journeying toward Jerusalem.

23 Then one said to him, Lord, are there few that be saved? And he said to them,

24 Strive to enter in at the strait gate: for many, I say to you, will seek to enter in, and shall not be able.

25 When once the master of the house has risen up, and has shut to the door, and you begin to stand without, and to knock at the door, saying, Lord, Lord, open to us; and he shall answer and say to you, I do not know from where you have come:

26 Then you shall begin to say, We have eaten and drunk in your presence, and you have taught in our streets.

27 But he shall say, I tell you, I do not know from where you have come; depart from me, all you workers of iniquity.

28 There shall be weeping and gnashing of teeth, when you shall see Abraham, and Isaac, and Jacob, and all the prophets, in the kingdom of God, and you yourselves thrust out.

29 And they shall come from the east, and from the west, and from the north, and from the south, and shall sit down in the kingdom of God.

30 And, look, there are last which shall be first, and there are first which shall be last.

7.21 Herod the fox (Judea beyond the Jordan) Luke 13:31-35

Luke 13:31-35

31 The same day there came certain of the Pharisees, saying to him, Get out, and depart from here: for Herod will kill you.

32 And he said to them, Go, and tell that fox, Look, I cast out devils, and I do cures today and tomorrow, and the third day I shall be perfected.

33 Nevertheless I must walk today, and tomorrow, and the day following: for it cannot be that a prophet perish out of Jerusalem.

34 O Jerusalem, Jerusalem, which kills the prophets, and stones those who are sent to you; how often would I have gathered your children together, as a hen does gather her brood under her wings, and you would not!

35 Look, your house is left to you desolate: and truly I say to you, You shall not see me, until the time

comes when you shall say, Blessed is he who comes in the name of the Lord.

7.22 Eats at a Pharisee's; heals a man of dropsy; parables of the best seats and great supper
Luke 14:1-24

Luke 14:1-24

[66]**1** And it happened, as he went into the house of one of the chief Pharisees to eat bread on the Sabbath, that they watched him.

2 And, look, there was a certain man before him who had the dropsy (edema).

3 And Jesus answering spoke to the lawyers and Pharisees, saying, Is it lawful to heal on the Sabbath?

4 And they held their peace. And he took him, and healed him, and let him go;

5 And he answered them, saying, Which of you shall have a donkey or an ox fall into a pit, and will not straightaway pull him out on the Sabbath?

6 And again they could not answer him these things.

[67]**7** And he presented a parable to those who had been invited, when he marked how they chose out the best seats; saying to them,

8 When you are invited by any man to a wedding, do not sit down in the best seat; lest a more honourable man than you is invited by him;

9 And he who invited you and him come and say to you, Give place to this man; and you begin with shame to take the lowest seat.

10 But when you are invited, go and sit down in the lowest seat; that when he who invited you comes, he may say to you, Friend, go up higher: then shall you have honour in the presence of those who sit to eat with you.

11 For whoever exalts himself shall be abased; and he who humbles himself shall be exalted.

12 Then he also said to him who invited him, When you make a dinner or a supper, do not call your friends, or your brethren, neither your kinsmen, nor your rich neighbours; lest they also invite you in return, and you are rewarded.

13 But when you make a feast, call the poor, the maimed, the lame, the blind:

14 And you shall be blessed; for they cannot recompense you: for you shall be recompensed at the resurrection of the just.

[68]**15** And when one of those who sat to eat with him heard these things, he said to him, Blessed is he who shall eat bread in the kingdom of God.

16 Then he said to him, A certain man made a great supper, and invited many:

17 And sent his servant at suppertime to say to those who were invited, Come; because all things are now ready.

---

[66] Healing miracle 33 (of 37). Man with dropsy. Lu 14:1-6.

[67] Parable 23. The best seats. Lu 14:7-11.

[68] Parable 24. The great supper. Lu 14:15-24.

18 And all of them with one consent began to make excuses. The first said to him, I have bought a piece of ground, and I must go and see it: Please have me excused.

19 And another said, I have bought five yoke of oxen, and I go to prove them: Please have me excused.

20 And another said, I have married a wife, and therefore I cannot come.

21 So that servant came, and showed his lord these things. Then the master of the house being angry said to his servant, Go out quickly into the streets and lanes of the city, and bring in here the poor, and the maimed, and the halt, and the blind.

22 And the servant said, Lord, it is done as you have commanded, and yet there is room.

23 And the lord said to the servant, Go out into the highways and hedges, and compel them to come in, that my house may be filled.

24 For I say to you, That none of those men who were invited shall taste of my supper.

7.23 Cost of discipleship (Judea beyond the Jordan) Luke 14:25-35

Luke 14:25-35

25 And great multitudes went with him: and he turned, and said to them,

26 If anyone comes to me, and does not hate his father, and mother, and wife, and children, and brothers, and sisters, yes, and his own life also, he cannot be my disciple.

27 And whoever does not carry his cross, and come after me, cannot be my disciple.

28 For which of you, intending to build a tower, does not first sit down, and count the cost, whether he has sufficient to finish it?

29 Lest perhaps, after he has laid the foundation, and is not able to finish it, all that look at it begin to mock him,

30 Saying, This man began to build, and was not able to finish.

31 Or what king, going to make war against another king, does not first sit down, and consult whether he is able with ten thousand to meet him that comes against him with twenty thousand?

32 Or else, while the other is yet a great way off, he sends a message, and desires conditions of peace.

33 So likewise, whoever among you does not forsake all that he has, he cannot be my disciple.

34 Salt is good: but if the salt has lost its flavour, with what shall it be seasoned?

35 It is neither fit for the land, nor yet for the dump; but men cast it out. He who has ears to hear, let him hear.

8: Judea beyond the Jordan (part 2)

8.01 Parable of the lost sheep Luke 15:1-7, Matthew 18:12-14

Luke 15:1-3

1 Then all the tax collectors and sinners drew near to him to hear him.

2 And the Pharisees and scribes murmured, saying, This man receives sinners, and eats with them.

[69]3 And he spoke this parable to them, saying,

Luke 15:4-7	Matthew 18:12-14
4 Which of you, having a hundred sheep, if he loses one of them, does not leave the ninety and nine in the wilderness, and go after that which is lost, until he finds it?	12 What do you think? if a man has a hundred sheep, and one of them has gone astray, dos he not leave the ninety and nine, and go into the mountains, and seek that which has gone astray?
5 And when he has found it, he lays it on his shoulders, rejoicing.	13 And if it happens that he finds it, truly I say to you, he rejoices more over that sheep, than over the ninety and nine that did not go astray.
6 And when he comes home, he calls together his friends and neighbours, saying to them, Rejoice with me; for I have found my sheep which was lost.	
7 I say to you, that likewise joy shall be in heaven over one sinner who repents, more than over ninety and nine just persons, who do not need to repent.	
	14 Even so it is not the will of your Father who is in heaven, that one of these little ones should perish.

8.02 Parable of the lost silver coin Luke 15:8-10

Luke 15:8-10

[70]8 Or what woman having ten pieces of silver, if she loses one piece, dos not light a candle, and sweep the house, and seek diligently till she finds it?

9 And when she has found it, she calls her friends and her neighbours together, saying, Rejoice with me; for I have found the piece which I had lost.

10 Likewise, I say to you, there is joy in the presence of the angels of God over one sinner who repents.

8.03 Parable of the prodigal son Luke 15:11-32

Luke 15:11-32

[71]11 And he said, A certain man had two sons:

12 And the younger of them said to his father, Father, give me the portion of goods that falls to me.

---

[69] Parable 25. The lost sheep. Lu 15:1-7, Mt 18:12-14.

[70] Parable 26. The lost silver coin. Lu 15:8-10.

[71] Parable 27. The prodigal son. Lu 15:11-32.

And he divided to them his goods.

13 And not many days after the younger son gathered all together, and took his journey into a far country, and there wasted his substance with riotous living.

14 And when he had spent all, there arose a mighty famine in that land; and he began to be in want.

15 And he went and joined himself to a citizen of that country; and he sent him into his fields to feed pigs.

16 And he would gladly have filled his belly with the husks that the swine did eat: and no man gave to him.

17 And when he came to himself, he said, How many hired servants of my father's have bread enough and to spare, and I perish with hunger!

18 I will arise and go to my father, and will say to him, Father, I have sinned against heaven, and before you,

19 And am no more worthy to be called your son: make me as one of your hired servants.

20 And he arose, and came to his father. But when he was yet a great way off, his father saw him, and had compassion, and ran, and fell on his neck, and kissed him.

21 And the son said to him, Father, I have sinned against heaven, and in your sight, and am no more worthy to be called your son.

22 But the father said to his servants, Bring forth the best robe, and put it on him; and put a ring on his hand, and shoes on his feet:

23 And bring here the fatted calf, and kill it; and let us eat, and be merry:

24 For this my son was dead, and is alive again; he was lost, and is found. And they began to be merry.

25 Now his elder son was in the field: and as he came and drew near to the house, he heard music and dancing.

26 And he called one of the servants, and asked what these things meant.

27 And he said to him, Your brother has come; and your father has killed the fatted calf, because he has received him safe and sound.

28 And he was angry, and would not go in: therefore his father came out, and entreated him.

29 And he answering said to his father, Look, these many years I have served you, neither have I at any time transgressed your commandment: and yet you never gave me a kid, that I might make merry with my friends:

30 But as soon as this your son had come, who has devoured your goods with harlots, you have killed the fatted calf for him.

31 And he said to him, Son, you are ever with me, and all that I have is yours.

32 It was necessary that we should make merry, and be glad: for this your brother was dead, and is alive again; and was lost, and is found.

8.04 Parable of the wasteful steward Luke 16:1-13

Luke 16:1-13

[72]1 And he said also to his disciples, There was a certain rich man, who had a steward; and the same was accused to him that he had wasted his goods.

---

[72] Parable 28. The wasteful steward. Lu 16:1-13.

2 And he called him, and said to him, How is it that I hear this of you? Give an account of your stewardship; for you may no longer be steward.

3 Then the steward said within himself, What shall I do? For my lord takes away from me the stewardship: I cannot dig; and I am ashamed to beg.

4 I have resolved what to do, that, when I am put out of the stewardship, they may receive me into their houses.

5 So he called every one of his lord's debtors to him, and said to the first, How much do you owe to my lord?

6 And he said, A hundred measures of oil. And he said to him, Take your bill, and sit down quickly, and write fifty.

7 Then said he to another, And how much do you owe? And he said, A hundred measures of wheat. And he said to him, Take your bill, and write fourscore.

8 And the lord commended the unjust steward, because he had done wisely: for the children of this world are in their generation wiser than the children of light.

9 And I say to you, Make to yourselves friends of the mammon of unrighteousness; that, when you fail, they may receive you into everlasting habitations.

10 He who is faithful in that which is least is faithful also in much: and he who is unjust in the least is unjust also in much.

11 If therefore you have not been faithful in the unrighteous mammon, who will commit to your trust the true riches?

12 And if you have not been faithful in that which is another man's, who shall give you that which is your own?

13 No servant can serve two masters: for either he will hate the one, and love the other; or else he will hold to the one, and despise the other. You cannot serve God and mammon.

8.05 Responds to the Pharisees' derision Luke 16:14-18

Luke 16:14-18

14 And the Pharisees also, who were covetous, heard all these things: and they derided him.

15 And he said to them, You are those who justify yourselves before men; but God knows your hearts: for that which is highly esteemed among men is abomination in the sight of God.

16 The law and the prophets were until John: since that time the kingdom of God is preached, and every man presses into it.

17 And it is easier for heaven and earth to pass, than one tittle of the law to fail.

18 Whoever puts away his wife, and marries another, commits adultery: and whoever marries her that is put away from her husband commits adultery.

8.06 Parable of the rich man and Lazarus Luke 16:19-31

Luke 16:19-31

[73]**19** There was a certain rich man, who was clothed in purple and fine linen, and fared sumptuously every day:

20 And there was a certain beggar named Lazarus, who was laid at his gate, full of sores,

21 And desiring to be fed with the crumbs which fell from the rich man's table: moreover the dogs came and licked his sores.

22 And it happened, that the beggar died, and was carried by the angels into Abraham's bosom: the rich man also died, and was buried;

23 And in hell he lift up his eyes, being in torment, and seeing Abraham afar off, and Lazarus in his bosom.

24 And he cried and said, Father Abraham, have mercy on me, and send Lazarus, that he may dip the tip of his finger in water, and cool my tongue; for I am tormented in this flame.

25 But Abraham said, Son, remember that you in your lifetime received your good things, and likewise Lazarus evil things: but now he is comforted, and you are tormented.

26 And beside all this, between us and you there is a great gulf fixed: so that those who would pass from here to you cannot; neither can they pass to us, that would come from there.

27 Then he said, I pray you therefore, father, that you would send him to my father's house:

28 For I have five brethren; that he may testify to them, lest they also come into this place of torment.

29 Abraham said to him, They have Moses and the prophets; let them hear them.

30 And he said, No, father Abraham: but if one went to them from the dead, they will repent.

31 And he said to him, If they do not hear Moses and the prophets, neither will they be persuaded, though one rose from the dead.

8.07 Offences and faith to forgive offences Luke 17:1-6

Luke 17:1-6

1 Then said he to the disciples, It is impossible but that offences will come: but woe to him, through whom they come!

2 It would be better for him that a millstone were hung about his neck, and he were cast into the sea, than that he should offend one of these little ones.

3 Take heed to yourselves: If your brother trespass against you, rebuke him; and if he repent, forgive him.

4 And if he trespass against you seven times in a day, and seven times in a day turns again to you, saying, I repent; you shall forgive him.

5 And the apostles said to the Lord, Increase our faith.

6 And the Lord said, If you had faith as a grain of mustard seed, you might say to this sycamore tree, Be

---

[73] Parable 29. The rich man and Lazarus. Lu 16:19-31.

plucked up by the root, and be planted in the sea; and it should obey you.

8.08 Parable of faith as a servant. Luke 17:7-10

Luke 17:7-10

[74]7 But which of you, having a servant plowing or feeding cattle, will say to him by and by, when he has come from the field, Go and sit down to eat?

8 And will not rather say to him, Make ready my supper, and gird yourself, and serve me, till I have eaten and drunk; and afterward you shall eat and drink?

9 Does he thank that servant because he did the things that were commanded him? I do not think so.

10 So likewise you, when you shall have done all those things which are commanded you, say, We are unprofitable servants: we have done that which was our duty to do.

8.09 The days of the Son of man Luke 17:20-37

Luke 17:20-37

[75]20 And when the Pharisees demanded from him when the kingdom of God should come, he answered them and said, The kingdom of God does not come with observation:

21 Neither shall they say, Look here! or, look there! for, look, the kingdom of God is within you.

22 And he said to the disciples, The days will come, when you shall desire to see one of the days of the Son of man, and you shall not see it.

23 And they shall say to you, See here; or, see there: do not go after them, or follow them.

24 For as the lightning, that flashes out of the one part under heaven, shines to the other part under heaven; so also shall the Son of man be in his day.

25 But first he must suffer many things, and be rejected by this generation.

26 And as it was in the days of Noah, so shall it be also in the days of the Son of man.

27 They did eat, they drank, they married wives, they were given in marriage, until the day that Noah entered into the ark, and the flood came, and destroyed them all.

28 Likewise also as it was in the days of Lot; they did eat, they drank, they bought, they sold, they planted, they built;

29 But the same day that Lot went out of Sodom it rained fire and brimstone from heaven, and destroyed them all.

30 Even so shall it be in the day when the Son of man is revealed.

31 In that day, he who shall be upon the housetop, and his stuff in the house, let him not come down to take it away: and he who is in the field, let him likewise not return.

32 Remember Lot's wife.

33 Whoever shall seek to save his life shall lose it; and whoever shall lose his life shall preserve it.

---

[74] Parable 30. Faith as a servant. Lu 17:7-10.

[75] Parable 31. The coming of the kingdom of God. Lu 17:20-37

34 I tell you, in that night there shall be two men in one bed; the one shall be taken, and the other shall be left.

35 Two women shall be grinding together; the one shall be taken, and the other left.

36 Two men shall be in the field; the one shall be taken, and the other left.

37 And they answered and said to him, Where, Lord? And he said to them, Wherever the body is, there will the eagles be gathered together.

8.10 Parable of the persistent widow Luke 18:1-8

Luke 18:1-8

[76]1 And he spoke a parable to them to this end, that men ought always to pray, and not to faint;

2 Saying, There was in a city a judge, who did not fear God, neither regarded man:

3 And there was a widow in that city; and she came to him, saying, Avenge me of my adversary.

4 And he would not for a while: but afterward he said within himself, Though I do not fear God, nor regard man;

5 Yet because this widow troubles me, I will give her justice, lest by her continual coming she wearies me.

6 And the Lord said, Hear what the unjust judge said.

7 And shall not God avenge his own elect, who cry day and night to him, though he bears long with them?

8 I tell you that he will avenge them speedily. Nevertheless when the Son of man comes, shall he find faith on the earth?

8.11 Parable of the Pharisee and the tax collector Luke 18:9-14

Luke 18:9-14

[77]9 And he spoke this parable to certain who trusted in themselves that they were righteous, and despised others:

10 Two men went up into the temple to pray; the one a Pharisee, and the other a tax collector.

11 The Pharisee stood and prayed thus with himself, God, I thank you, that I am not as other men are, extortioners, unjust, adulterers, or even as this tax collector.

12 I fast twice in the week, I give tithes of all that I possess.

13 And the tax collector, standing afar off, would not lift up so much as his eyes to heaven, but smote his breast, saying, God be merciful to me a sinner.

14 I tell you, this man went down to his house justified rather than the other: for every one that exalts himself shall be abased; and he who humbles himself shall be exalted.

---

[76] Parable 32. The persistent widow. Lu 18:1-8.

[77] Parable 33. The Pharisee and the tax collector. Lu 18:9-14.

8.12 Divorce and remarriage Mark 10:1-12, Matthew 19:1-12

Mark 10:1-12	Matthew 19:1-12
1 And he arose from there, and came into the coasts of Judea by the farther side of Jordan: and the people resorted to him again; and, as was his habit, he taught them again.	1 And it happened, that when Jesus had finished these sayings, he departed from Galilee, and came into the coasts of Judea beyond Jordan; 2 And great multitudes followed him; and he healed them there.
2 And the Pharisees came to him, and asked him, Is it lawful for a man to put away his wife? tempting him.	3 The Pharisees also came to him, tempting him, and saying to him, Is it lawful for a man to put away his wife for any reason?
3 And he answered and said to them, What did Moses command you?	
4 And they said, Moses allowed us to write a bill of divorce, and to put her away.	7 They said to him, Why did Moses then command to give a writing of divorce, and to put her away?
5 And Jesus answered and said to them, Because of the hardness of your heart he wrote you this precept.	8 He said to them, Moses because of the hardness of your hearts allowed you to put away your wives: but from the beginning it was not so.
6 But from the beginning of the creation God made them male and female.	4 And he answered and said to them, Have you not read, that he who made them at the beginning made them male and female,
7 For this cause shall a man leave his father and mother, and cleave to his wife;	5 And said, For this cause shall a man leave father and mother, and shall cleave to his wife: and the two shall be one flesh?
8 And the two shall be one flesh: so then they are no more two, but one flesh.	6 Therefore they are no more two, but one flesh. What therefore God has joined together, let not man put asunder.
9 What therefore God has joined together, let not man put asunder.	
10 And in the house his disciples asked him again about the same matter.	
11 And he said to them, Whoever puts away his wife, and marries another, commits adultery against her.	9 And I say to you, Whoever shall put away his wife, except it be for fornication, and shall marry another, commits adultery: and whoever marries her which is put away does commit adultery.
12 And if a woman shall put away her husband, and be married to another, she commits adultery.	
	10 His disciples said to him, If the case of the man

	is so with his wife, it is not good to marry.
	11 But he said to them, All men cannot receive this saying, except they to whom it is given.
	12 For there are some eunuchs, which were so born from their mother's womb: and there are some eunuchs, which were made eunuchs of men: and there be eunuchs, which have made themselves eunuchs for the kingdom of heaven's sake. He who is able to receive it, let him receive it.

8.13 Jesus blesses children (Judea beyond the Jordan) Mark 10:13-16, Luke 18:15-17, Matthew 19:13-15

Mark 10:13-16	Luke 18:15-17	Matthew 19:13-15
13 And they brought young children to him, that he should touch them: and his disciples rebuked those who brought them.	15 And they also brought to him infants, that he would touch them: but when his disciples saw it, they rebuked them.	13 Then there were brought to him little children, that he should put his hands on them, and pray: and the disciples rebuked them.
14 But when Jesus saw it, he was much displeased, and said to them, Allow the little children to come to me, and do not forbid them: for of such is the kingdom of God.	16 But Jesus called them to him, and said, Allow the little children to come to me, and do not forbid them: for of such is the kingdom of God.	14 But Jesus said, Allow the little children, and do not forbid them, to come to me: for of such is the kingdom of heaven.
15 Truly I say to you, Whoever shall not receive the kingdom of God as a little child, he shall not enter into it.	17 Truly I say to you, Whoever shall not receive the kingdom of God as a little child shall in no wise enter therein.	
16 And he took them up in his arms, put his hands upon them, and blessed them.		15 And he laid his hands on them, and departed from there.

8.14 A certain ruler asks about eternal life (Judea beyond the Jordan) Mark 10:17-31, Luke 18:18-30, Matthew 19:16-30

Mark 10:17-31	Luke 18:18-30	Matthew 19:16-30
17 And when he had begun his journey, there came one running, and knelt to him, and	18 And a certain ruler asked him, saying, Good Master, what shall I do to inherit eternal life?	16 And, look, one came and said to him, Good Master, what good thing shall I do, that I may

asked him, Good Master, what shall I do that I may inherit eternal life?		have eternal life?
18 And Jesus said to him, Why do you call me good? There is none good but one, that is, God.	19 And Jesus said to him, Why do you call me good? None is good, except one, that is, God.	17 And he said to him, Why do you call me good? There is none good but one, that is, God: but if you will enter into life, keep the commandments.
19 You know the commandments, Do not commit adultery, Do not kill, Do not steal, Do not bear false witness, Do not defraud, Honour your father and mother.	20 You know the commandments, Do not commit adultery, Do not kill, Do not steal, Do not bear false witness, Honour your father and your mother.	18 He said to him, Which? Jesus said, You shall do no murder, You shall not commit adultery, You shall not steal, You shall not bear false witness, 19a Honour your father and your mother:
		19b and, You shall love your neighbour as yourself.
20 And he answered and said to him, Master, all these I have observed from my youth.	21 And he said, All these I have kept from my youth up.	20 The young man said to him, All these things have I kept from my youth up: what do I yet lack?
21 Then Jesus looking at him loved him, and said to him, One thing you lack: go your way, sell whatever you have, and give to the poor, and you shall have treasure in heaven: and come, take up the cross, and follow me.	22 Now when Jesus heard these things, he said to him, Yet you lack one thing: sell all that you have, and distribute to the poor, and you shall have treasure in heaven: and come, follow me.	21 Jesus said to him, If you will be perfect, go and sell what you have, and give to the poor, and you shall have treasure in heaven: and come and follow me.
22 And he was sad at that saying, and went away grieved: for he had great possessions.	23 And when he heard this, he was very sorrowful: for he was very rich.	22 But when the young man heard that saying, he went away sorrowful: for he had great possessions.
23 And Jesus looked round about, and said to his disciples, How hardly shall those who have riches enter into the kingdom of God!	24 And when Jesus saw that he was very sorrowful, he said, How hardly shall those who have riches enter into the kingdom of God!	23 Then said Jesus to his disciples, Truly I say to you, That a rich man shall hardly enter into the kingdom of heaven.

24 And the disciples were astonished at his words. But Jesus answered again, and said to them, Children, how hard is it for those who trust in riches to enter into the kingdom of God!		
25 It is easier for a camel to go through the eye of a needle, than for a rich man to enter into the kingdom of God.	25 For it is easier for a camel to go through a needle's eye, than for a rich man to enter into the kingdom of God.	24 And again I say to you, It is easier for a camel to go through the eye of a needle, than for a rich man to enter into the kingdom of God.
26 And they were astonished beyond measure, saying among themselves, Who then can be saved?	26 And those who heard it said, Who then can be saved?	25 When his disciples heard it, they were exceedingly amazed, saying, Who then can be saved?
27 And Jesus looking upon them said, With men it is impossible, but not with God: for with God all things are possible.	27 And he said, The things which are impossible with men are possible with God.	26 But Jesus looked at them, and said to them, With men this is impossible; but with God all things are possible.
28 Then Peter began to say to him, Look, we have left all, and have followed you.	28 Then Peter said, Look, we have left all, and followed you.	27 Then Peter answered and said to him, Look, we have forsaken all, and followed you; what shall we have therefore?
		28 And Jesus said to them, Truly I say to you, That you which have followed me, in the regeneration when the Son of man shall sit in the throne of his glory, you also shall sit upon twelve thrones, judging the twelve tribes of Israel.
29 And Jesus answered and said, Truly I say to you, There is no man that has left house, or brethren, or sisters, or father, or mother, or wife, or children, or lands, for my sake, and the	29 And he said to them, Truly I say to you, There is no man that has left house, or parents, or brethren, or wife, or children, for the kingdom of God's sake,	29a, b And every one that has forsaken houses, or brethren, or sisters, or father, or mother, or wife, or children, or lands, for my name's sake,

gospel's,		
30 But he shall receive a hundredfold now in this time, houses, and brethren, and sisters, and mothers, and children, and lands, with persecutions; and in the world to come eternal life.	30 Who shall not receive many times more in this present time, and in the world to come life everlasting.	29c shall receive a hundredfold, and shall inherit everlasting life.
31 But many that are first shall be last; and the last first.		30 But many that are first shall be last; and the last shall be first.

8.15 Parable of the labourers in the vineyard Matthew 20:1-16

Matthew 20:1-16

[78]1 For the kingdom of heaven is like a man that is a landowner, who went out early in the morning to hire labourers into his vineyard.

2 And when he had agreed with the labourers for a penny a day, he sent them into his vineyard.

3 And he went out about the third hour, and saw others standing idle in the marketplace,

4 And said to them; You also go into the vineyard, and whatever is right I will give you. And they went their way.

5 Again he went out about the sixth and ninth hour, and did similarly.

6 And about the eleventh hour he went out, and found others standing idle, and said to them, Why do you stand here all the day idle?

7 They said to him, Because no man has hired us. He said to them, You also go into the vineyard; and whatever is right, you shall receive.

8 So when evening had come, the lord of the vineyard said to his steward, Call the labourers, and give them their wages, beginning from the last to the first.

9 And when those who were hired about the eleventh hour came, they each received a penny.

10 But when the first came, they supposed that they should have received more; and they likewise received every man a penny.

11 And when they had received it, they murmured against the landowner,

12 Saying, These last have worked but one hour, and you have made them equal to us, which have borne the burden and heat of the day.

13 But he answered one of them, and said, Friend, I do you no wrong: did you not agree with me for a penny?

14 Take what is yours, and go your way: I will give to this last, even as to you.

15 Is it not lawful for me to do what I will with mine own? Is your eye evil, because I am good?

---

[78] Parable 34. Labourers in the vineyard. Mt 20:1-16.

16 So the last shall be first, and the first last: for many are called, but few chosen.

8.16 Jesus foretells His death and resurrection (Near Jordan) Mark 10:32-34, Luke 18:31-34, Matthew 20:17-19

Mark 10:32-34	Luke 18:31-34	Matthew 20:17-19
32 As they were on the way going up to Jerusalem; and Jesus went before them: and they were amazed; and as they followed, they were afraid. And he took again the twelve, and began to tell them what things should happen to him,		17 And Jesus going up to Jerusalem took the twelve disciples apart in the way, and said to them,
33 Saying, Look, we go up to Jerusalem; and the Son of man shall be delivered to the chief priests, and to the scribes; and they shall condemn him to death, and shall deliver him to the Gentiles:	31 Then he took to him the twelve, and said to them, Look, we go up to Jerusalem, and all things that are written by the prophets concerning the Son of man shall be accomplished.	18 Look, we are going up to Jerusalem; and the Son of man shall be betrayed to the chief priests and to the scribes, and they shall condemn him to death,
34 And they shall mock him, and shall scourge him, and shall spit upon him, and shall kill him: and the third day he shall rise again.	32 For he shall be delivered to the Gentiles, and shall be mocked, and spitefully entreated, and spit on: 33 And they shall scourge him, and put him to death: and the third day he shall rise again.	19 And shall deliver him to the Gentiles to mock, and to scourge, and to crucify him: and the third day he shall rise again.
	34 And they understood none of these things: and this saying was hidden from them, neither did they understand the things which were spoken.	

8.17 Grant that we may each sit on your right and left Mark 10:35-45, Matthew 20:20-28

Mark 10:35-45	Matthew 20:20-28
35 And James and John, the sons of Zebedee, came to him, saying, Master, we would that you should do for us whatever we shall desire.	20 Then the mother of Zebedee's children came to him with her sons, worshipping him, and desiring a certain thing of him.

36 And he said to them, What would you that I should do for you?	21a And he said to her, What do you want?
37 They said to him, Grant to us that we may sit, one on your right hand, and the other on your left hand, in your glory.	21b, c She said to him, Grant that these my two sons may sit, the one on your right hand, and the other on the left, in your kingdom.
38 But Jesus said to them, You do not know what you ask: can you drink of the cup that I drink of? And be baptized with the baptism that I am baptized with?	22a, b But Jesus answered and said, You do not know what you ask. Are you able to drink of the cup that I shall drink of, and to be baptized with the baptism that I am baptized with?
39 And they said to him, We can. And Jesus said to them, You shall indeed drink of the cup that I drink of; and with the baptism that I am baptized with you shall be baptized:	22c They said to him, We are able. 23a, b And he said to them, You shall drink indeed of my cup, and be baptized with the baptism that I am baptized with:
40 But to sit on my right hand and on my left hand is not mine to give; but it shall be given to them for whom it is prepared.	23c, d but to sit on my right hand, and on my left, is not mine to give, but it shall be given to those for whom it is prepared by my Father.
41 And when the ten heard it, they began to be much displeased with James and John.	24 And when the ten heard it, they were moved with indignation against the two brothers.
42 But Jesus called them to him, and said to them, You know that those who are counted as rulers over the Gentiles exercise lordship over them; and their great ones exercise authority upon them.	25 But Jesus called them to him, and said, You know that the princes of the Gentiles exercise dominion over them, and those who are great exercise authority upon them.
43 But so shall it not be among you: but whoever will be great among you, shall be your minister:	26 But it shall not be so among you: but whoever will be great among you, let him be your minister;
44 And whoever of you will be the chief, shall be servant of all.	27 And whoever will be chief among you, let him be your servant:
45 For even the Son of man came not to be ministered to, but to minister, and to give his life a ransom for many.	28 Even as the Son of man came not to be ministered to, but to minister, and to give his life a ransom for many.

8.18 Heals Bartimeus and another blind man (Jericho) Mark 10:46-52, Luke 18:35-43, Matthew 20:29-34

Mark 10:46-52	Luke 18:35-43	Matthew 20:29-34
[79]46 And they came to Jericho: and as he went out of Jericho with his disciples and a great	35 And it happened, that as he came near to Jericho, a certain blind man sat by the way side	29 And as they departed from Jericho, a great multitude followed him.

---

[79] Healing miracle 34 (of 37). Blind Bartimeus. Mr 10:46-52, Lu 18:35-43, Mt 20:29-34.

number of people, blind Bartimaeus, the son of Timaeus, sat by the highway side begging.	begging:	30a And, look, two blind men were sitting by the way side,
	36 And hearing the multitude pass by, he asked what it meant. 37 And they told him, that Jesus of Nazareth was passing by.	
47 And when he heard that it was Jesus of Nazareth, he began to cry out, and say, Jesus, you Son of David, have mercy on me.	38 And he cried, saying, Jesus, you Son of David, have mercy on me.	30b when they heard that Jesus passed by, cried out, saying, Have mercy on us, O Lord, you Son of David.
48 And many charged him that he should hold his peace: but he cried the more a great deal, You Son of David, have mercy on me.	39 And those who went before rebuked him, that he should hold his peace: but he cried so much the more, You Son of David, have mercy on me.	31 And the multitude rebuked them, because they wanted them to hold their peace: but they cried the more, saying, Have mercy on us, O Lord, you Son of David.
49 And Jesus stood still, and commanded him to be called. And they called the blind man, saying to him, Be of good comfort, rise; he calls you.	40 And Jesus stood, and commanded him to be brought to him:	32a And Jesus stood still, and called them,
50 And he, casting away his garment, rose, and came to Jesus.	40c and when he had come near, he asked him,	
51 And Jesus answered and said to him, What do you want me to do for you? The blind man said to him, Lord, that I might receive my sight.	41 Saying, What do you want me to do for you? And he said, Lord, that I may receive my sight.	32b and said, What do you want me to do for you? 33 They say to him, Lord, that our eyes may be opened.

[80]**52** And Jesus said to him, Go your way; your faith has made you whole. And immediately he received his sight, and followed Jesus in the way.	42 And Jesus said to him, Receive your sight: your faith has saved you. 43 And immediately he received his sight, and followed him, glorifying God: and all the people, when they saw it, gave praise to God.	34 So Jesus had compassion on them, and touched their eyes: and immediately their eyes received sight, and they followed him.

8.19 Zacchaeus (Jericho) Luke 19:1-10

Luke 19:1-10

1 And Jesus entered and passed through Jericho.

2 And, look, there was a man named Zacchaeus, who was the chief among the tax collectors, and he was rich.

3 And he sought to see who Jesus was; and could not for the crowd, because he was small in stature.

4 And he ran ahead, and climbed up into a sycamore tree to see him: for he was to pass that way.

5 And when Jesus came to the place, he looked up, and saw him, and said to him, Zacchaeus, make haste, and come down; for today I must abide at your house.

6 And he hurried, and came down, and received him joyfully.

7 And when they saw it, they all murmured, saying, That he had gone to be guest with a man who was a sinner.

8 And Zacchaeus stood, and said to the Lord; Look, Lord, half of my goods I will give to the poor; and if I have taken anything from any man by false accusation, I will restore it to him fourfold.

9 And Jesus said to him, This day has salvation come to this house, inasmuch as he also is a son of Abraham.

10 For the Son of man has come to seek and to save that which was lost.

8.20 Parable of the ten minas (pounds) (Jericho) Luke 19:11-27

Luke 19:11-27

[81]**11** And as they heard these things, he added and spoke a parable, because he was near to Jerusalem, and because they thought that the kingdom of God should immediately appear.

12 He said therefore, A certain nobleman went into a far country to receive for himself a kingdom, and to return.

13 And he called his ten servants, and delivered them ten pounds, and said to them, Occupy till I come.

14 But his citizens hated him, and sent a message after him, saying, We will not have this man to reign over us.

---

[80] Your faith has made you well (according to your faith) 7 (of 8). Mr 10:52, Lu 18:42.

[81] Parable 35. The ten minas (pounds). Lu 19:11-27.

15 And it happened, that when he returned, having received the kingdom, he commanded these servants to be called to him, to whom he had given the money, that he might know how much every man had gained by trading.

16 Then came the first, saying, Lord, your pound has gained ten pounds.

17 And he said to him, Well, you good servant: because you have been faithful in a very little, you have authority over ten cities.

18 And the second came, saying, Lord, your pound has gained five pounds.

19 And he said similarly to him, You also be over five cities.

20 And another came, saying, Lord, look, here is your pound, which I have kept laid up in a napkin:

21 For I feared you, because you are an austere man: you take up what you did not lay down, and reap what you did not sow.

22 And he said to him, Out of your own mouth will I judge you, you wicked servant. you knew that I was an austere man, taking up what I did not lay down, and reaping that I did not sow:

23 Why then did you not put my money into the bank, that at my coming I might have gotten back my own with interest?

24 And he said to those who stood by, Take the pound from him, and give it to him who has ten pounds.

25 (And they said to him, Lord, he has ten pounds.)

26 For I say to you, That to everyone who has shall more be given; and from him who has not, even what he has shall be taken away from him.

27 But those mine enemies, who would not have me reign over them, bring here, and slay them before me.

8.21 Raises Lazarus back to life (Bethany) John 11:1-44

John 11:1-44

[82]1 Now a certain man was sick, named Lazarus, of Bethany, the town of Mary and her sister Martha.

2 (It was that Mary who anointed the Lord with ointment, and wiped his feet with her hair, whose brother Lazarus was sick.)

3 Therefore his sisters sent to him, saying, Lord, look, he whom you love is sick.

4 When Jesus heard that, he said, This sickness is not to death, but for the glory of God, that the Son of God might be glorified thereby.

5 Now Jesus loved Martha, and her sister, and Lazarus.

6 When he had heard therefore that he was sick, he stayed two days still in the same place where he was.

7 Then after that he said to his disciples, Let us go into Judea again.

8 His disciples said to him, Master, the Jews of late sought to stone you; and do you go there again?

9 Jesus answered, Are there not twelve hours in the day? If any man walk in the day, he does not stumble, because he sees the light of this world.

---

[82] Healing miracle 35 (of 37). Lazarus. Joh 11:1-44.

10 But if a man walks in the night, he stumbles, because there is no light in him.

11 These things he said: and after that he said to them, Our friend Lazarus sleeps; but I go, that I may wake him out of sleep.

12 Then his disciples said, Lord, if he sleeps, he shall be well.

13 However Jesus spoke of his death: but they thought that he had spoken of taking a rest in sleep.

14 Then said Jesus to them plainly, Lazarus is dead.

15 And I am glad for your sakes that I was not there, to the intent you may believe; nevertheless let us go to him.

16 Then said Thomas, which is called Didymus, to his fellow disciples, Let us also go, that we may die with him.

17 Then when Jesus came, he found that he had lain in the grave four days already.

18 Now Bethany was near to Jerusalem, about fifteen furlongs (two miles) off:

19 And many of the Jews came to Martha and Mary, to comfort them concerning their brother.

20 Then Martha, as soon as she heard that Jesus was coming, went and met him: but Mary sat still in the house.

21 Then said Martha to Jesus, Lord, if you had been here, my brother would not have died.

22 But I know, that even now, whatever you will ask of God, God will give it to you.

23 Jesus said to her, Your brother shall rise again.

24 Martha said to him, I know that he shall rise again in the resurrection at the last day.

25 Jesus said to her, I am the resurrection, and the life: he who believes in me, though he were dead, yet shall he live:

26 And whoever lives and believes in me shall never die. Do you believe this?

27 She said to him, Yes, Lord: I believe that you are the Christ, the Son of God, who should come into the world.

28 And when she had so said, she went her way, and called Mary her sister secretly, saying, The Master is come, and calls for you.

29 As soon as she heard that, she arose quickly, and came to him.

30 Now Jesus had not yet come into the town, but was in that place where Martha met him.

31 Then the Jews who were with her in the house, and comforted her, when they saw Mary, that she rose up hastily and went out, followed her, saying, She goes to the grave to weep there.

32 Then when Mary had come where Jesus was, and saw him, she fell down at his feet, saying to him, Lord, if you had been here, my brother would not have died.

33 Therefore, when Jesus saw her weeping, and the Jews also weeping who came with her, he groaned in the spirit, and was troubled,

34 And said, Where have you laid him? They said to him, Lord, come and see.

35 Jesus wept.

36 Then said the Jews, Look how he loved him!

37 And some of them said, Could not this man, who opened the eyes of the blind, have caused that even this man should not have died?

38 Jesus therefore again groaning in himself came to the grave. It was a cave, and a stone lay upon it.

39 Jesus said, Take away the stone. Martha, the sister of he who was dead, said to him, Lord, by this time he stinks: for he has been dead four days.

[83]**40** Jesus said to her, Did I not say to you, that, if you would believe, you would see the glory of God?

41 Then they took away the stone from the place where the dead was laid. And Jesus lifted up his eyes, and said, Father, I thank you that you have heard me.

42 And I knew that you hear me always: but because of the people who stand by I said it, that they may believe that you have sent me.

43 And when he had thus spoken, he cried with a loud voice, Lazarus, come forth.

44 And he who was dead came forth, bound hand and foot with grave clothes: and his face was bound about with a napkin. Jesus said to them, Loose him, and let him go.

8.22 Jesus withdraws to Ephraim John 11:45-57

John 11:45-57

45 Then many of the Jews who had come to Mary, and had seen the things which Jesus did, believed on him.

46 But some of them went their ways to the Pharisees, and told them what things Jesus had done.

47 Then the chief priests and the Pharisees gathered a council, and said, What do we do? For this man does many miracles.

48 If we let him alone thus, all men will believe on him: and the Romans shall come and take away both our place and nation.

49 And one of them, named Caiaphas, being the high priest that same year, said to them, You know nothing at all,

50 Nor consider that it is expedient for us, that one man should die for the people, and that the whole nation not perish.

51 And this he spoke not of himself: but being high priest that year, he prophesied that Jesus should die for that nation;

52 And not for that nation only, but that also he should gather together in one the children of God that were scattered abroad.

53 Then from that day on they took counsel together to put him to death.

54 Jesus therefore walked no more openly among the Jews; but went away to a country near the wilderness, into a city called Ephraim, and there continued with his disciples.

55 And the Jews' Passover was very near: and many went out of the country up to Jerusalem before the Passover, to purify themselves.

56 Then they searched for Jesus, and spoke among themselves, as they stood in the temple, What do you think, that he will not come to the feast?

57 Now both the chief priests and the Pharisees had given a commandment, that, if any man knew

---

[83] If you would believe (according to your faith) 8 (of 8). Joh 11:40.

where he was, he should show it, that they might arrest him.

8.23 Anointed by Mary (Bethany) John 12:1-8

John 12:1-8

1 Then Jesus six days before the Passover came to Bethany, where Lazarus was who had been dead, whom he raised from the dead.

2 There they made him a supper; and Martha served: but Lazarus was one of those who sat at the table with him.

3 Then Mary took a pound of ointment of spikenard, very costly, and anointed the feet of Jesus, and wiped his feet with her hair: and the house was filled with the fragrance of the ointment.

4 Then one of his disciples, Judas Iscariot, Simon's son, who would betray him, said,

5 Why was this ointment not sold for three hundred pence, and given to the poor?

6 This he said, not because he cared for the poor; but because he was a thief, and had the bag, and took what was put in it.

7 Then Jesus said, Leave her alone: against the day of my burial she has kept this.

8 For the poor you always have with you; but me you do not have always.

8.24 Plot to kill Lazarus (Bethany) John 12:9-11

John 12:9-11

9 Many of the Jews therefore knew that he was there: and they came not for Jesus' sake only, but that they might see Lazarus also, whom he had raised from the dead.

10 But the chief priests consulted that they might put Lazarus to death also;

11 Because on account of him many of the Jews went away, and believed on Jesus.

9: Jesus' last week in Jerusalem

9.01 Triumphal entry (Sunday, Jerusalem) Mark 11:1-11, Luke 19:28-44, Matthew 21:1-9, John 12:12-19

Mark 11:1-3	Luke 19:28-31	Matthew 21:1-5	John 12:12, 14c, 15
1 And when they came near to Jerusalem, to Bethphage and Bethany, at the mount of Olives, he sent two of his disciples,	28 And when he had thus spoken, he went ahead, ascending up to Jerusalem. 29 And it happened, when he had come near to Bethphage and Bethany, at the mount	1 And when they drew near to Jerusalem, and were come to Bethphage, to the mount of Olives, then Jesus sent two disciples,	12 On the next day many people that had come to the feast, when they heard that Jesus was coming to Jerusalem,

	called the mount of Olives, he sent two of his disciples,		
2 And said to them, Go your way into the village over against you: and as soon as you have entered into it, you shall find a colt tied, on which no man has ever sat; loose him, and bring him.	30 Saying, You go into the village over against you; which at your entering you shall find a colt tied, on which no man has ever sat: loose him, and bring him here.	2 Saying to them, Go into the village over against you, and straightaway you shall find a donkey tied, and a colt with her: loose them, and bring them to me.	
3 And if any man says to you, Why do you do this? You say that the Lord has need of him; and straightaway he will send him here.	31 And if any man asks you, Why do you loose him? So you shall say to him, Because the Lord has need of him.	3 And if any man says anything to you, you shall say, The Lord has need of them; and straightaway he will send them.	
		4 All this was done, that it might be fulfilled which was spoken by the prophet (Micah), saying,	14c as it iswritten,
		5 You tell the daughter of Zion, Look, your King comes to you, meek, and sitting upon a donkey, and a colt the foal of a donkey.	15 Do not fear, daughter of Zion: look, your King comes, sitting on a donkey's colt.

Mark 11:4-10	Luke 19:32-38	Matthew 21:6-9	John 12:13, 14a, b
4 And they went their way, and found the colt tied by the door outside in a place where two ways met; and they loosed him.	32 And those who were sent went their way, and found (things) even as he had said to them.		
5 And some of them who stood there said to	33 And as they were loosening the colt, its		

them, What are you doing, loosening the colt?	owners said to them, Why do you loose the colt?		
6 And they said to them even as Jesus had commanded: and they let them go.	34 And they said, The Lord has need of him.	6 And the disciples went, and did as Jesus commanded them,	
7 And they brought the colt to Jesus, and cast their garments on him; and he sat upon him.	35 And they brought him to Jesus: and they cast their garments upon the colt, and they set Jesus on it.	7 And brought the donkey, and the colt, and put on them their clothes, and they set him on it.	14a, b And Jesus, when he had found a young donkey, sat on it;
8 And many spread their garments in the way: and others cut down branches off the trees, and strewed them in the way.	36 And as he went, they spread their clothes in the way.	8 And a very great multitude spread their garments in the way; others cut down branches from the trees, and strewed them in the way.	13a Took branches of palm trees, and went to meet him,
9 And those who went before, and those who followed, cried, saying, Hosanna; Blessed is he who comes in the name of the Lord:	37 And when he had come near, even now at the descent of the mount of Olives, the whole multitude of the disciples began to rejoice and praise God with a loud voice for all the mighty works that they had seen;	9 And the multitudes that went before, and that followed, cried, saying, Hosanna to the Son of David: Blessed is he who comes in the name of the Lord; Hosanna in the highest.	13b and cried, Hosanna: Blessed is the King of Israel that comes in the name of the Lord.
10 Blessed be the kingdom of our father David, that comes in the name of the Lord: Hosanna in the highest.	38 Saying, Blessed be the King that comes in the name of the Lord: peace in heaven, and glory in the highest.		

John 12:16-19

16 These things his disciples did not understand at first: but when Jesus was glorified, then they remembered that these things were written about him, and that they had done these things to him.

17 Therefore, the people who were with him when he called Lazarus out of his grave, and raised him from the dead, testified.
18 For this cause the people also met him, for they heard that he had done this miracle.
19 The Pharisees therefore said among themselves, Perceive how you prevail nothing? Look, the world is gone after him.

Luke 19:39-43
39 And some of the Pharisees from among the multitude said to him, Master, rebuke your disciples.
40 And he answered and said to them, I tell you that, if these should hold their peace, the stones would immediately cry out.
41 And when he had come near, he beheld the city, and wept over it,
42 Saying, If you had known, even thou, at least in this your day, the things which belong to your peace! But now they are hid from your eyes.
43 For the days shall come upon you, that your enemies shall cast a trench about you, and compass you round, and keep you in on every side,

Mark 11:11	Luke 19:44
	44 And shall lay you even with the ground, and your children within you; and they shall not leave in you one stone upon another; because you did not know the time of your visitation.
11 And Jesus entered into Jerusalem, and into the temple: and when he had looked round about upon all things, and now the eventide was come, he went out to Bethany with the twelve.	

9.02 The fig tree with nothing but leaves (Monday; between Bethany and Jerusalem) Mark 11:12-14, Luke 19:45-48, Matthew 21:17-19, 10-16

Mark 11:12-14	Matthew 21:17-19, 10-11
12 And on the morrow, when they had come from Bethany, he was hungry:	17 And he left them, and went out of the city into Bethany; and he lodged there. 18 Now in the morning as he returned into the city, he was hungry.
13 And seeing a fig tree afar off having leaves, he came, if perhaps he might find anything thereon: and when he came to it, he found nothing but leaves; for it was not yet the time of figs.	
14 And Jesus answered and said to it, No man eat	19 And when he saw a fig tree in the way, he came

fruit of you hereafter forever. And his disciples heard it.	to it, and found nothing thereon, but leaves only, and said to it, Let no fruit grow on you henceforth forever. And presently the fig tree withered away.
	10 And when he had come into Jerusalem, all the city was moved, saying, Who is this?
	11 And the multitude said, This is Jesus the prophet of Nazareth of Galilee.

9.03 Cleansing the Temple (Monday; Jerusalem) Mark 11:15-18, Luke 19:45-48, Matthew 21:12-16

Mark 11:15-17	Luke 19:45-46	Matthew 21:12-13
15 And they came to Jerusalem: and Jesus went into the temple, and began to cast out those who sold and bought in the temple, and overthrew the tables of the moneychangers, and the seats of those who sold doves;	45 And he went into the temple, and began to cast out those who sold in it, and those who bought;	12 And Jesus went into the temple of God, and cast out all those who sold and bought in the temple, and overthrew the tables of the moneychangers, and the seats of those who sold doves,
16 And would not allow that any man should carry any vessel through the temple.		
17 And he taught, saying to them, Is it not written, My house shall be called of all nations the house of prayer? But you have made it a den of thieves.	46 Saying to them, It is written, My house is the house of prayer: but you have made it a den of thieves.	13 And said to them, It is written, My house shall be called the house of prayer; but you have made it a den of thieves.

Matthew 21:14-16
[84]**14** And the blind and the lame came to him in the temple; and he healed them.
15 And when the chief priests and scribes saw the wonderful things that he did, and the children crying in the temple, and saying, Hosanna to the Son of David; they were very displeased,
16 And said to him, Do you hear what these are saying? And Jesus said to them, Yes; have you never read, Out of the mouth of babes and nursing infants you have perfected praise?

---

[84] Healing miracle 36 (of 37). Blind and lame in the temple. Mt 21:12-16.

Mark 11:18	Luke 19:47-48
18 And the scribes and chief priests heard it, and sought how they might destroy him: for they feared him, because all the people were astonished at his doctrine.	47 And he taught daily in the temple. But the chief priests and the scribes and the chief of the people sought to destroy him,
	48 And could not find what they might do: for all the people were very attentive to hear him.

9.04 Greeks want to see Jesus; death of a grain of wheat (Jerusalem) John 12:20-50

John 12:20-50

20 And there were certain Greeks among those who came up to worship at the feast:

21 The same came to Philip, who was from Bethsaida of Galilee, and asked him, saying, Sir, we want to see Jesus.

22 Philip came and told Andrew: and again Andrew and Philip told Jesus.

23 And Jesus answered them, saying, The hour has come, that the Son of man should be glorified.

24 Very Truly, I say to you, Except a grain of wheat falls into the ground and dies, it abides alone: but if it dies, it brings forth much fruit.

25 He who loves his life shall lose it; and he who hates his life in this world shall keep it to life eternal.

26 If any man serves me, let him follow me; and where I am, there also shall my servant be: if any man serves me, him will my Father honour.

27 Now is my soul troubled; and what shall I say? Father, save me from this hour: but for this cause I came to this hour.

28 Father, glorify your name. Then there came a voice from heaven, saying, I have both glorified it, and will glorify it again.

29 Therefore the people, who stood by, and heard it, said that it thundered: others said, An angel spoke to him.

30 Jesus answered and said, This voice did not come because of me, but for your sakes.

31 Now is the judgment of this world: now shall the prince of this world be cast out.

32 And I, if I am lifted up from the earth, I will draw all men to me.

33 This he said, signifying what death he should die.

34 The people answered him, We have heard out of the law that Christ abides forever: and how do you say, The Son of man must be lifted up? Who is this Son of man?

35 Then Jesus said to them, Yet a little while the light is with you. Walk while you have the light, lest darkness come upon you: for he who walks in darkness does not know where he is going.

36 While you have light, believe in the light, that you may be the children of light. These things Jesus spoke, then departed, and hid himself from them.

37 But though he had done so many miracles in their presence, yet they did not believe on him:

38 That the saying of Isaiah the prophet might be fulfilled, which he spoke, Lord, who has believed our report? And to whom has the arm of the Lord been revealed?

39 Therefore they could not believe, because Isaiah said again,

40 He has blinded their eyes, and hardened their heart; that they should not see with their eyes, nor understand with their heart, and be converted, that I should heal them.

41 These things said Isaiah, when he saw his glory, and spoke of him.

42 Nevertheless among the chief rulers also many believed on him; but because of the Pharisees they did not confess him, lest they should be put out of the synagogue:

43 For they loved the praise of men more than the praise of God.

44 Jesus cried and said, He who believes on me, believes not on me, but on him who sent me.

45 And he who sees me sees him who sent me.

46 I have come as a light into the world, that whoever believes on me should not abide in darkness.

47 And if any man hears my words, and does not believe, I do not judge him: for I did not come to judge the world, but to save the world.

48 He who rejects me, and does not receive my words, has one who judges him: the words that I have spoken, the same shall judge him in the last day.

49 For I have not spoken of myself; but the Father who sent me, he gave me a commandment, what I should say, and what I should speak.

50 And I know that his commandment is life everlasting: whatever I speak therefore, even as the Father said to me, so I speak.

9.05 The withered fig tree (Tuesday; between Bethany and Jerusalem) Mark 11:19-26, Matthew 21:19d-22

Mark 11:19-26	Matthew 21:19d-22
19 And when evening had come, he went out of the city.	
20 And in the morning, as they passed by, they saw the fig tree dried up from the roots.	19d And presently the fig tree withered away.
21 And Peter calling to remembrance said to him, Master, look, the fig tree which you cursed has withered away.	20 And when the disciples saw it, they marvelled, saying, How soon has the fig tree withered away!
22 And Jesus answering said to them, Have faith in God.	21a Jesus answered and said to them,
23 For truly I say to you, That whoever shall say to this mountain, Be removed, and be cast into the sea; and shall not doubt in his heart, but shall believe that those things which he says shall come to pass; he shall have whatever he says.	21b-d Truly I say to you, If you have faith, and do not doubt, you shall not only do what has been done to the fig tree, but also if you shall say to this mountain, Be removed, and be cast into the sea; it shall be done.
24 Therefore I say to you, Whatever you desire,	22 And all things, whatever you shall ask in

when you pray, believe that you receive them, and you shall have them.	prayer, believing, you shall receive.
25 And when you stand praying, forgive, if you have anything against anyone: that your Father also which is in heaven may forgive you your trespasses.	
26 But if you do not forgive, neither will your Father who is in heaven forgive your trespasses.	

9.06 By whose authority do you do these things? (Jerusalem) Mark 11:27-33, Luke 20:1-8, Matthew 21:23-27

Mark 11:27-33	Luke 20:1-8	Matthew 21:23-27
27 And they came again to Jerusalem: and as he was walking in the temple, there came to him the chief priests, and the scribes, and the elders,	1 And it happened, that on one of those days, as he taught the people in the temple, and preached the gospel, the chief priests and the scribes came to him with the elders,	23a, b And when he had come into the temple, the chief priests and the elders of the people came to him as he was teaching,
28 And said to him, By whose authority do you do these things? And who gave you this authority to do these things?	2 And spoke to him, saying, Tell us, by whose authority do you do these things? Or who gave you this authority?	23c and said, By whose authority do you do these things? And who gave you this authority?
29 And Jesus answered and said to them, I will also ask of you one question, and answer me, and I will tell you by whose authority I do these things.	3 And he answered and said to them, I will also ask you one thing; and answer me:	24 And Jesus answered and said to them, I also will ask you one thing, which if you tell me, I in like manner will tell you by whose authority I do these things.
30 The baptism of John, was it from heaven, or from men? Answer me.	4 The baptism of John, was it from heaven, or from men?	25a The baptism of John, where was it from? From heaven, or from men?
31 And they reasoned with themselves, saying, If we shall say, From heaven; he will say, Why then did you not believe him?	5 And they reasoned with themselves, saying, If we shall say, From heaven; he will say, Why then did you not believe him?	25b And they reasoned with themselves, saying, If we shall say, From heaven; he will say to us, Why then did you not believe him?
32 But if we shall say, From men; they feared the people: for	6 But and if we say, From men; all the people will stone us: for	26 But if we shall say, From men; we fear the people; for all

all men counted that John was a prophet indeed.	they were persuaded that John was a prophet.	hold John as a prophet.
33a, b And they answered and said to Jesus, We cannot tell.	7 And they answered, that they could not tell from where it came.	27a, b And they answered Jesus, and said, We cannot tell.
33c, d And Jesus answering said to them, Neither will I tell you by whose authority I do these things.	8 And Jesus said to them, Neither will I tell you by whose authority I do these things.	27c, d And he said to them, Neither will I tell you by whose authority I do these things.

9.07 Parable of the two sons (Jerusalem) Matthew 21:28-32

Matthew 21:28-32

[85]**28** But what do you think? A certain man had two sons; and he came to the first, and said, Son, go work today in my vineyard.

29 He answered and said, I will not: but afterward he repented, and went.

30 And he came to the second, and said likewise. And he answered and said, I go, sir: and did not go.

31 Which of the two did the will of his father? They said to him, The first. Jesus said to them, Truly I say to you, That the tax collectors and the harlots go into the kingdom of God before you.

32 For John came to you in the way of righteousness, and you did not believe him: but the tax collectors and the harlots believed him: and, when you had seen it, you did not repent afterward, that you might believe him.

9.08 Parable of the landlord and farmers (Jerusalem) Mark 12:1-12, Luke 20:9-19, Matthew 21:33-46

Mark 12:1-12	Luke 20:9-19	Matthew 21:33-46
1 And he began to speak to them in parables. A certain man planted a vineyard, and set a hedge about it, and dug a place for the grape juice, and built a tower, and let it out to farmers, and went into a far country.	9 Then he began to speak to the people this parable; A certain man planted a vineyard, leased it to farmers, and went into a far country for a long time.	[86]**33** Hear another parable: There was a certain landlord, who planted a vineyard, and hedged it round about, and dug a winepress in it, and built a tower, and let it out to farmers, and went into a far country:
2 And at the season, he sent a servant to the farmers, that he	10a, b And at the season, he sent a servant to the farmers, that	34 And when the time of the fruit drew near, he sent his

---

[85] Parable 36. The two sons. Mt 21:28-32.

[86] Parable 37. The vineyard leased to vinedressers. Mt 21:33-46, Mr 12:1-12, Lu 20:9-19.

might receive from the farmers of the fruit of the vineyard.	they should give him of the fruit of the vineyard:	servants to the farmers, that they might receive the fruits of it.
3 And they caught him, beat him, and sent him away empty.	10c but the farmers beat him, and sent him away empty.	35 And the farmers took his servants, beat one, killed another, and stoned another.
4 And again he sent another servant to them; and at him they cast stones, wounded him in the head, and sent him away shamefully handled. 5 And again he sent another; and him they killed, and many others; beating some, and killing some.	11 And again he sent another servant: and they beat him also, and treated him shamefully, and sent him away empty. 12 And again he sent a third: and they wounded him also, and cast him out.	36 Again, he sent other servants more than the first: and they did similarly to them.
	13a Then the lord of the vineyard said, What shall I do?	
6 Having yet therefore one son, his well beloved, he also sent him to them last, saying, They will reverence my son.	13b-c I will send my beloved son: it may be they will revere him when they see him.	37 But last of all, he sent his son to them, saying, They will revere my son.
7 But those farmers said among themselves, This is the heir; come, let us kill him, and the inheritance shall be ours.	14 But when the farmers saw him, they reasoned among themselves, saying, This is the heir: come, let us kill him, that the inheritance may be ours.	38 But when the farmers saw the son, they said among themselves, This is the heir; come, let us kill him, and let us seize on his inheritance.
8 And they took him and killed him, and cast him out of the vineyard.	15a, b So they cast him out of the vineyard, and killed him.	39 And they caught him, and cast him out of the vineyard, and slew him.
9a Therefore what shall the lord of the vineyard do?	15c Therefore what shall the lord of the vineyard do to them?	40 Therefore when the lord of the vineyard comes, what will he do to those farmers?
9b He will come and destroy the farmers, and will give the vineyard to others.	16 He shall come and destroy these farmers, and shall give the vineyard to others. And when they heard it, they said, God forbid.	41 They said to him, He will miserably destroy those wicked men, and will let out his vineyard to other farmers, who shall render him the fruits in their seasons.
10 And have you not read this	17 And he beheld them, and	42 Jesus said to them, Did you

scripture; The stone which the builders rejected is become the head of the corner: 11 This was the Lord's doing, and it is marvellous in our eyes?	said, What is this then that is written, The stone which the builders rejected, the same is become the head of the corner?	never read in the scriptures, The stone which the builders rejected, the same is become the head of the corner: this is the Lord's doing, and it is marvellous in our eyes?
		43 Therefore I say to you, The kingdom of God shall be taken from you, and given to a nation bringing forth its fruits.
	18 Whoever shall fall upon that stone shall be broken; but on whomever it shall fall, it will grind him to powder.	44 And whoever shall fall on this stone shall be broken: but on whomever it shall fall, it will grind him to powder.
12 And they sought to lay hold on him, but feared the people: for they knew that he had spoken the parable against them: and they left him, and went their way.	19 And the chief priests and the scribes that same hour sought to lay hands on him; and they feared the people: for they perceived that he had spoken this parable against them.	45 And when the chief priests and Pharisees had heard his parables, they perceived that he spoke of them.
		46 But when they sought to lay hands on him, they feared the multitude, because they took him for a prophet.

9.09 Parable of the marriage of the king's son (Jerusalem) Matthew 22:1-14

Matthew 22:1-14

[87]1 And Jesus answered and spoke to them again by parables, and said,

2 The kingdom of heaven is like a certain king, who made a marriage for his son,

3 And sent forth his servants to call those who were invited to the wedding: and they would not come.

4 Again, he sent forth other servants, saying, Tell those who are invited, Look, I have prepared my dinner: my oxen and my fatlings are killed, and all things are ready: come to the marriage.

5 But they made light of it, and went their ways, one to his farm, another to his merchandise:

6 And the remnant took his servants, and treated them spitefully, and slew them.

7 But when the king heard of it, he was angry: and he sent forth his armies, and destroyed those murderers, and burned up their city.

---

[87] Parable 36. Marriage of the King's Son. Mt 22:1-14.

8 Then he said to his servants, The wedding is ready, but those who were invited were not worthy.

9 Go therefore into the highways, and as many as you shall find, invite to the marriage.

10 So those servants went out into the highways, and gathered together all, as many as they could find, both bad and good: and the wedding was furnished with guests.

11 And when the king came in to see the guests, he saw there a man who did not have on a wedding garment:

12 And he said to him, Friend, how did you come here not having a wedding garment? And he was speechless.

13 Then said the king to the servants, Bind him hand and foot, and take him away, and cast him into outer darkness; there shall be weeping and gnashing of teeth.

14 For many are called, but few are chosen.

9.10 Tribute to Caesar (Jerusalem) Mark 12:13-17, Luke 20:20-26, Matthew 22:15-22

Mark 12:13-17	Luke 20:20-26	Matthew 22:15-22
13 And they sent to him certain of the Pharisees and of the Herodians, to catch him in his words.	20 And they watched him, and sent forth spies, who would pretend to be just men, that they might take hold of his words, that so they might deliver him to the power and authority of the governor.	15 Then the Pharisees went, and took counsel how they might entangle him in his talk.
14a, b And when they had come, they said to him, Master, we know that you are true, and care for no man: for you do not regard the person of men, but teach the way of God in truth:	21 And they asked him, saying, Master, we know that you say and teach rightly, neither do you accept the person of any, but teach the way of God truly:	16 And they sent their disciples out to him with the Herodians, saying, Master, we know that you are true, and teach the way of God in truth, neither do you care for any man: for you do not regard the person of men.
14c Is it lawful to give tribute to Caesar, or not? 15a Shall we give, or shall we not give?	22 Is it lawful for us to give tribute to Caesar, or not?	17 Tell us therefore, What do you think? Is it lawful to give tribute to Caesar, or not?
15b, c But he, knowing their hypocrisy, said to them, Why do you tempt me?	23 But he perceived their craftiness, and said to them, Why do you tempt me?	18 But Jesus perceived their wickedness, and said, Why do you tempt me, you hypocrites?
15d Bring me a penny, that I may see it.	24a Show me a penny.	19 Show me the tribute money. And they brought a penny to him.
16 And they brought it. And he	24b , c Whose image and	20 And he said to them, Whose

sad to them, Whose is this image and superscription? And they said to him, Caesar's.	superscription has it? They answered and said, Caesar's.	is this image and superscription?
17 And Jesus answering said to them, Render to Caesar the things that are Caesar's, and to God the things that are God's. And they marvelled at him.	25 And he said to them, Render therefore to Caesar the things which are Caesar's, and to God the things which are God's.	21 They said to him, Caesar's. Then said he to them, Render therefore to Caesar the things which are Caesar's; and to God the things that are God's.
	26 And they could not take hold of his words before the people: and they marvelled at his answer, and held their peace.	22 When they had heard these words, they marvelled, left him, and went their way.

9.11 Sadducees question the resurrection (Jerusalem) Mark 12:18-27, Luke 20:27-40, Matthew 22:23-33

Mark 12:18-27	Luke 20:27-40	Matthew 22:23-33
18 Then the Sadducees, who say there is no resurrection, came to him; and they asked him, saying,	27 Then certain of the Sadducees, who deny that there is any resurrection, came to him; and they asked him,	23 The same day the Sadducees came to him, who say that there is no resurrection, and asked him,
19 Master, Moses wrote to us, that if a man's brother dies, leaves his wife behind, and leaves no children, his brother should take his wife, and raise up seed to his brother.	28 Saying, Master, Moses wrote to us, If any man's brother dies, having a wife, and he dies without children, that his brother should take his wife, and raise up seed to his brother.	24 Saying, Master, Moses said, If a man dies, having no children, his brother shall marry his wife, and raise up seed to his brother.
20 Now there were seven brethren: and the first took a wife, and dying left no seed.	29 There were therefore seven brothers: and the first took a wife, and died without children.	25 Now there were with us seven brothers: and the first, when he had married a wife, deceased, and, having no children, left his wife to his brother:
21 And the second took her, and died, neither left he any seed: and the third likewise.	30 And the second took her to wife, and he died childless.	26 Likewise the second also, and the third, to the seventh.
22 And the seven had her, and left no seed: last of all the woman died also.	31 And the third took her; and in like manner the seven also: and they left no children, and died.	27 And last of all the woman died also.

	32 Last of all the woman died also.	
23 In the resurrection therefore, when they shall rise, whose wife shall she be of them? For the seven had her as wife.	33 Therefore in the resurrection whose wife of them is she? For seven had her as wife.	28 Therefore in the resurrection whose wife of the seven shall she be? For they all had her.
24 And Jesus answering said to them, Do you not therefore err, because you do not know the scriptures, neither the power of God?		29 Jesus answered and said to them, You do err, not knowing the scriptures, nor the power of God.
	34 And Jesus answering said to them, The children of this world marry, and are given in marriage:	
25a, b For when they shall rise from the dead, they neither marry, nor are given in marriage;	35 But they which shall be counted worthy to obtain that world, and the resurrection from the dead, neither marry, nor are given in marriage:	30a, b For in the resurrection they neither marry, nor are given in marriage,
	36 Neither can they die any more: for they are equal to the angels; and are the children of God, being the children of the resurrection.	30c but are as the angels of God in heaven.
26 And as touching the dead, that they rise: have you not read in the book of Moses, how in the bush God spoke to him, saying, I am the God of Abraham, and the God of Isaac, and the God of Jacob?	37 Now that the dead are raised, even Moses showed at the bush, when he called the Lord the God of Abraham, and the God of Isaac, and the God of Jacob.	31 But as touching the resurrection of the dead, have you not read that which was spoken to you by God, saying, 32a I am the God of Abraham, and the God of Isaac, and the God of Jacob?
	38 For he is not a God of the dead, but of the living: for all live to him.	32b God is not the God of the dead, but of the living.
	39 Then certain of the scribes answering said, Master, you have	33 And when the multitude heard this, they were

	well said.	astonished at his doctrine
27 He is not the God of the dead, but the God of the living: therefore, you do greatly err.	40 And after that they dared not ask him any question at all.	

9.12 The great commandment in the law (Jerusalem) Mark 12:28-34, Matthew 22:34-40

Mark 12:28-31	Matthew 22:34-40
28a-d And one of the scribes came, and having heard them reasoning together, and perceiving that he had answered them well, asked him,	34 But when the Pharisees had heard that he had put the Sadducees to silence, they were gathered together.
	35 Then one of them, who was a lawyer, asked him a question, tempting him, and saying,
28e Which is the first commandment of all?	36 Master, which is the great commandment in the law?
29 And Jesus answered him, The first of all the commandments is, Hear, O Israel; The Lord our God is one Lord:	37a Jesus said to him,
30a-d And you shall love the Lord your God with all your heart, with all your soul, with all your mind, and with all your strength:	37b-d You shall love the Lord your God with all your heart, with all your soul, and with all your mind.
30e this is the first commandment.	38 This is the first and great commandment.
31a, b And the second is like, namely this, You shall love your neighbour as yourself.	39 And the second is like it, You shall love your neighbour as yourself.
31c There is no other commandment greater than these.	40 On these two commandments hang all the law and the prophets.

Mark 12:32-34
32 And the scribe said to him, Well, Master, you have said the truth: for there is one God; and there is none other but he:
33 And to love him with all the heart, and with all the understanding, and with all the soul, and with all the strength, and to love his neighbour as himself, is more than all whole burnt offerings and sacrifices.
34 And when Jesus saw that he answered discreetly, he said to him, You are not far from the kingdom of God. And no man after that dared ask him any question.

9.13 Is Christ David's Son or Lord? (Jerusalem) Mark 12:35-37, Luke 20:41-44, Matthew 22:41-46

Mark 12:35-37	Luke 20:41-44	Matthew 22:41-46
		41 While the Pharisees were gathered together, Jesus asked them,
35 And Jesus answered and said, while he taught in the temple, Why do the scribes say that Christ is the Son of David?	41 And he said to them, How do they say that Christ is David's son?	42 Saying, What do you think of Christ? Whose son is he? They say to him, The Son of David.
		43 He said to them, How then does David in spirit call him Lord, saying,
36 For David himself said by the Holy Spirit, The LORD said to my Lord, You sit on my right hand, till I make your enemies your footstool.	42 And David himself said in the book of Psalms, The LORD said to my Lord, You sit on my right hand, 43 Till I make your enemies your footstool.	44 The LORD said to my Lord, You sit on my right hand, till I make your enemies your footstool?
37a, b Therefore David himself called him Lord; Why is he then his son?	44 David therefore called him Lord, how is he then his son?	45 If David then calls him Lord, how is he his son?
37c And the common people heard him gladly.		46 And no man was able to answer him a word, neither dared any man from that day forth ask him any more questions.

9.14 Beware of the scribes (Jerusalem) Mark 12:38-40, Luke 20:45-47, Matthew 23:1-12

Mark 12:38-40	Luke 20:45-47	Matthew 23:1-2a
	45 Then in the audience of all the people he said to his disciples,	1 Then Jesus spoke to the multitude, and to his disciples, 2a Saying,
38 And he said to them in his doctrine, Beware of the scribes, who love to go in long clothing, and love salutations in the marketplaces,	46 Beware of the scribes, which desire to walk in long robes, and love greetings in the markets, and the highest seats in the synagogues, and the best seats at	

39 And the chief seats in the synagogues, and the best places at feasts:	feasts;	
40 Which devour widows' houses, and for a pretence make long prayers: these shall receive greater damnation.	47 Which devour widows' houses, and for a show make long prayers: the same shall receive greater damnation.	

Matthew 23:2b -12
2b The scribes and the Pharisees sit in Moses' seat:
3 Therefore all they bid you observe, those observe and do; but do not do their works: for they say, and do not do.
4 For they bind heavy burdens, grievous to be borne, and lay them on men's shoulders; but they themselves will not move them with one of their fingers.
5 But all their works they do to be seen of men: they make broad their phylacteries, and enlarge the borders of their garments,
6 And love the uppermost rooms at feasts, and the chief seats in the synagogues,
7 And greetings in the markets, and to be called of men, Rabbi, Rabbi.
8 But do not be called Rabbi: for one is your Master, even Christ; and you are all brethren.
9 And call no man your father upon the earth: for one is your Father, who is in heaven.
10 Neither be called masters: for one is your Master, even Christ.
11 But he who is greatest among you shall be your servant.
12 And whoever shall exalt himself shall be abased; and he who shall humble himself shall be exalted.

9.15 Woe to the scribes and Pharisees (Jerusalem) Matthew 23:13-39

Matthew 23:13-39

13 But woe to you, scribes and Pharisees, hypocrites! For you shut up the kingdom of heaven against men: for you neither go in yourselves, neither do you allow those that are entering to go in.

14 Woe to you, scribes and Pharisees, hypocrites! For you devour widows' houses, and for a pretence make long prayer: therefore you shall receive the greater damnation.

15 Woe to you, scribes and Pharisees, hypocrites! For you compass sea and land to make one proselyte, and when he is made, you make him twofold more the child of hell than yourselves.

16 Woe to you, you blind guides, who say, Whoever shall swear by the temple, it is nothing; but whoever shall swear by the gold of the temple, he is a debtor!

17 You blind fools: for which is greater, the gold, or the temple that sanctifies the gold?

18 And, Whoever shall swear by the altar, it is nothing; but whoever swears by the gift that is upon it, he is guilty.

19 You blind fools: for which is greater, the gift, or the altar that sanctifies the gift?

20 Whoever therefore shall swear by the altar, swears by it, and by all things on it.

21 And whoever shall swear by the temple, swears by it, and by he who dwells in it.

22 And he who shall swear by heaven, swears by the throne of God, and by he who sits on it.

23 Woe to you, scribes and Pharisees, hypocrites! For you pay tithe of mint and anise and cummin, and have omitted the weightier matters of the law, judgment, mercy, and faith: these you ought to have done, and not left the other undone.

24 You blind guides, who strain at a gnat, and swallow a camel.

25 Woe to you, scribes and Pharisees, hypocrites! For you make clean the outside of the cup and of the platter, but within you are full of extortion and excess.

26 You blind Pharisee, first cleanse that which is within the cup and platter, that their outside may be clean also.

27 Woe to you, scribes and Pharisees, hypocrites! For you are like whitened graves, which indeed appear beautiful outward, but within are full of dead men's bones, and of all uncleanness.

28 Even so you also outwardly appear righteous to men, but within you are full of hypocrisy and iniquity.

29 Woe to you, scribes and Pharisees, hypocrites! Because you build the tombs of the prophets, and garnish the graves of the righteous,

30 "and say, 'If we had lived in the days of our fathers, we would not have been partakers with them in the blood of the prophets.'

31 "Therefore you are witnesses against yourselves that you are sons of those who murdered the prophets.

32 "Fill up, then, the measure of your fathers' guilt.

33 "Serpents, brood of vipers! How can you escape the condemnation of hell?

34 "Therefore, indeed, I send you prophets, wise men, and scribes: some of them you will kill and crucify, and some of them you will scourge in your synagogues and persecute from city to city,

35 "that on you may come all the righteous blood shed on the earth, from the blood of righteous Abel to the blood of Zechariah, son of Berechiah, whom you murdered between the temple and the altar.

36 "Assuredly, I say to you, all these things will come upon this generation.

37 "O Jerusalem, Jerusalem, the one who kills the prophets and stones those who are sent to her! How often I wanted to gather your children together, as a hen gathers her chicks under her wings, but you were not willing!

38 "See! Your house is left to you desolate;

39 "for I say to you, you shall see me no more till you say, 'Blessed is He who comes in the name of the LORD!'"

9.16 The widows two mites (Jerusalem) Mark 12:41-44, Luke 21:1-4

Mark 12:41-44	Luke 21:1-4
41 And Jesus sat over against the treasury, and	1 And he looked up, and saw the rich men casting

watched how the people cast money into the treasury: and many that were rich cast in much.	their gifts into the treasury.
42 And there came a certain poor widow, and she threw in two mites, which make a farthing.	2 He also saw a certain poor widow casting in there two mites.
43 And he called to him his disciples, and said to them, Truly I say to you, That this poor widow has cast more in, than all those who have cast into the treasury:	3 And he said, Of a truth I say to you, that this poor widow has cast in more than all of them:
44 For they all did cast in from their abundance; but she from her want did cast in all that she had, even all her living.	4 For all these have from their abundance cast in to the offerings of God: but she of her extreme poverty has cast in all the living that she had.

9.17 There shall not be one stone left upon another (Mount of Olives) Mark 13:1-27, Luke 21:5-28, Matthew 24:1-31

Mark 13:1-17	Luke 21:5-24	Matthew 24:1-19
1 And as he went out of the temple, one of his disciples said to him, Master, see what manner of stones and what buildings are here!	5 And as some spoke of the temple, how it was adorned with goodly stones and gifts, he said,	1 And Jesus went out, and departed from the temple: and his disciples came to him to show him the buildings of the temple.
2 And Jesus answering said to him, Do you see these great buildings? There shall not be left one stone upon another, that shall not be thrown down.	6 As for these things which you see, the days will come, in which there shall not be left one stone upon another, that shall not be thrown down.	2 And Jesus said to them, Do you not see all these things? Truly I say to you, There shall not be left here one stone upon another, that shall not be thrown down.
3 And as he sat upon the mount of Olives over against the temple, Peter and James and John and Andrew asked him privately,	7a And they asked him, saying,	3a, b And as he sat upon the mount of Olives, the disciples came to him privately, saying,
4 Tell us, when shall these things be? And what shall be the sign when all these things shall be fulfilled?	7b, c Master, but when shall these things be? And what sign will there be when these things shall happen?	3c Tell us, when shall these things be?
		3c and what shall be the sign of your coming, and of the end of the world?

5 And Jesus answering them began to say, Take heed lest any man deceive you:	8a And he said, Take heed that you are not deceived:	4 And Jesus answered and said to them, Take heed that no man deceive you.
6 For many shall come in my name, saying, I am Christ; and shall deceive many.	8b-d for many shall come in my name, saying, I am Christ; and the time draws near: therefore do not go after them.	5 For many shall come in my name, saying, I am Christ; and shall deceive many.
7 And when you shall hear of wars and rumours of wars, do not be troubled: for such things must of necessity be; but the end shall not be yet.	9 But when you shall hear of wars and commotions, do not be terrified: for these things must first come to pass; but the end is not soon.	6 And you shall hear of wars and rumours of wars: see that you are not troubled: for all these things must come to pass, but the end is not yet.
8a-c For nation shall rise against nation, and kingdom against kingdom: and there shall be earthquakes in various places, and there shall be famines and troubles:	10 Then he said to them, Nation shall rise against nation, and kingdom against kingdom: 11a And great earthquakes shall be in various places, and famines,	7 For nation shall rise against nation, and kingdom against kingdom: and there shall be famines, and pestilences, and earthquakes, in various places.
	11b, c and pestilences; and fearful sights and great signs shall there be from heaven.	
8d these are the beginnings of sorrows.		8 All these are the beginning of sorrows.
	12 But before all these, they shall lay their hands on you, and persecute you, delivering you up to the synagogues, and into prisons, being brought before kings and rulers for my name's sake.	9 Then they shall deliver you up to be afflicted, and shall kill you: and you shall be hated of all nations for my name's sake.
9 But take heed to yourselves: for they shall deliver you up to councils; and in the synagogues you shall be beaten: and you shall be brought before rulers and kings for my sake, for a testimony against them.	13 And it shall turn to you for a testimony.	
10 And the gospel must first be published among all nations.		

11 But when they shall lead you, and deliver you up, take no thought beforehand what you shall say, neither premeditate: but whatever shall be given you in that hour, that speak: for it is not you who speaks, but the Holy Spirit.	14 Settle it therefore in your hearts, not to meditate ahead of time what you shall answer:	
	15 For I will give you a mouth and wisdom, which all your adversaries shall not be able to contradict nor resist.	
12 Now brother shall betray brother to death, and the father the son; and children shall rise up against their parents, and shall cause them to be put to death.	16 And you shall be betrayed both by parents, and family, and kindred, and friends; and some of you they shall cause to be put to death.	10 And then shall many be offended, and shall betray one another, and shall hate one another.
		11 And many false prophets shall rise, and shall deceive many.
		12 And because iniquity shall abound, the love of many shall wax cold.
13 And you shall be hated of all men for my name's sake: but he who shall endure to the end, shall be saved.	17 And you shall be hated of all men for my name's sake.	13 But he who shall endure to the end, the same shall be saved.
	18 But there shall not a hair of your head perish.	
	19 In your patience possess your souls.	
		14 And this gospel of the kingdom shall be preached in all the world for a witness to all nations; and then the end shall come.
	20 And when you shall see	

	Jerusalem compassed with armies, then know that its desolation is near.	
14 But when you shall see the abomination of desolation, spoken of by Daniel the prophet, standing where it ought not, (let him that reads understand,) then let those in Judea flee to the mountains:	21a Then let those which are in Judea flee to the mountains;	15 Therefore when you shall see the abomination of desolation, spoken of by Daniel the prophet, stand in the holy place, (let whoever reads understand:) 16 Then let those who are in Judea flee into the mountains:
	21b and let those in the midst of it depart; and let not those in the countries enter in.	
15 And let him who is on the housetop not go down into the house, neither enter in, to take anything out of his house:		17 Let him who is on the housetop not come down to take anything out of his house:
16 And let him who is in the field not turn back again to take up his garment.		18 Neither let him who is in the field return to take his clothes.
	22 For these are the days of vengeance, that all things which are written may be fulfilled.	
17 But woe to those who are with child, and to those who are nursing infants in those days!	23 But woe to those who are with child, and to those who are nursing infants, in those days! For there shall be great distress in the land, and wrath upon this people.	19 And woe to those who are with child, and to those who are nursing infants in those days!
	24 And they shall fall by the edge of the sword, and shall be led away captive into all nations: and Jerusalem shall be trodden down by the Gentiles, until the times of the Gentiles is fulfilled.	

Mark 13:18-24	Matthew 24:20-29
18 And pray that your flight is not in winter.	20 But pray that your flight is not in winter,

	neither on the Sabbath:
19 For in those days there shall be affliction, such as was not from the beginning of the creation which God created to this time, neither shall there be (after it).	21 For then shall be great tribulation, such as was not since the beginning of the world to this time, no, nor ever shall be.
20 And except the Lord had shortened those days, no flesh would be saved: but for the elect's sake, whom he has chosen, he shortened the days.	22 And except those days should be shortened, no flesh shall be saved: but for the elect's sake those days shall be shortened.
21 And then if any man shall say to you, Look, here is Christ; or, look, he is there; do not believe him:	23 Then if any man shall say to you, Look, here is Christ, or there; believe it not.
22 For false Christs and false prophets shall rise, and shall show signs and wonders, to seduce, if it were possible, even the elect.	24 For there shall arise false Christs, and false prophets, and shall show great signs and wonders; so much so that, if it were possible, they shall deceive the very elect.
23 But you take heed: look, I have foretold you all things.	25 Look, I have told you ahead of time.
	26 Therefore if they shall say to you, Look, he is in the desert; do not go there: look, he is in the secret chambers; do not believe it.
	27 For as the lightning comes out of the east, and shines even to the west; also shall the coming of the Son of man be.
	28 For wherever the carcass is, there will the eagles be gathered together.
24 But in those days, after that tribulation, the sun shall be darkened, and the moon shall not give her light,	29 Immediately after the tribulation of those days the sun shall be darkened, and the moon shall not give her light, and the stars shall fall from heaven, and the powers of the heavens shall be shaken:

Mark 13:25-27	Luke 21:25-28	Matthew 24:30-31
25 And the stars of heaven shall fall, and the powers that are in heaven shall be shaken.		
	25 And there shall be signs in the sun, and in the moon, and in the stars; and upon the earth distress of nations, with	

	perplexity; the sea and the waves roaring;	
	26 Men's hearts failing them for fear, and for looking after those things which are coming on the earth: for the powers of heaven shall be shaken.	
26 And then shall they see the Son of man coming in the clouds with great power and glory.	27 And then shall they see the Son of man coming in a cloud with power and great glory.	30 And then the sign of the Son of man shall appear in heaven: and then shall all the tribes of the earth mourn, and they shall see the Son of man coming in the clouds of heaven with power and great glory.
27 And then shall he send his angels,		31a And he shall send his angels
		31b with a great sound of a trumpet,
27b-d and shall gather together his elect from the four winds, from the uttermost part of the earth to the uttermost part of heaven.		And they shall gather together his elect from the four winds, from one end of heaven to the other.
	28 And when these things begin to come to pass, then look up, and lift up your heads; for your redemption draws near.	

9.18 Parable of the fig tree leafing (Mount of Olives) Mark 13:28-33, Luke 21:29-36, Matthew 24:32-36

Mark 13:28-33	Luke 21:29-33	Matthew 24:32-36
[88]28 Now learn a parable of the fig tree; When her branch is yet tender, and puts forth leaves, you know that summer is near:	29 And he spoke a parable to them; Look at the fig tree, and all the trees; 30 When they now shoot forth, you see and know of your own selves that summer is now near	32 Now learn a parable of the fig tree; When its branch is yet tender, and puts forth leaves, you know that summer is near:

---

[88] Parable 39. The fig tree leafing. Mr 13:28-31, Lu 21:29-33, Mt 24:32-35.

	at hand.	
29 So you also, when you shall see these things come to pass, know that it is near, even at the doors.	31 So likewise you, when you see these things come to pass, know that the kingdom of God is near at hand.	33 So likewise you, when you shall see all these things, know that it is near, even at the doors.
30 Truly I say to you, that this generation shall not pass, till all these things are done.	32 Truly I say to you, This generation shall not pass away, till all are fulfilled.	34 Truly I say to you, This generation shall not pass, till all these things are fulfilled.
31 Heaven and earth shall pass away: but my words shall not pass away.	33 Heaven and earth shall pass away: but my words shall not pass away.	35 Heaven and earth shall pass away, but my words shall not pass away.
32 But no man knows that day and that hour, no, not the angels who are in heaven, neither the Son, only the Father.		36 But no man knows that day and hour, no, not the angels of heaven, but my Father only.
33 You take heed, watch and pray: for you do not know when the time is.		

Luke 21:34-36
34 And take heed to yourselves, lest at any time your hearts be overcharged with surfeiting, and drunkenness, and cares of this life, and so that day come upon you unawares.
35 For as a snare shall it come on all those who dwell on the face of the whole earth.
36 Therefore, you watch and pray always, that you may be counted worthy to escape all these things that shall come to pass, and to stand before the Son of man.

9.19 Parable about the returning master (Mount of Olives) Mark 13:34-37, Matthew 24:37-44

Mark 13:34-37

[89]**34** For the Son of man is like a man taking a far journey, who left his house, and gave authority to his servants, and to every man his work, and commanded the porter to watch.

35 You therefore watch: for you do not know when the master of the house comes, at evening, or at midnight, or at the cockcrowing, or in the morning:

36 Lest coming suddenly he find you sleeping.

37 And what I say to you I say to all, Watch.

---

[89] Parable 40. The returning master Mr 13:33-37, Lu 21:34-36, Mt 24:37-44

Matthew 24:37-44

37 But as the days of Noah were, so also shall the coming of the Son of man be.

38 For as in the days that were before the flood they were eating and drinking, marrying and giving in marriage, until the day that Noah entered into the ark,

39 And did not know until the flood came, and took them all away; so also shall the coming of the Son of man be.

40 Then shall two be in the field; the one shall be taken, and the other left.

41 Two women shall be grinding at the mill; the one shall be taken, and the other left.

42 Watch therefore: for you do not know what hour your Lord does come.

43 But know this, that if the owner of the house had known in what watch the thief would come, he would have watched, and would not have allowed his house to be broken into.

44 Therefore you also be ready: for in such an hour as you do not think the Son of man comes.

9.20 Parable about the faithful and wise servant (Mount of Olives) Matthew 24:45-51

Matthew 24:45-51

[90]**45** Who then is a faithful and wise servant, whom his lord has made ruler over his household, to give them food in due season?

46 Blessed is that servant, whom his lord when he comes shall find so doing.

47 Truly I say to you, That he shall make him ruler over all his goods.

48 But if that evil servant shall say in his heart, My lord delays his coming;

49 And shall begin to smite his fellow servants, and to eat and drink with the drunken;

50 The lord of that servant shall come in a day when he is not looking for him, and in an hour that he is not aware of,

51 And shall cut him asunder, and appoint him his portion with the hypocrites: there shall be weeping and gnashing of teeth.

9.21 Parable of the ten virgins (Mount of Olives) Matthew 25:1-46

Matthew 25:1-13

[91]**1** Then shall the kingdom of heaven be likened to ten virgins, who took their lamps, and went forth to meet the bridegroom.

2 And five of them were wise, and five were foolish.

3 Those who were foolish took their lamps, and took no oil with them:

4 But the wise took oil in their vessels with their lamps.

5 While the bridegroom delayed, they all slumbered and slept.

6 And at midnight there was a cry made, Look, the bridegroom is coming; go out to meet him.

---

[90] Parable 41. The faithful and wise servant versus the evil servant. Mt 24:45-51, Lu 12:41-48

[91] Parable 42. The ten virgins. Mt 25:1-13.

7 Then all those virgins arose, and trimmed their lamps.

8 And the foolish said to the wise, Give us some of your oil; for our lamps have gone out.

9 But the wise answered, saying, Not so; lest there is not enough for us and you: but go rather to those who sell, and buy for yourselves.

10 And while they went to buy, the bridegroom came; and those who were ready went in with him to the marriage: and the door was shut.

11 Afterward came also the other virgins, saying, Lord, Lord, open to us.

12 But he answered and said, Truly I say to you, I do not know you.

13 Watch therefore, for you know neither the day nor the hour in which the Son of man comes.

9.22 Parable of the talents (Mount of Olives) Matthew 25:14-30

Matthew 25:14-30

[92]**14** For the kingdom of heaven is as a man travelling into a far country, who called his own servants, and delivered to them his goods.

15 And to one he gave five talents, to another two, and to another one; to every man according to his individual ability; and straightaway took his journey.

16 Then he who had received the five talents went and traded with the same, and made them five other talents.

17 And likewise he who had received two, he also gained two others.

18 But he who had received one went and dug in the earth, and hid his lord's money.

19 After a long time the lord of those servants came, and reckoned with them.

20 And so he who had received five talents came and brought five other talents, saying, Lord, you delivered to me five talents: look, I have gained beside them five talents more.

21 His lord said to him, Well done, good and faithful servant: you have been faithful over a few things, I will make you ruler over many things: you enter into the joy of your lord.

22 He also who had received two talents came and said, Lord, you delivered to me two talents: look, I have gained two other talents besides them.

23 His lord said to him, Well done, good and faithful servant; you have been faithful over a few things, I will make you ruler over many things: you enter into the joy of your lord.

24 Then he who had received the one talent came and said, Lord, I knew you, that you are a hard man, reaping where you have not sown, and gathering where you have not strewn:

25 And I was afraid, and went and hid your talent in the earth: look, there you have what is yours.

26 His lord answered and said to him, you wicked and slothful servant, you knew that I reap where I did not sow, and gather where I have not strewn:

27 You ought therefore to have put my money with the exchangers, and then at my coming I should have received mine own with interest.

---

[92] Parable 43. The talents. Mt 25:14-30.

28 Take therefore the talent from him, and give it to him who has ten talents.

29 For to everyone who has shall (more) be given, and he shall have abundance: but from him who does not have shall be taken away even that which he has.

30 And cast the unprofitable servant into outer darkness: there shall be weeping and gnashing of teeth.

9.23 Parable of the sheep and goats (Mount of Olives) Matthew 25:31-46

Matthew 25:31-46

[93]**31** When the Son of man shall come in his glory, and all the holy angels with him, then shall he sit upon the throne of his glory:

32 And before him shall be gathered all nations: and he shall separate them one from another, as a shepherd divides his sheep from the goats:

33 And he shall set the sheep on his right hand, but the goats on the left.

34 Then shall the King say to them on his right hand, Come, you blessed of my Father, inherit the kingdom prepared for you from the foundation of the world:

35 For I was hungry, and you gave me meat: I was thirsty, and you gave me drink: I was a stranger, and you took me in:

36 Naked, and you clothed me: I was sick, and you visited me: I was in prison, and you came to me.

37 Then shall the righteous answer him, saying, Lord, when did we see you hungry, and fed you? Or thirsty, and gave you drink?

38 When did we see you a stranger, and took you in? Or naked, and clothed you?

39 Or when did we see you sick, or in prison, and came to you?

40 And the King shall answer and say to them, Truly I say to you, Inasmuch as you have done it to one of the least of these my brethren, you have done it to me.

41 Then shall he say also to those on the left hand, Depart from me, you cursed, into everlasting fire, prepared for the devil and his angels:

42 For I was hungry, and you gave me no meat: I was thirsty, and you gave me no drink:

43 I was a stranger, and you did not take me in: naked, and you did not clothe me: sick, and in prison, and you did not visit me.

44 Then shall they also answer him, saying, Lord, when did we see you hungry, or thirsty, or a stranger, or naked, or sick, or in prison, and did not minister to you?

45 Then shall he answer them, saying, Truly I say to you, Inasmuch as you did not do it to one of the least of these, you did not do it to me.

46 And these shall go away into everlasting punishment: but the righteous into life eternal.

Luke 21:37, 38

---

[93] Parable 44. The sheep and the goats. Mt 25:31-46.

37 And in the daytime he was teaching in the temple; and at night he went out, and abode in the mount that is called the Mount of Olives.

38 And all the people came early in the morning to him in the temple, to hear him.

9.24 Jesus tells date of crucifixion Mark 14:1, 2, Luke 22:1, 2, Matthew 26:1-5

Mark 14:1, 2	Luke 22:1, 2	Matthew 26:1-5
		1 And it happened, when Jesus had finished all these sayings, he said to his disciples,
1a After two days was the feast of the Passover, and of unleavened bread:	1 Now the feast of unleavened bread drew near, which is called the Passover.	2 You know that after two days is the feast of the Passover, and the Son of man is betrayed to be crucified.
		3 Then assembled together the chief priests, and the scribes, and the elders of the people, to the palace of the high priest, who was called Caiaphas,
1b and the chief priests and the scribes sought how they might take him craftily, and put him to death.	2 And the chief priests and scribes sought how they might kill him; for they feared the people.	4 And consulted that they might take Jesus by subtlety, and kill him.
2 But they said, Not on the feast day, lest there be an uproar of the people.		5 But they said, Not on the feast day, lest there be an uproar among the people.

9.25 Anointed by woman at Simon's house (Bethany) Mark 14:3-9, Matthew 26:6-13

Mark 14:3-9	Matthew 26:6-13
3 And being in Bethany in the house of Simon the leper, as he sat to eat, there came a woman having an alabaster box of ointment of spikenard very precious; and she broke the box, and poured it on his head.	6 Now when Jesus was in Bethany, in the house of Simon the leper,
	7 There came to him a woman having an alabaster box of very precious ointment, and poured it on his head, as he sat to eat.
4 And there were some that were indignant	8 But when his disciples saw it, they were

183

among themselves, and said, Why was this waste of the ointment made?	indignant, saying, To what purpose is this waste?
5 For it might have been sold for more than three hundred pence, and given to the poor. And they murmured against her.	9 For this ointment might have been sold for much, and given to the poor.
6 And Jesus said, Let her alone; why do you trouble her? She has worked a good work on me.	10 When Jesus understood it, he said to them, Why do you trouble the woman? For she has wrought a good work upon me.
7 For you have the poor with you always, and whenever you will you may do them good: but me you do not have always.	11 For you have the poor always with you; but me you do not have always.
8 She has done what she could: she is come beforehand to anoint my body to the burying.	12 For in that she has poured this ointment on my body, she did it for my burial.
9 Truly I say to you, Wherever this gospel shall be preached throughout the whole world, this also that she has done shall be spoken of for a memorial of her.	13 Truly I say to you, Wherever this gospel shall be preached in the whole world, there also shall this, that this woman has done, be told for a memorial of her.

9.26 Judas offers to betray Jesus Mark 14:10-11, Luke 22:3-6, Matthew 26:14-16

Mark 14:10-11	Luke 22:3-6	Matthew 26:14-16
	3 Then Satan entered Judas, surnamed Iscariot, who was numbered among the twelve.	
10 Then Judas Iscariot, one of the twelve, went to the chief priests to betray Him to them.	4 So he went his way and conferred with the chief priests and captains, how he might betray Him to them.	Then one of the twelve, called Judas Iscariot, went to the chief priests
11 And when they heard it, they were glad, and promised to give him money. So he sought how he might conveniently betray Him.	5 And they were glad, and agreed to give him money.	
		15 and said, "What are you willing to give me if I deliver Him to you?" And they counted out to him thirty pieces of silver.
	6 So he promised and sought opportunity to betray Him to	16 So from that time he sought opportunity to betray Him.

	them in the absence of the multitude.	

10: Last week in Jerusalem (Wednesday - Friday)

10.01 Last Supper and washing of disciples' feet (Wednesday; Jerusalem) John 13:1-20

John 13:1-20

1 Now before the feast of the Passover, when Jesus knew that his hour had come that he should depart out of this world to the Father, having loved his own which were in the world, he loved them to the end.

2 And supper being ended, the devil having now put into the heart of Judas Iscariot, Simon's son, to betray him;

3 Jesus knowing that the Father had given all things into his hands, that he had come from God, and was going back to God;

4 He rose from supper, and laid aside his garments; and took a towel, and girded himself.

5 After that he poured water into a basin, and began to wash the disciples' feet, and to wipe them with the towel with which he was girded.

6 Then he came to Simon Peter: and Peter said to him, Lord, do you wash my feet?

7 Jesus answered and said to him, What I do you do not know now; but you shall know hereafter.

8 Peter said to him, You shall never wash my feet. Jesus answered him, If I do not wash you, you have no part with me.

9 Simon Peter said to him, Lord, not my feet only, but also my hands and my head.

10 Jesus said to him, He who is washed need not wash except to wash his feet, but is clean every bit: and you are clean, but not all.

11 For he knew who should betray him; therefore he said, You are not all clean.

12 So after he had washed their feet, and had taken his garments, and had sat down again, he said to them, Do you know what I have done to you?

13 You call me Master and Lord: and you say well; for so I am.

14 If I then, your Lord and Master, have washed your feet; you also ought to wash one another's feet.

15 For I have given you an example, that you should do as I have done to you.

16 Very Truly, I say to you, The servant is not greater than his lord; neither he who is sent greater than he who sent him.

17 If you know these things, happy are you if you do them.

18 I do not speak of all of you: I know whom I have chosen: but that the scripture may be fulfilled, He who eats bread with me has lifted up his heel against me.

19 Now I tell you before it happens, that, when it happens , you may believe that I am he.

20 Very Truly, I say to you, He who receives whomever I send receives me; and he who receives me

receives him who sent me.

10.02 The betrayer revealed John 13:21-30

John 13:21-30

21 When Jesus had said this, he was troubled in spirit, and testified, and said, Very Truly, I say to you, that one of you shall betray me.

22 Then the disciples looked to one another, doubting of whom he spoke.

23 Now there was leaning on Jesus' bosom one of his disciples, whom Jesus loved.

24 Simon Peter therefore beckoned to him, that he should ask who it should be of whom he spoke.

25 He then lying on Jesus' breast said to him, Lord, who is it?

26 Jesus answered, It is he, to whom I shall give a sop, when I have dipped it. And when he had dipped the sop, he gave it to Judas Iscariot, the son of Simon.

27 And after the sop Satan entered into him. Then Jesus said to him, What you do, do quickly.

28 Now no man at the table knew why he spoke this to him.

29 For some of them thought, because Judas had the bag, that Jesus had said to him, Buy those things that we have need of against the feast; or, that he should give something to the poor.

30 He then having received the sop went immediately out: and it was night.

10.03 A new commandment John 13:31-38

John 13:31-38

31 Therefore, when he had gone out, Jesus said, Now is the Son of man glorified, and God is glorified in him.

32 If God is glorified in him, God shall also glorify him in himself, and shall straightaway glorify him.

33 Little children, yet a little while I am with you. You shall seek me: and as I said to the Jews, Where I go, you cannot come; so now I say to you.

34 A new commandment I give to you, That you love one another; as I have loved you, that you also love one another.

35 By this shall all men know that you are my disciples, if you love one to another.

36 Simon Peter said to him, Lord, where are you going? Jesus answered him, Where I go, you cannot follow me now; but you shall follow me afterwards.

37 Peter said to him, Lord, why can I not follow you now? I will lay down my life for your sake.

38 Jesus answered him, Will you lay down your life for my sake? Very Truly, I say to you, The cock shall not crow, till you have denied me thrice.

10.04 Preparation for the Passover (Thursday, Jerusalem) Mark 14:12-16, Luke 22:7-13, Matthew 26:17-19

Mark 14:12-16	Luke 22:7-13	Matthew 26:17-19
12 And on the first day of	7 Then came the day of	17 Now the first day of the feast

unleavened bread, when they killed the Passover, his disciples said to him, Where do you want us to go and prepare that you may eat the Passover?	unleavened bread, when the Passover must be killed. 8 And he sent Peter and John, saying, Go and prepare us the Passover, that we may eat. 9 And they said to him, Where do you want us to prepare?	of unleavened bread the disciples came to Jesus, saying to him, Where do you want us to prepare for you to eat the Passover?
13 And he sent forth two of his disciples, and said to them, You go into the city, and there you shall meet a man bearing a pitcher of water: follow him.	10 And he said to them, Look, when you have entered into the city, there shall a man meet you, bearing a pitcher of water; follow him into the house he enters.	
14 And wherever he shall go in, you say to the owner of the house, The Master says, Where is the guest chamber, where I shall eat the Passover with my disciples?	11 And you shall say to the owner of the house, The Master says to you, Where is the guest chamber, where I shall eat the Passover with my disciples?	18 And he said, Go into the city to such a man, and say to him, The Master says, My time is at hand; I will keep the Passover at your house with my disciples.
15 And he will show you a large upper room furnished and prepared: there make ready for us.	12 And he shall show you a large upper room furnished: there make ready.	
16 And his disciples went forth, and came into the city, and found as he had said to them: and they made ready the Passover.	13 And they went, and found as he had said to them: and they made ready the Passover.	19 And the disciples did as Jesus had appointed them; and they made ready the Passover.

10.05 Passover eaten (Upper room, Jerusalem) Mark 14:17, Luke 22:14-16, Matthew 26:20

Mark 14:17	Luke 22:14-16	Matthew 26:20
17 And in the evening he came with the twelve.		
	14 And when the hour had come, he sat down, and the twelve apostles with him.	20 Now when it was evening, he sat down with the twelve.
	15 And he said to them, With desire I have desired to eat this	

	Passover with you before I suffer:	
	16 For I say to you, I will not any more eat of it, until it is fulfilled in the kingdom of God.	

10.06 Another warning of betrayal (Upper room) Mark 14:18-21, Luke 22:21-23, Matthew 26:21-25

Mark 14:18-21	Luke 22:21-23	Matthew 26:21-25
18 And as they sat and did eat, Jesus said, Truly I say to you, One of you who eats with me shall betray me.	21 But, look, the hand of him who betrays me is with me on the table.	21 And as they did eat, he said, Truly I say to you, that one of you shall betray me.
19 And they began to be sorrowful, and to say to him one by one, Is it I? and another said, Is it I?	23 And they began to enquire among themselves, which of them it was that should do this thing.	22 And they were exceeding sorrowful, and began every one of them to say to him, Lord, is it I?
20 And he answered and said to them, It is one of the twelve, that dips with me in the dish.		23 And he answered and said, He who dips his hand with me in the dish, the same shall betray me.
21 The Son of man indeed goes, as it is written of him: but woe to that man by whom the Son of man is betrayed! It would have been good for that man if he had never been born.	22 And truly the Son of man goes, as it was determined: but woe to that man by whom he is betrayed!	24 The Son of man goes as it is written of him: but woe to that man by whom the Son of man is betrayed! It had been good for that man if he had not been born.
		25 Then Judas, who betrayed him, answered and said, Master, is it I? He said to him, You have said.

10.07 The Lord's Supper instituted (Upper room) Mark 14:22-25, Luke 22:19-20, 17-18, Matthew 26:26-29

Mark 14:22-25	Luke 22:17-20	Matthew 26:26-29
22 And as they did eat, Jesus took bread, and blessed, and broke it, and gave to them, and	19a-c And he took bread, and gave thanks, and broke it, and gave to them, saying, This is my	26 And as they were eating, Jesus took bread, and blessed it, and broke it, and gave it to the

said, Take, eat: this is my body.	body	disciples, and said, Take, eat; this is my body.
	19d-e which is given for you: this do in remembrance of me.	
23 And he took the cup, and when he had given thanks, he gave it to them: and they all drank of it.	17 And he took the cup, and gave thanks, and said, Take this, and divide it among yourselves:	27 And he took the cup, and gave thanks, and gave it to them, saying, Drink you all of it;
24 And he said to them, This is my blood of the new testament, which is shed for many.	20 Likewise also the cup after supper, saying, This cup is the new testament in my blood, which is shed for you.	28 For this is my blood of the new testament, which is shed for many for the remission of sins.
25 Truly I say to you, I will no more drink of the fruit of the vine, until that day that I drink it new in the kingdom of God.	18 For I say to you, I will not drink of the fruit of the vine, until the kingdom of God shall come.	29 But I say to you, henceforth I will not drink of this fruit of the vine, until that day when I drink it new with you in my Father's kingdom.

10.08 You shall deny me thrice (Upper room), Mark 14:27-31, Luke 22:31-38, Matthew 26:31-35

Mark 14:27-31	Luke 22:31-34	Matthew 26:31-35
27 And Jesus said to them, All of you shall be offended because of me this night: for it is written, I will smite the shepherd, and the sheep shall be scattered.		31 Then Jesus said to them, All of you shall be offended because of me this night: for it is written, I will smite the shepherd, and the sheep of the flock shall be scattered abroad.
28 But after I have risen, I will go before you into Galilee.		32 But after I have risen again, I will go before you into Galilee.
	31 And the Lord said, Simon, Simon, look, Satan has desired to have you, that he may sift you as wheat:	
	32 But I have prayed for you, that your faith does not fail; and when you are converted, strengthen your brethren.	
29a But Peter said to him,	33 And he said to him, Lord, I	33a Peter answered and said to

189

	am ready to go with you, both into prison, and to death.	him,
29b, c Although all shall be offended, yet I will not.		33b Though all men shall be offended because of you, yet will I never be offended.
30 And Jesus said to him, Truly I say to you, That this day, even in this night, before the cock crows twice, you shall deny me thrice.	34 And he said, I tell you, Peter, the cock shall not crow this day, before you shall thrice deny that you know me.	34 Jesus said to him, Truly I say to you, That this night, before the cock crows, you shall deny me thrice.
31 But he spoke the more vehemently, If I should die with you, I will not deny you in any wise. Also, they all said likewise.		35 Peter said to him, Though I should die with you, yet will I not deny you. Likewise said all the disciples.

Luke 22:35-38
35 And he said to them, When I sent you without purse, and money, and shoes, did you lack any thing? And they said, Nothing.
36 Then said he to them, But now, he who has a purse, let him take it, and likewise his money: and he who has no sword, let him sell his garment, and buy one.
37 For I say to you, that what is written must yet be accomplished in me, And he was reckoned among the transgressors: for the things concerning me have an end.
38 And they said, Lord, look, here are two swords. And he said to them, It is enough.

10.09 The greatest as the younger; the chief as one who serves (Upper room) Luke 22:24-30

Luke 22:24-30

24 And there was also strife among them, which of them should be counted the greatest.

25 And he said to them, The kings of the Gentiles exercise lordship over them; and those who exercise authority over them are called benefactors.

26 But you shall not be so: but he who is greatest among you, let him be as the younger; and he who is chief, as he who serves.

27 For which is greater, he who sits to eat, or he who serves? Is it not he who sits to eat? But I am among you as he who serves.

28 You are those who have continued with me in my temptations.

29 And I appoint to you a kingdom, as my Father has appointed to me;

30 That you may eat and drink at my table in my kingdom, and sit on thrones judging the twelve tribes of Israel.

10.10 Jesus, the way, truth and life (Upper room, Jerusalem) John 14:1-11

John 14:1-11

1 Let not your heart be troubled: you believe in God, believe also in me.

2 In my Father's house are many mansions: if it were not so, I would have told you. I go to prepare a place for you.

3 And if I go and prepare a place for you, I will come again, and receive you to myself; that where I am, there you may be also.

4 And where I go you know, and the way you know.

5 Thomas said to him, Lord, we do not know where you go; and how can we know the way?

6 Jesus said to him, I am the way, the truth, and the life: no man comes to the Father, but by me.

7 If you had known me, you should have known my Father also: and from henceforth you know him, and have seen him.

8 Philip said to him, Lord, show us the Father, and it will be sufficient for us.

9 Jesus said to him, I have been with you for such a long time, and yet you have not known me, Philip? He who has seen me has seen the Father; and how do you then say, Show us the Father?

10 Do you not believe that I am in the Father, and the Father in me? The words that I speak to you I do not speak of myself: but the Father that dwells in me, he does the works.

11 Believe me that I am in the Father, and the Father in me: or else believe me for the very works' sake.

10.11 Another Comforter (Upper room, Jerusalem) John 14:12-31

John 14:12-31

[94]**12** Very Truly, I say to you, He who believes on me, the works that I do shall he do also; and greater works than these he shall do; because I go to my Father.

13 And whatever you shall ask in my name, that I will do, that the Father may be glorified in the Son.

14 If you shall ask anything in my name, I will do it.

15 If you love me, keep my commandments.

16 And I will pray the Father, and he shall give you another Comforter, that he may abide with you forever;

17 Even the Spirit of truth; whom the world cannot receive, because it does not see him, neither knows him: but you know him; for he dwells with you, and shall be in you.

18 I will not leave you comfortless: I will come to you.

19 Yet a little while, and the world sees me no more; but you see me: because I live, you shall live also.

20 At that day you shall know that I am in my Father, and you in me, and I in you.

21 He who has my commandments, and keeps them, he it is that loves me: and he who loves me shall be loved of my Father, and I will love him, and will manifest myself to him.

22 Judas said to him, not Iscariot, Lord, how is it that you will manifest yourself to us, and not to the

---

[94] The disciple's power and authority 7 (of 10). Joh 14:12-31.

world?

23 Jesus answered and said to him, If a man loves me, he will keep my words: and my Father will love him, and we will come to him, and make our abode with him.

24 He who does not love me does not keep my sayings: and the word which you hear is not mine, but the Father's who sent me.

25 These things I have spoken to you, being yet present with you.

26 But the Comforter, who is the Holy Ghost, whom the Father will send in my name, he shall teach you all things, and bring all things to your remembrance, whatever I have said to you.

27 Peace I leave with you, my peace I give to you: not as the world gives, I give to you. Do not let your heart be troubled, neither let it be afraid.

28 You have heard how I said to you, I go away, and come again to you. If you loved me, you would rejoice, because I said, I go to the Father: for my Father is greater than I.

29 And now I have told you before it happens, that, when it happens, you might believe.

30 Hereafter I will not talk much with you: for the prince of this world comes, and has nothing in me.

31 But that the world may know that I love the Father; and as the Father gave me commandment, even so I do. Arise, let us go from here.

[It was at this point that Judas left to get a band of men, and officers.]

10.12 Departure for Gethsemane Mark 14:26, Luke 22:39, Matthew 26:30

Mark 14:26	Luke 22:39	Matthew 26:30
26a And when they had sung n hymn,		30a And when they had sung a hymn,
26b they went out into the mount of Olives.	39 And he came out, and went, as was his habit, to the mount of Olives; and his disciples also followed him.	30b they went out to the mount of Olives.

10.13 Parable of the true vine (en route to Gethsemane) John 15:1-8

John 15:1-8

[95]1 I am the true vine, and my Father is the farmer.

2 Every branch in me that does not bear fruit he takes away: and every branch that bears fruit, he purges it, that it may bring forth more fruit.

3 Now you are clean through the word which I have spoken to you.

4 Abide in me, and I in you. As the branch cannot bear fruit of itself, except it abides in the vine; no more can you, except you abide in me.

---

[95] Parable 45. The true vine. Joh 15:1-8.

5 I am the vine, you are the branches: He who abides in me, and I in him, the same brings forth much fruit: for without me you can do nothing.

6 If a man does not abide in me, he is cast forth as a branch, and is withered; and men gather them, and cast them into the fire, and they are burned.

7 If you abide in me, and my words abide in you, you shall ask what you will, and it shall be done to you.

8 Herein is my Father glorified, that you bear much fruit; so you shall be my disciples.

10.14 Love one another John 15:9-17

John 15:9-17

9 As the Father has loved me, so have I loved you: continue in my love.

10 If you keep my commandments, you shall abide in my love; even as I have kept my Father's commandments, and abide in his love.

11 These things have I spoken to you, that my joy might remain in you, and that your joy might be full.

12 This is my commandment, That you love one another, as I have loved you.

13 Greater love has no man than this, that a man lay down his life for his friends.

14 You are my friends, if you do whatever I command you.

15 Henceforth I do not call you servants; for the servant does not know what his lord does: but I have called you friends; for all things that I have heard of my Father I have made known to you.

16 You have not chosen me, but I have chosen you, and ordained you, that you should go and bring forth fruit, and that your fruit should remain: that whatever you shall ask the Father in my name, he may give it to you.

17 These things I command you, that you love one another.

10.15 The world's triple hatred John 15:18-27

John 15:18-27

18 If the world hates you, you know that it hated me before it hated you.

19 If you were of the world, the world would love its own: but because you are not of the world, but I have chosen you out of the world, therefore the world hates you.

20 Remember the word that I said to you, The servant is not greater than his lord. If they have persecuted me, they will also persecute you; if they have kept my saying, they will keep yours also.

21 But all these things they will do to you for my name's sake, because they do not know him who sent me.

22 If I had not come and spoken to them, they would not have had sin: but now they have no cloak for their sin.

23 He who hates me hates my Father also.

24 If I had not done among them the works which no other man did, they would not have had sin: but now they have seen and hated both me and my Father.

25 But this happened, that the word might be fulfilled that is written in their law, They hated me without a cause.

26 But when the Comforter has come, whom I will send to you from the Father, even the Spirit of truth, who proceeds from the Father, he shall testify of me:

27 And you also shall bear witness, because you have been with me from the beginning.

10.16 I will send you the Comforter John 16:1-15

John 16:1-15

1 These things I have spoken to you, that you should not be offended.

2 They shall put you out of the synagogues: yes, the time is coming, that whoever kills you will think that he does God service.

3 And these things will they do to you, because they have not known the Father, nor me.

4 But these things I have told you, that when the time shall come, you may remember that I told you of them. And these things I did not say to you at the beginning, because I was with you.

5 But now I go my way to him who sent me; and none of you asks me, Where are you going?

6 But because I have said these things to you, sorrow has filled your heart.

7 Nevertheless I tell you the truth; It is expedient for you that I go away: for if I do not go away, the Comforter will not come to you; but if I depart, I will send him to you.

8 And when he is comes, he will reprove the world of sin, and of righteousness, and of judgment:

9 Of sin, because they do not believe on me;

10 Of righteousness, because I go to my Father, and you see me no more;

11 Of judgment, because the prince of this world is judged.

12 I have yet many things to say to you, but you cannot bear them now.

13 However when he, the Spirit of truth, has come, he will guide you into all truth: for he shall not speak of himself; but whatever he shall hear, that shall he speak: and he will show you things to come.

14 He shall glorify me: for he shall receive of mine, and shall show it to you.

15 All things that the Father has are mine: therefore I said, that he shall take of mine, and shall show it to you.

10.17 You will not see me, then you will see me John 16:16-22

John 16:16-22

16 A little while, and you shall not see me: and again, a little while, and you shall see me, because I go to the Father.

17 Then said some of his disciples among themselves, What is this that he said to us, A little while, and you shall not see me: and again, a little while, and you shall see me: and, Because I go to the Father?

18 They said therefore, What is this that he said, A little while? We cannot tell what he said.

19 Now Jesus knew that they were desirous to ask him, and said to them, Do you enquire among yourselves of that I said, A little while, and you shall not see me: and again, a little while, and you shall

see me?

20 Very Truly, I say to you, That you shall weep and lament, but the world shall rejoice: and you shall be sorrowful, but your sorrow shall be turned into joy.

21 A woman when she is in labour has sorrow, because her hour has come: but as soon as she has delivered the child, she remembers no more the anguish, for joy that a child is born into the world.

22 And you now therefore have sorrow: but I will see you again, and your heart shall rejoice, and your joy no man takes from you.

10.18 Ask in my name John 16:23-33

John 16:23-33

23 And in that day you shall ask me nothing. Very Truly, I say to you, Whatever you shall ask the Father in my name, he will give it to you.

24 Until now you have asked nothing in my name: ask, and you shall receive, that your joy may be full.

25 These things have I spoken to you in proverbs: but the time is coming, when I shall no more speak to you in proverbs, but I shall show you plainly of the Father.

26 At that day you shall ask in my name: and I do not say to you, that I will pray the Father for you:

27 For the Father himself loves you, because you have loved me, and have believed that I came out from God.

28 I came forth from the Father, and have come into the world: again, I leave the world, and go to the Father.

29 His disciples said to him, Look, now you speak plainly, and speak no proverb.

30 Now are we sure that you know all things, and does not need that any man should ask you: by this we believe that you came forth from God.

31 Jesus answered them, Do you now believe?

32 Look, the hour is coming, yes, has now come, that you shall be scattered, every man to his own, and shall leave me alone: and yet I am not alone, because the Father is with me.

33 These things I have spoken to you, that in me you might have peace. In the world you shall have tribulation: but be of good cheer; I have overcome the world.

10.19 Glorify your son John 17:1-5

John 17:1-5

1 After speaking these words, Jesus lifted up his eyes to heaven, and said, Father, the hour has come; glorify your Son, that your Son also may glorify you:

2 As you have given him power over all flesh, that he should give eternal life to as many as you have given him.

3 And this is life eternal, that they might know you the only true God, and Jesus Christ, whom you have sent.

4 I have glorified you on the earth: I have finished the work which you gave me to do.

5 And now, O Father, glorify me together with yourself with the glory which I had with you before the world was.

10.20 I have manifested your name John 17:6-8

John 17:6-8

6 I have manifested your name to the men whom you gave me out of the world: yours they were, and you gave them to me; and they have kept your word.

7 Now they have known that all things whatever you have given me are of you.

8 For I have given to them the words which you gave me; and they have received them, and have known surely that I came out from you, and they have believed that you did send me.

10.21 Jesus prays for his disciples John 17:9-26

John 17:9-26

9 I pray for them: I do not pray for the world, but for them whom you have given me; for they are yours.

10 And all mine are yours, and yours are mine; and I am glorified in them.

11 And now I am no more in the world, but these are in the world, and I come to you. Holy Father, keep through your own name those whom you have given me, that they may be one, as we are.

12 While I was with them in the world, I kept them in your name: those that you gave me I have kept, and none of them is lost, but the son of perdition; that the scripture might be fulfilled.

13 And now I come to you; and these things I speak in the world, that they might have my joy fulfilled in themselves.

14 I have given them your word; and the world has hated them, because they are not of the world, even as I am not of the world.

15 I do not pray that you should take them out of the world, but that you should keep them from the evil.

16 They are not of the world, even as I am not of the world.

17 Sanctify them through your truth: your word is truth.

18 As you have sent me into the world, even so have I also sent them into the world.

19 And for their sakes I sanctify myself, that they also might be sanctified through the truth.

20 Neither do I pray for these alone, but for them also which shall believe on me through their word;

21 That they all may be one; as you, Father, are in me, and I in you, that they also may be one in us: that the world may believe that you have sent me.

22 And the glory which you gave me I have given them; that they may be one, even as we are one:

23 I in them, and you in me, that they may be made perfect in one; and that the world may know that you have sent me, and have loved them, as you have loved me.

24 Father, I will that they also, whom you have given me, be with me where I am; that they may see my glory, which you have given me: for you loved me before the foundation of the world.

25 O righteous Father, the world has not known you: but I have known you, and these have known that you have sent me.

26 And I have declared to them your name, and will declare it: that the love with which you have loved me may be in them, and I in them.

10.22 Pressed (Gethsemane) Mark 14:32-42, Luke 22:40-46, Matthew 26:36-46, John 18:1

John 18:1
1 When Jesus had spoken these words, he went forth with his disciples over the brook Kidron, where there was a garden, into which he and his disciples entered,

Mark 14:32-38	Luke 22:40-46	Matthew 26:36-41
32 And they came to a place which was named Gethsemane: and he said to his disciples, Sit here, while I shall pray.	40 And when he was at the place, he said to them, Pray that you do not enter into temptation.	36 Then Jesus came with them to a place called Gethsemane, and said to the disciples, Sit here, while I go and pray yonder.
33 And he took with him Peter and James and John, and began to be extremely amazed, and to be very heavy;		37 And he took with him Peter and the two sons of Zebedee, and began to be sorrowful and very heavy.
34 And said to them, My soul is exceeding sorrowful to death: you wait here, and watch.		38 Then he said to them, My soul is exceeding sorrowful, even to death: You wait here, and watch with me.
35 And he went forward a little, and fell on the ground, and prayed that, if it were possible, the hour might pass from him. 36 And he said, Abba, Father, all things are possible to you; take away this cup from me: nevertheless not what I will, but what you will.	41 And he was withdrawn from them about a stone's throw, and kneeled down, and prayed, 42 Saying, Father, if you are willing, remove this cup from me: nevertheless not my will, but yours, be done.	39 And he went a little further, and fell on his face, and prayed, saying, O my Father, if it is possible, let this cup pass from me: nevertheless not as I will, but as you will.
	43 And there appeared an angel to him from heaven, strengthening him.	
	44 And being in an agony he prayed more earnestly: and his	

	sweat was as it were great drops of blood falling down to the ground.	
37 And he came, and found them sleeping, and said to Peter, Simon, are you sleeping? Could you not watch one hour?	45 And when he rose up from prayer, and came to his disciples, he found them sleeping for sorrow,	40 And he came to the disciples, and found them asleep, and said to Peter, What, could you not watch with me one hour?
38 Watch and pray, lest you enter into temptation. The spirit truly is ready, but the flesh is weak.	46 And said to them, Why do you sleep? Rise and pray, lest you enter into temptation.	41 Watch and pray, that you do not enter into temptation: the spirit indeed is willing, but the flesh is weak.

Mark 14:39-42	Matthew 26:42-46
39 And again he went away, and prayed, and spoke the same words.	42 He went away again the second time, and prayed, saying, O my Father, if this cup may not pass away from me, except I drink it, your will be done.
40 And when he returned, he found them asleep again, (for their eyes were heavy,) neither did they know what to answer him.	43 And he came and found them asleep again: for their eyes were heavy.
	44 And he left them, went away again, and prayed the third time, saying the same words.
41 And he came the third time, and said to them, Sleep on now, and take your rest: it is enough, the hour has come; look, the Son of man is betrayed into the hands of sinners.	45 Then he came to his disciples, and said to them, Sleep on now, and take your rest: look, the hour is at hand, and the Son of man is betrayed into the hands of sinners.
42 Rise up, let us go; lo, he who betrays me is at hand.	46 Rise, let us be going: look, he is at hand that does betray me.

10.23 Arrested and deserted (Friday Gethsemane) Mark 14:43-52, Luke 22:47-53, Matthew 26:47-56, John 18:2-11

Mark 14:43	Luke 22:47	Matthew 26:47-50a	John 18:2-3
			2 And Judas also, who betrayed him, knew the place: for Jesus often resorted there with his disciples.
43 And immediately,	47a And while he yet	47 And while he yet	3 Judas then, having

while he yet spoke, Judas, one of the twelve came, and with him a great multitude with swords and staves, from the chief priests and the scribes and the elders.	spoke, look a multitude,	spoke, look, Judas, one of the twelve, came, and with him a great multitude with swords and staves, from the chief priests and elders of the people.	received a band of men and officers from the chief priests and Pharisees, came there with lanterns and torches and weapons.

Mark 14:44-45	Luke 22:47-48	Matthew 26:48-50a
44 And he who betrayed him had given them a sign, saying, Whomever I shall kiss, the same is he; take him, and lead him away safely.		48 Now he who betrayed him gave them a sign, saying, Whomever I shall kiss, that same is he: hold him fast.
45 And as soon as he had come, he went straightaway to him, and said, Master, master; and kissed him.	47b and he who was called Judas, one of the twelve, went before them, and drew near to Jesus to kiss him.	49 And forthwith he came to Jesus, and said, Hail, master; and kissed him.
	48a But Jesus said to him,	50a And Jesus said to him, Friend, where have you come from?
	48b Judas, do you betray the Son of man with a kiss?	

John 18.4-9
4 Jesus therefore, knowing all things that should come upon him, went forth, and said to them, Whom do you seek?
5 They answered him, Jesus of Nazareth. Jesus said to them, I am he. And Judas also, who betrayed him, stood with them.
6 As soon then as he had said to them, I am he, they went backward, and fell to the ground.
7 Then he asked them again, Whom do you seek? And they said, Jesus of Nazareth.
8 Jesus answered, I have told you that I am he: if therefore you seek me, let these go their way:
9 That the saying might be fulfilled, which he spoke, Of them whom you gave me I have lost none.

Mark 14:46-47	Luke 22:49-51	Matthew 26:50b-51	John 18:10-11
46 And they laid their hands on him, and took him.		50b Then they came, and laid hands on Jesus, and took him.	

199

	[96]**49** When those who were about him saw what would follow, they said to him, Lord, shall we smite with the sword?		
47 And one of those who stood by drew a sword, and struck a servant of the high priest, and cut off his ear.	50 And one of them struck the servant of the high priest, and cut off his right ear.	51 And, look, one of them who was with Jesus stretched out his hand, and drew his sword, and struck a servant of the high priest's, and smote off his ear.	10 Then Simon Peter having a sword drew it, and struck the high priest's servant, and cut off his right ear. The servant's name was Malchus.
	51 And Jesus answered and said,		11 Then Jesus said to Peter, Put your sword into its sheath: the cup which my Father has given me, shall I not drink it?

Mark 14:48-52	Luke 22:51-53	Matthew 26:52-56
	51b-d Allow this also. And he touched his ear, and healed him.	
		52 Then said Jesus to him, Put up again your sword into his place: for all those who take the sword shall perish with the sword.
		53 Do you think that I cannot now pray to my Father, and he shall presently give me more than twelve legions of angels?
		54 But how then shall the scriptures be fulfilled, that it must be so?
48 And Jesus answered and said	52 Then Jesus said to the chief	55a, b In that same hour Jesus

[96] Healing miracle 37 (of 37). Ear of the high priest's servant. Lu 21:49-51.

to them, Have you come out, as against a thief, with swords and with staves to take me?	priests, and captains of the temple, and the elders, which were come to him, Have you come out, as against a thief, with swords and staves?	said to the multitudes, Have you come out as against a thief with swords and staves to take me?
49 I was daily with you in the temple teaching, and you did not take me: but the scriptures must be fulfilled.	53 When I was daily with you in the temple, you stretched forth no hands against me: but this is your hour, and the power of darkness.	55c, d I sat daily with you teaching in the temple, and you did not lay hold of me.
50 And they all forsook him, and fled.		56 But all this was done, that the scriptures of the prophets might be fulfilled. Then all the disciples forsook him, and fled.
51 And there followed him a certain young man, having a linen cloth cast about his naked body; and the young men laid hold of him:		
52 And he left the linen cloth, and fled from them naked.		

10.24 First examined by Annas (Jerusalem) John 18:12-14, 19-23

John 18:12-14

12 Then the band and the captain and officers of the Jews took Jesus, and bound him,

13 And led him away to Annas first; for he was father in law to Caiaphas, who was the high priest that same year.

14 Now Caiaphas was he, who gave counsel to the Jews, that it was expedient that one man should die for the people.

John 18:19-23

19 The high priest then asked Jesus of his disciples, and of his doctrine.

20 Jesus answered him, I spoke openly to the world; I always taught in the synagogue, and in the temple, where the Jews always gather; and in secret I have said nothing.

21 Why do you ask me? Ask those who heard me, what I have said to them: look, they know what I said.

22 And when he had thus spoken, one of the officers who stood by struck Jesus with the palm of his hand, saying, Do you answer the high priest so?

23 Jesus answered him, If I have spoken evil, bear witness of the evil: but if well, why do you strike me?

10.25 Tried and condemned by Caiaphas and the council (Jerusalem) Mark 14:53-65, Luke 22:54-55, 63-65, Matthew 26:57-68, John 18:24, 15-16

Mark 14:53-54	Luke 22:54-55	Matthew 26:57-58	John 18:24, 15-16
53a And they led Jesus away to the high priest:	54a Then they took him, and led him, and brought him into the high priest's house.	57 And those who had laid hold on Jesus led him away to Caiaphas the high priest, where the scribes and the elders were assembled.	24 Now Annas had sent him bound to Caiaphas the high priest.
53b and with him were assembled all the chief priests and the elders and the scribes.			
54 And Peter followed him afar off,	54b And Peter followed afar off.	58a But Peter followed him afar off	15 And Simon Peter followed Jesus, and so did another disciple: that disciple was known to the high priest, and went in with Jesus into the palace of the high priest.
			16 But Peter stood at the door outside. Then that other disciple went out, who was known to the high priest, and spoke to her that kept the door, and brought in Peter.
54b even into the palace of the high priest:		58b to the high priest's palace, and went in, and sat with the servants, to see the end.	
54c and he sat with the servants, and warmed himself at the fire.	55 And when they had kindled a fire in the midst of the hall, and		

	had sat down together, Peter sat down among them.		

Mark 14:55-64	Matthew 26:59-66
55 And the chief priests and all the council sought for witness against Jesus to put him to death; and found none.	59 Now the chief priests, and elders, and all the council, sought false witness against Jesus, to put him to death;
56 For many bore false witness against him, but their witness did not agree together.	60 But found none: yes, though many false witnesses came, yet found they none. At the last came two false witnesses,
57 And there arose certain, and bore false witness against him, saying,	
58 We heard him say, I will destroy this temple that is made with hands, and within three days I will build another made without hands.	61 And said, This fellow said, I am able to destroy the temple of God, and to build it in three days.
59 But not even then did their witness agree.	
60 And the high priest stood up in the midst, and asked Jesus, saying, Do you answer nothing? What is it which these witness against you?	62 And the high priest arose, and said to him, Do you answer nothing? What is it which these witness against you?
61 But he held his peace, and answered nothing. Again the high priest asked him, and said to him, Are you the Christ, the Son of the Blessed?	63 But Jesus held his peace. And the high priest answered and said to him, I adjure you by the living God, that you tell us whether you are the Christ, the Son of God.
62 And Jesus said, I am: and you shall see the Son of man sitting on the right hand of power, and coming in the clouds of heaven.	64 Jesus said to him, You have said: nevertheless I say to you, Hereafter you shall see the Son of man sitting on the right hand of power, and coming in the clouds of heaven.
63 Then the high priest tore his clothes, and said, What need we any further witnesses?	65 Then the high priest tore his clothes, saying, He has spoken blasphemy; what further need have we of witnesses? Look, now you have heard his blasphemy.
64 You have heard the blasphemy: what do you think? And they all condemned him to be guilty of death.	66 What do you think? They answered and said, He is guilty of death.

Mark 14:65	Luke 22:63-65	Matthew 26:67-68
	63 And the men that held Jesus	67 Then did they spit in his face,

	mocked him, and struck him.	and buffeted him; and others struck him with the palms of their hands,
65 And some began to spit on him, to cover his face, to buffet him, and to say to him, Prophesy: and the servants did strike him with the palms of their hands.	64 And when they had blindfolded him, they struck him on the face, and asked him, saying, Prophesy, who is it that struck you?	68 Saying, Prophesy to us, Christ, Who is he who struck you?
	65 And many other things blasphemously they spoke against him.	

10.26 Peter's triple denial (Jerusalem) Mark 14:66-72, Luke 22:56-62, Matthew 26:69-75, John 18:17-18, 25-27

Mark 14:66-72	Luke 22:56-62	Matthew 26:69-75	John 18.17-18, 25-27
66 And as Peter was beneath in the palace, there came one of the maids of the high priest:			
67 And when she saw Peter warming himself, she looked upon him, and said, You also were with Jesus of Nazareth.	56 But a certain maid looked at him as he sat by the fire, and looked earnestly at him, and said, This man was also with him.	69 Now Peter sat without in the palace: and a young girl came to him, saying, You also were with Jesus of Galilee.	17a, b Then said the damsel that kept the door to Peter, Are you not also one of this man's disciples?
68 But he denied, saying, I do not know, neither do I understand what you are saying. And he went out into the porch; and the cock crowed.	57 And he denied, saying, Woman, I do not know him.	70 But he denied before all of them, saying, I do not know what you are saying.	17c He said, I am not. 18 And the servants and officers stood there, who had made a fire of coals; for it was cold: and they warmed themselves: and Peter stood with them, and warmed himself. 25a And Simon Peter stood and warmed

			himself.
69 And a maid saw him again, and began to say to those who stood by, This is one of them.	58 And after a little while another saw him, and said, You are also of them. And Peter said, Man, I am not.	71 And when he had gone out onto the porch, another maid saw him, and said to those who were there, This man was also with Jesus of Nazareth.	25b They said therefore to him, Are you not also one of his disciples? He denied it, and said, I am not.
70a And he denied it again.		72 And again he denied with an oath, I do not know the man.	
70b-d And a little after, those who stood by said again to Peter, Surely you are one of them: for you are a Galilean, and your speech sounds like theirs.	59 And after about one hour another confidently affirmed, saying, Of a truth this fellow also was with him: for he is a Galilean.	73 And after a while those who stood by came to him, and said to Peter, Surely you also are one of them; for your speech betrays you.	26 One of the servants of the high priest, being his kinsman whose ear Peter cut off, said, Did I not see you in the garden with him?
71 But he began to curse and to swear, saying, I do not know this man of whom you speak. 72a And the second time the cock crowed.	60 And Peter said, Man, I do not know what you are saying. And immediately, while he yet spoke, the cock crowed.	74 Then he began to curse and to swear, saying, I do not know the man. And immediately the cock crowed.	27 Peter then denied again: and immediately the cock crowed.
72b-d And Peter remembered the word that Jesus said to him, Before the cock crows twice, you shall deny me thrice.	61 And the Lord turned, and looked at Peter. And Peter remembered the word of the Lord, how he had said to him, Before the cock crows, you shall deny me thrice.	75a-b And Peter remembered the word of Jesus, who said to him, Before the cock crows, you shall deny me thrice..	
72e And when he thought on it, he wept.	62 And Peter went out, and wept bitterly.	75c And he went out, and wept bitterly	

10.27 Are You the Christ? (Jerusalem) Mark 15:1, Luke 22:66-71, Matthew 27:1

Mark 15:1	Luke 22:66-71	Matthew 27:1
1a And straightaway in the morning the chief priests held a consultation with the elders and scribes and the whole council,	66 And as soon as it was day, the elders of the people and the chief priests and the scribes came together, and led him into their council, saying,	1 When the morning was come, all the chief priests and elders of the people took counsel against Jesus to put him to death:

Luke 22:67-61
67 Are you the Christ? Tell us. And he said to them, If I tell you, you will not believe:
68 And if I also ask you, you will not answer me, nor let me go.
69 Hereafter shall the Son of man sit on the right hand of the power of God.
70 Then said they all, Are you then the Son of God? And he said to them, You say that I am.
71 And they said, What need we any further witness? For we ourselves have heard of his own mouth.

10.28 Judas commits suicide (Jerusalem) Matthew 27:3-10

Matthew 27:3-10

3 Then Judas, who had betrayed him, when he saw that he was condemned, repented, and brought again the thirty pieces of silver to the chief priests and elders,

4 Saying, I have sinned in that I have betrayed the innocent blood. And they said, What is that to us? You see to that.

5 And he cast down the pieces of silver in the temple, and departed, and went and hung himself.

6 And the chief priests took the silver pieces, and said, It is not lawful to put them into the treasury, because they are the price of blood.

7 And they took counsel, and bought with them the potter's field, to bury strangers in.

8 Therefore that field was called, The field of blood, to this day.

9 Then was fulfilled that which was spoken by Jeremiah the prophet, saying, And they took the thirty pieces of silver, the price of him who was valued, whom they of the children of Israel did value;

10 And gave them for the potter's field, as the Lord appointed me.

10.29 Are you the king of the Jews? (Jerusalem) Mark 15:1-5, Luke 23:1-5, Matthew 27:2, 11-14, John 18:28-38

Mark 15:1b	Luke 23:1	Matthew 27:2, 11-	John 18:28
1b, c and bound Jesus, and carried him away, and delivered him to Pilate.	1 And the whole multitude of them arose, and led him to Pilate.	2 And when they had bound him, they led him away, and delivered him to	28 Then they led Jesus from Caiaphas to the hall of judgment: and it was early; and they

		Pontius Pilate the governor.	themselves did not go into the judgment hall, lest they should be defiled; but that they might eat the Passover.

John 18:29-32

29 Pilate then went out to them, and said, What accusation do you bring against this man?

30 They answered and said to him, If he were not a malefactor, we would not have delivered him up to you.

31 Then Pilate said to them, You take him, and judge him according to your law. The Jews therefore said to him, It is not lawful for us to put any man to death:

32 That the saying of Jesus might be fulfilled, which he spoke, signifying what death he should die.

Luke 23:2	John 18:33-36
2 And they began to accuse him, saying, We found this fellow perverting the nation, and forbidding to give tribute to Caesar, saying that he himself is Christ a King.	
	33 Then Pilate entered into the judgment hall again, and called Jesus, and said to him, Are you the King of the Jews?
	34 Jesus answered him, Do you say this thing of yourself, or did others tell it to you of me?
	35 Pilate answered, Am I a Jew? Your own nation and the chief priests have delivered you to me: what have you done?
	36 Jesus answered, My kingdom is not of this world: if my kingdom were of this world, then would my servants fight, that I should not be delivered to the Jews: but now is my kingdom not from here.

Mark 15:1b-5	Luke 23:3-5	Matthew 27:2, 11-14	John 18:28-38
2 And Pilate asked him, Are you the King of the Jews? And he answering said to him,	3 And Pilate asked him, saying, Are you the King of the Jews? And he answered him	11 And Jesus stood before the governor: and the governor asked him, saying, Are you	37 Pilate therefore said to him, Are you a king then? Jesus answered, you say that I am a

You said it.	and said, You said it.	the King of the Jews? And Jesus said to him, You say.	king. To this end was I born, and for this cause I came into the world, that I should bear witness to the truth. Every one that is of the truth hears my voice.
	4 Then Pilate said to the chief priests and to the people, I find no fault in this man.		38 Pilate said to him, What is truth? And when he had said this, he went out again to the Jews, and said to them, I find in him no fault at all.
3 And the chief priests accused him of many things: but he answered nothing.		12 And when he was accused by the chief priests and elders, he answered nothing.	
4 And Pilate asked him again, saying, Do you answer nothing? Look how many things they witness against you.		13 Then Pilate said to him, Do you not hear how many things they witness against you?	
5 But Jesus yet answered nothing; so that Pilate marvelled.		14 And he never answered him a word; so much so that the governor marvelled greatly.	
	5 And they were the more fierce, saying, He stirs up the people, teaching throughout all Judea, and beginning from Galilee to this place.		

10.30 Before Herod (Jerusalem) Luke 23:6-12

Luke 23:6-12

6 When Pilate heard of Galilee, he asked whether the man were a Galilean.

7 And as soon as he knew that he belonged to Herod's jurisdiction, he sent him to Herod, who himself also was at Jerusalem at that time.

8 And when Herod saw Jesus, he was exceeding glad: for he had desired to see him for a long time, because he had heard many things of him; and he hoped to have seen some miracle done by him.

9 Then he questioned with him in many words; but he answered him nothing.

10 And the chief priests and scribes stood and vehemently accused him.

11 And Herod with his men of war despised him, and mocked him, and arrayed him in a gorgeous robe, and sent him back to Pilate.

12 And the same day Pilate and Herod were made friends: for before they were at enmity with each other.

10.31 Crucify him (Jerusalem) Mark 15:6-14, Luke 23:13-17, 19, 18, 20-22, Matthew 27:15-23, John 18:39-40

Luke 23:13-16
13 And Pilate, when he had called together the chief priests and the rulers and the people,
14 Said to them, You have brought this man to me, as one who perverts the people: and, look, I, having examined him before you, have found no fault in this man touching those things of which you accuse him:
15 No, nor yet Herod: for I sent you to him; and, look, nothing worthy of death is done to him.
16 I will therefore chastise him, and release him.

Mark 15:6-14	Luke 23:17, 19, 18	Matthew 27:15-18	John 18:39-40
6 Now at that feast he released to them one prisoner, whom they desired.	17 (For of necessity he must release one to them at the feast.)	15 Now at that feast the governor was in the habit of releasing to the people a prisoner, whom they wanted	39a But you have a custom, that I should release to you one at the Passover:
7 And there was one named Barabbas, who lay bound with those who had committed insurrection with him, who had committed murder in the	19 (Who for a certain sedition made in the city, and for murder, was cast into prison.)	16 And they had then a notable prisoner, called Barabbas.	

insurrection.			
8 And the multitude crying aloud began to desire him to do as he had always done to them.			
9 But Pilate answered them, saying, Will you that I release to you the King of the Jews?		17 Therefore when they were gathered together, Pilate said to them, Whom do you want me to release to you? Barabbas, or Jesus which is called Christ?	39b will you therefore that I release to you the King of the Jews?
10 For he knew that the chief priests had delivered him because of envy.		18 For he knew that because of envy they had delivered him.	
11 But the chief priests moved the people, that he should rather release Barabbas to them.	18 And they cried out all at once, saying, Away with this [man], and release Barabbas to us:		40 Then they all cried again, saying, Not this man, but Barabbas. Now Barabbas was a robber.

Matthew 27:19-21
19 When he had sat down on the judgment seat, his wife sent to him, saying, Have nothing to do with that just man: for I have suffered many things this day in a dream because of him.
20 But the chief priests and elders persuaded the multitude that they should ask for Barabbas, and destroy Jesus.
21 The governor answered and said to them, Which of the two do you want me to release to you? They said, Barabbas.

Mark 15:12-14	Luke 23:20-22	Matthew 27:22-23
12 And Pilate answered and said again to them, What then do you want me to do to him whom you call the King of the Jews? 13 And they cried out again, Crucify him.		22 Pilate said to them, What shall I do then with Jesus which is called Christ? They all said to him, Let him be crucified.

	20 Pilate therefore, willing to release Jesus, spoke again to them.	
	21 But they cried, saying, Crucify him, crucify him.	
14 Then Pilate said to them, Why, what evil has he done? And they cried out the more exceedingly, Crucify him.	22 And he said to them the third time, Why, what evil has he done? I have found no cause of death in him: I will therefore chastise him, and let him go.	23 And the governor said, Why, what evil has he done? But they cried out the more, saying, Let him be crucified.

10.32 Scourged John 19:1-5

John 19:1-5

1 Pilate therefore took Jesus, and scourged him.

2 And the soldiers plaited a crown of thorns, and put it on his head, and they put a purple robe on him,

3 And said, Hail, King of the Jews! And they struck him with their hands.

4 Pilate went out again, and said to them, Look, I bring him out to you, that you may know that I find no fault in him.

5 Then Jesus came out, wearing the crown of thorns, and the purple robe. And Pilate said to them, Behold the man!

10.33 Behold your king John 19:6-15, Luke 23:23

John 19:6-15

6 When the chief priests therefore and officers saw him, they cried out, saying, Crucify him, crucify him. Pilate said to them, You take him, and crucify him: for I find no fault in him.

7 The Jews answered him, We have a law, and by our law he ought to die, because he made himself the Son of God.

8 When Pilate therefore heard that saying, he was the more afraid;

9 And went again into the judgment hall, and said to Jesus, Where did You come from? But Jesus did not answer him.

10 Then Pilate said to Him, Will you not speak to me? Don't you know that I have power to crucify you, and power to release you?

11 Jesus answered, You would have no power at all over me, except it were given you from above: therefore he who delivered me to you has the greater sin.

12 And from then on Pilate sought to release him: but the Jews cried out, saying, If you let this man go, you are not Caesar's friend: whoever makes himself a king speaks against Caesar.

13 When Pilate therefore heard that saying, he brought Jesus forth, and sat down in the judgment seat in a place that is called the Pavement, but in the Hebrew, Gabbatha.

14 And it was the preparation of the Passover, and about the sixth hour: and he said unto the Jews, Behold your King!

Luke 23:23	John 19:15
23 And they were instant with loud voices, requiring that he might be crucified. And their voices and those of the chief priests prevailed.	15 But they cried out, Away with him, away with him, crucify him. Pilate said to them, Shall I crucify your King? The chief priests answered, We have no king but Caesar.

10.34 Sentenced to death Mark 15:15, Luke 23:24-25, Matthew 27:24-26, John 19:16

Mark 15:15	Luke 23:24-25	Matthew 27:24-26	John 19:16
		24 When Pilate saw that he could not prevail, but that rather a tumult was made, he took water, and washed his hands before the multitude, saying, I am innocent of the blood of this just person: you see to it.	
		25 Then all the people answered and said, His blood be on us, and on our children.	
	24 And Pilate gave sentence that it should be as they required.		
15 And so Pilate, willing to please the people, released Barabbas to them, and delivered Jesus, when he had scourged him, to be crucified.	25 And he released to them he who for sedition and murder was cast into prison, whom they had desired; but he delivered Jesus to their will.	26 Then released he Barabbas to them: and when he had scourged Jesus, he delivered him to be crucified.	
			16 Then he delivered

			him therefore to them to be crucified. And they took Jesus, and led him away.

10.35 Mocked by Roman soldiers (Jerusalem) Mark 15:16-19, Matthew 27:27-30

Mark 15:16-19	Matthew 27:27-30
16 And the soldiers led him away into the hall, called Praetorium; and they called together the whole band.	27 Then the soldiers of the governor took Jesus into the common hall, and gathered to him the whole band of soldiers.
17 And they clothed him with purple, and platted a crown of thorns, and put it about his head,	28 And they stripped him, and put on him a scarlet robe.
18 And began to salute him, Hail, King of the Jews!	29 And when they had plaited a crown of thorns, they put it on his head, and a reed in his right hand: and they bowed the knee before him, and mocked him, saying, Hail, King of the Jews!
19 And they struck him on the head with a reed, and did spit upon him, and bowing their knees worshipped him.	30 And they spat on him, took the reed, and struck him on the head.

11: Crucifixion, resurrection, and ascension

11.01 Crucified at Golgotha (Jerusalem) Mark 15:20-23, 27-28, Luke 23:26-33, Matthew 27:31-34, 38, John 19:17-18

Mark 15:20-23, 27-28	Luke 23:26-33	Matthew 27:31-34, 38	John 19:17a
20 And when they had mocked him, they took off the purple from him, put his own clothes on him, and led him out to crucify him.		31 And after they had mocked him, they took the robe off from him, and put his own garments on him, and led him away to crucify him.	
			17a And he bearing his cross went forth
21 And they compelled one Simon a Cyrenian, who passed by, coming out of the country, the	26 And as they led him away, they laid hold upon one Simon, a Cyrenian, coming out	32 And as they came out, they found a man of Cyrene, Simon by name: they compelled	

| father of Alexander and Rufus, to bear his cross. | of the country, and they laid the cross on him, that he might bear it after Jesus. | him to bear his cross. | |

Luke 23:27-32
27 And there followed him a great company of people, and of women, who also wailed and lamented after him.
28 But Jesus turning to them said, Daughters of Jerusalem, do not weep for me, but weep for yourselves, and for your children.
29 For, look, the days are coming, in which they shall say, Blessed are the barren, and the wombs that never bore, and the breasts which never nursed an infant.
30 Then shall they begin to say to the mountains, Fall on us; and to the hills, Cover us.
31 For if they do these things in a green tree, what shall be done in the dry?
32 And there were also two other, malefactors, led with him to be put to death.

Mark 15:22-23, 27-28	Luke 23:33	Matthew 27:33-34, 38	John 19:17b-18
22 And they brought him to the place, Golgotha, which is, being interpreted, The place of a skull.		33 And when they had come to a place called Golgotha, that is to say, a place of a skull,	17b, c into a place called the place of a skull, which is called in the Hebrew Golgotha:
23 And they gave him wine mingled with myrrh to drink: but he did not receive it.		34 They gave him vinegar to drink mingled with gall: and when he had tasted it, he would not drink.	
	33a And when they had come to the place, which is called Calvary, there they crucified him,		18a Where they crucified him,
27 And with him they crucified two thieves; the one on his right hand, and the other on his left.	33b and the malefactors, one on the right hand, and the other on the left.	38 Then there were two thieves crucified with him, one on the right hand, and another on the left.	18b and two others with him, one on either side, and Jesus in the middle.
28 And the scripture was fulfilled, which			

said, And he was numbered with the transgressors.			

11.02 On the cross (Golgotha) Mark 15:24-32, Luke 23:34-43, Matthew 27:35-44, John 19:19-27

Mark 15:24-32	Luke 23:34-43	Matthew 27:35-44	John 19:19-22
	34a, b Then Jesus said, Father, forgive them; for they know not what they do.		
24 And when they had crucified him, they parted his garments, casting lots upon them, what every man should take.	35c And they parted his garments, and cast lots.	35 And they crucified him, and parted his garments, casting lots: that it might be fulfilled which was spoken by the prophet, They parted my garments among them, and upon my apparel did they cast lots.	23 Then the soldiers, when they had crucified Jesus, took his garments, and made four parts, to every soldier a part; and also his coat: now the coat was without seam, woven from the top throughout.
			24 They said therefore among themselves, Let us not rend it, but cast lots for it, whose it shall be: that the scripture might be fulfilled, which said, They parted my garment among them, and for my apparel they did cast lots. These things therefore the soldiers did.
25 And it was the third hour, and they crucified him.			
		36 And sitting down	

		they watched him there;	
26 And the superscription of his accusation was written over (him), THE KING OF THE JEWS.	38 And an inscription also was written over him in letters of Greek, and Latin, and Hebrew, THIS IS THE KING OF THE JEWS.	37 And set up over his head his accusation written, THIS IS JESUS THE KING OF THE JEWS.	19 And Pilate wrote a title, and put it on the cross. And the writing was, JESUS OF NAZARETH THE KING OF THE JEWS.
			20 This title then many of the Jews read: for the place where Jesus was crucified was near the city: and it was written in Hebrew, and Greek, and Latin.
			21 Then said the chief priests of the Jews to Pilate, Do not write, The King of the Jews; but that he said, I am King of the Jews.
			22 Pilate answered, What I have written I have written.

Mark 15:29-32	Luke 23:35-43	Matthew 27:39-44
	35 And the people stood looking. And the rulers also with them derided him, saying, He saved others; let him save himself, if he is Christ, the chosen of God.	
	36 And the soldiers also mocked him, coming to him, and offering him vinegar,	
	37 And saying, If you are the king of the Jews, save yourself.	
29a And those who passed by railed on him, wagging their		39 And those who passed by reviled him, wagging their

heads, and saying, ,		heads,
29b Ah, you who would destroy the temple, and build it in three days 30 Save yourself, and come down from the cross.		40 And saying, You who would destroy the temple, and build it in three days, save yourself. If you are the Son of God, come down from the cross.
31 Likewise also the chief priests mocking said among themselves with the scribes,		41 Likewise also the chief priests mocking him, with the scribes and elders, said,
31b He saved others; himself he cannot save. 32 Let Christ the King of Israel descend now from the cross, that we may see and believe. And those who were crucified with him reviled him.		42 He saved others; himself he cannot save. If he is the King of Israel, let him now come down from the cross, and we will believe him.
		43 He trusted in God; let him deliver him now, if he will have him: for he said, I am the Son of God.
	39 And one of the malefactors who were hanged railed on him, saying, If you are Christ, save yourself and us.	44 The thieves also, who were crucified with him, cast the same in his teeth.

Luke 25:40-43

40 But the other answering rebuked him, saying, Do you not fear God, seeing you are in the same condemnation?

41 And we indeed justly; for we receive the due reward of our deeds: but this man has done nothing wrong.

42 And he said to Jesus, Lord, remember me when you come into your kingdom.

43 And Jesus said to him, Truly I say to you, Today you shall be with me in paradise.

John 19:25-27

25 Now there stood by the cross of Jesus his mother, and his mother's sister, Mary the wife of Cleophas, and Mary Magdalene.

26 When Jesus therefore saw his mother, and the disciple standing by, whom he loved, he said to his mother, Woman, look at your son!

27 Then he said to the disciple, Look at your mother! And from that hour that disciple took her to his own home.

11.03 Jesus' death (Golgotha) Mark 15:33-37, Luke 23:44-46, Matthew 27:45-50, John 19:28-30

Mark 15:33-37	Luke 23:44-46	Matthew 27:45-50	John 19:28-30
33 And when the sixth hour had come, there was darkness over the whole land until the ninth hour.	44 And it was about the sixth hour, and there was a darkness over all the earth until the ninth hour.	45 Now from the sixth hour there was darkness over all the land until the ninth hour.	
34 And at the ninth hour Jesus cried with a loud voice, saying, Eloi, Eloi, lama sabachthani? Which is, being interpreted, My God, my God, why have you forsaken me?		46 And about the ninth hour Jesus cried with a loud voice, saying, Eli, Eli, lama sabachthani? That is to say, My God, my God, why have you forsaken me?	
35 And some of those who stood by, when they heard it, said, Look, he calls Elijah.		47 Some of those who stood there, when they heard that, said, This man calls for Elijah.	
			28 After this, Jesus knowing that all things were now accomplished, that the scripture might be fulfilled, said, I thirst.
36a And one ran and filled a sponge full of vinegar, and put it on a reed, and gave him to drink, saying, down.		48 And straightaway one of them ran, took a sponge, filled it with vinegar, put it on a reed, and gave him to drink.	29 Now a vessel full of vinegar was nearby: and they filled a sponge with vinegar, and put it upon hyssop, and put it to his mouth.
36b Leave him alone; let us see whether		49 The rest said, Let him be, let us see	

Elijah will come to take him		whether Elijah will come to save him.	
			30 When Jesus therefore had received the vinegar, he said, It is finished: and he bowed his head, and gave up the ghost.
37 And Jesus cried with a loud voice, and gave up the ghost.	46 And when Jesus had cried with a loud voice, he said, Father, into your hands I commend my spirit: and having said this, he gave up the ghost.	50 Jesus, when he had cried again with a loud voice, yielded up the ghost.	

11.04 Events attending Jesus' death Mark 15:38-41, Luke 23:45, 47-49, Matthew 27:51-56

Mark 15:38-41	Luke 23:45, 47-49	Matthew 27:51-56
	45a And the sun was darkened,	
38 And the veil of the temple was torn in two from the top to the bottom.	45b and the veil of the temple was torn in the middle.	51 And, the veil of the temple was torn in two from the top to the bottom; and the earth did quake, and the rocks split;
		52 And the graves were opened; and many bodies of the saints which slept arose,
		53 And came out of the graves after his resurrection, and went into the holy city, and appeared to many.
39 And when the centurion, who stood over against him, saw that he so cried out, and gave up the ghost, he said, Truly this man was the Son of God.	47 Now when the centurion saw what was done, he glorified God, saying, Certainly this was a righteous man.	54 Now when the centurion watching Jesus, and those that were with him, saw the earthquake, and those things that were done, they feared greatly, saying, Truly this was the Son of God.
	48 And all the people that came	

219

	together to that sight, looking at the things which were done, struck their breasts, and returned.	
40 There were also women looking on afar off: among whom was Mary Magdalene, and Mary the mother of James the less and of Joses, and Salome;	49 And all his acquaintance, and the women that followed him from Galilee, stood afar off, looking at these things.	55 And many women were there looking from afar off, which followed Jesus from Galilee, ministering to him:
41 (Who also, when he was in Galilee, followed him, and ministered to him;) and many other women who came up with him to Jerusalem.		56 Among whom was Mary Magdalene, and Mary the mother of James and Joses, and the mother of Zebedee's children.

11.05 Jesus' burial (Jerusalem) Mark 15:42-46, Luke 23:50-54, Matthew 27:57-60, John 19:31-42

Mark 15:42	John 19:31
42 And now when it was evening, because it was the preparation, that is, the day before the Sabbath,	31 The Jews therefore, because it was the preparation, that the bodies should not remain upon the cross on the Sabbath, (for that Sabbath was a high day,) begged Pilate that their legs might be broken, and that they might be taken away.

why were legs broken

John 19:32-47
32 Then the soldiers came, and broke the legs of the first, and of the other who were crucified with him.
33 But when they came to Jesus, and saw that he was dead already, they did not break his legs:
34 But one of the soldiers with a spear pierced his side, and immediately there came out blood and water.
35 And he who saw it bore record, and his record is true: and he knows that he says the truth, that you might believe.
36 For these things were done, that the scripture should be fulfilled, A bone of his shall not be broken.
37 And again another scripture said, They shall look on him whom they pierced.

Mark 15:43-46	Luke 23:50-54	Matthew 27:57-60	John 19:38-42
	50a And, look, there was a man named Joseph,	57 When it was evening, there came a rich man of Arimathea, named Joseph, who also himself was Jesus' disciple:	
	50b a counsellor; and he was a good man, and a just:		
43 Joseph of Arimathea, an honourable counsellor, which also waited for the kingdom of God, came, and went in boldly to Pilate, and asked for the body of Jesus.	51 (The same had not consented to the counsel and their deed;) he was of Arimathea, a city of the Jews: who also himself waited for the kingdom of God.	58 He went to Pilate, and begged the body of Jesus. Then Pilate commanded the body to be delivered.	38a And after this Joseph of Arimathea, being a disciple of Jesus, but secretly for fear of the Jews, begged Pilate that he might take away the body of Jesus: and
	52 This man went to Pilate, and begged the body of Jesus.		
44 And Pilate wondered if he were already dead: and calling to him the centurion, he asked him whether he had been dead awhile.			
45 And when he confirmed it from the centurion, he gave the body to Joseph.			38b Pilate gave him leave. He came therefore, and took the body of Jesus.
			39 And there came also Nicodemus, who at the first came to Jesus by night, and brought a mixture of myrrh and

			aloes, about a hundred pound weight.
46 And he bought fine linen, took him down, and wrapped him in the linen, and laid him in a tomb which was hewn out of a rock, and rolled a stone to the door of the tomb.	53 And he took it down, and wrapped it in linen, and laid it in a tomb that was hewn in stone, in which no man had ever been laid.	59 And when Joseph had taken the body, he wrapped it in a clean linen cloth,	40 Then they took the body of Jesus, and wrapped it in linen clothes with the spices, as the manner of the Jews is to bury.
	54 And that day was the preparation, and the Sabbath drew near.		41 Now in the place where he was crucified there was a garden; and in the garden a new tomb, in which no man had ever been laid.
		60a And laid it in his own new tomb, which he had hewn out in the rock:	42 There laid they Jesus therefore because of the Jews' preparation day; for the tomb was near at hand.
		60b and he rolled a great stone to the door of the tomb, and departed.	

11.06 Women watch Mark 15:47, Luke 23:55-56, Matthew 27:61

Mark 15:47	Luke 23:55-56	Matthew 27:61
	55 And the women also, who came with him from Galilee, followed after, and took note of the tomb, and how his body was laid.	
47 And Mary Magdalene and Mary the mother of Joses took note of where he was laid.		61 And there was Mary Magdalene, and the other Mary, sitting over against the tomb.
	56 And they returned, and prepared spices and ointments;	

	and rested the Sabbath according to the commandment.	

11.07 Tomb sealed (Saturday) Matthew 27:62-66

Matthew 27:62-66

62 Now the next day, that followed the day of the preparation, the chief priests and Pharisees came together to Pilate,

63 Saying, Sir, we remember what that deceiver said, while he was yet alive, After three days I will rise again.

64 Command therefore that the tomb be made sure until the third day, lest his disciples come by night, and steal him away, and say to the people, He is risen from the dead: so the last error shall be worse than the first.

65 Pilate said to them, You have a guard: go your way, make it as sure as you can.

66 So they went, and made the tomb sure, sealing the stone, and setting a watch.

11.08 The stone is rolled away (Sunday) Matthew 28:1-4

Matthew 28:2-4

2 And, there was a great earthquake: for the angel of the Lord descended from heaven, and came and rolled back the stone from the door, and sat upon it.

3 His countenance was like lightning, and his raiment white as snow:

4 And for fear of him the keepers did shake, and became as dead men.

11.09 Mary Magdalene visits the tomb alone John 20:1

John 20:1

1 The first day of the week Mary Magdalene came early, when it was yet dark, to the tomb, and saw the stone taken away from the tomb.

11.10 Peter and John see the empty tomb Luke 24:12, John 20:2-10

Luke 24:12	John 20:2-6
	2 Then she ran, and came to Simon Peter, and to the other disciple, whom Jesus loved, and said to them, They have taken away the Lord out of the grave, and we do not know where they have laid him.
12a Then Peter arose, and ran to the grave;	3 Peter therefore went forth, and that other disciple, and came to the grave.

	4 So they both ran together: and the other disciple did outrun Peter, and came first to the grave.
	5 And he stooping down, and looking in, saw the linen clothes lying there; yet he did not go in.
12b and stooping down, he saw the linen clothes laid by themselves,	6 Then Simon Peter came following him, and went into the grave, and saw the linen clothes lying there,
12c and departed, wondering in himself at that which had happened.	

John 20:7-10
7 And the napkin, that was about his head, not lying with the linen clothes, but wrapped together in a place by itself.
8 Then that other disciple also went in, who came first to the grave, and he saw, and believed.
9 For as yet they did not know the scripture, that he must rise again from the dead.
10 Then the disciples went away again to their own home.

11.11 Jesus appears first to Mary Magdalene Mark 16:9, John 20:11-17

Mark 16:9	John 20:11
9 Now when Jesus had risen early the first day of the week, he appeared first to Mary Magdalene, out of whom he had cast seven devils.	
	11 But Mary stood without at the grave weeping: and as she wept, she stooped down, and looked into the grave,

John 20:12-17
12 And saw two angels in white sitting, the one at the head, and the other at the feet, where the body of Jesus had lain.
13 And they said to her, Woman, why are you crying? She said to them, Because they have taken away my Lord, and I do not know where they have laid him.
14 And when she had said this, she turned back, saw Jesus standing there and did not know that it was Jesus.
15 Jesus said to her, Woman, why do you weep? Whom do you seek? She, supposing him to be the gardener, said to him, Sir, if you have carried him away from here, tell me where you have laid him, and I will take him away.
16 Jesus said to her, Mary. She turned herself, and said to him, Rabboni; which is to say, Master.

17 Jesus said to her, Do not touch me; for I have not yet ascended to my Father: but go to my brethren, and say to them, I ascend to my Father, and your Father; and to my God, and your God.

11.12 Mary tells the disbelieving disciples Mark 16:10, 11, John 20:18

Mark 16:10, 11	John 20:18
	18 Mary Magdalene came and told the disciples that she had seen the Lord, and that he had spoken these things to her.
10 And she went and told those that had been with him, as they mourned and wept.	
11 And when they had heard that he was alive, and had been seen by her, they did not believe.	

11.13 Other women (and Mary) visit the tomb Mark 16:1-8, Luke 24:1-11, Matthew 28:1, 5-10

Mark 16:1	Luke 24:1	Matthew 28:1
1 And when the Sabbath had ended, Mary Magdalene, and Mary the mother of James, and Salome, had bought sweet spices, that they might come and anoint him.	1 Now on the first day of the week, very early in the morning, they came to the grave, bringing the spices which they had prepared, and certain others with them.	1 At the end of the Sabbath, as it began to dawn toward the first day of the week, Mary Magdalene and the other Mary came to see the grave.

Mark 16:2-3
2 And very early in the morning the first day of the week, they came to the grave at the rising of the sun.
3 And they said among themselves, Who shall roll us away the stone from the door of the grave?

Mark 16:4-5	Luke 24:2-3
4 And when they looked, they saw that the stone was rolled away: for it was very great.	2 And they found the stone rolled away from the grave.
5 And entering into the grave, they saw a young man sitting on the right side, clothed in a long white garment; and they were frightened.	3 And they entered in, and did not find the body of the Lord Jesus. 4 And it happened, as they were much perplexed thereabout, look, two men stood by them in shining garments:

Mark 16:6	Luke 24:5-6	Matthew 28: 5-6
6a And he said to them, Do not	5 And as they were afraid, and	5 And the angel answered and

be afraid: You seek Jesus of Nazareth, who was crucified:	bowed down their faces to the earth, they said to them, Why do you seek the living among the dead?	said to the women, Do not be afraid: for I know that you seek Jesus, who was crucified.
6b he is risen; he is not here: look at the place where they laid him.	6 He is not here, but is risen:	6 He is not here: for he is risen, as he said. Come, see the place where the Lord lay.

Luke 24:6-8

6b, c remember how he spoke to you when he was yet in Galilee,
7 Saying, The Son of man must be delivered into the hands of sinful men, and be crucified, and the third day rise again.
8 And they remembered his words,

Mark 16:7-8	**Matthew 28:7-10**
7 But go your way, tell his disciples and Peter that he goes before you into Galilee: there shall you see him, as he said to you.	7 And go quickly, and tell his disciples that he is risen from the dead; and, look, he goes before you into Galilee; there you shall see him: look, I have told you
8 And they went out quickly, and fled from the grave; for they trembled and were amazed: neither said they anything to any man; for they were afraid.	8 And they departed quickly from the grave with fear and great joy; and did run to bring his disciples word.
	9 And as they went to tell his disciples, look, Jesus met them, saying, All hail. And they came and held him by the feet, and worshipped him.
	10 Then said Jesus to them, Do not be afraid: go tell my brethren that they go into Galilee, and there shall they see me.

Luke 24:9-11

9 And returned from the grave, and told all these things to the eleven, and to all the rest.
10 It was Mary Magdalene, and Joanna, and Mary the mother of James, and other women that were with them, who told these things to the apostles.
11 And their words seemed to them as idle tales, and they did not believe them.

11.14 Guards report the resurrection Matthew 28:11-15

Matthew 28:11-15

11 Now when they were going, some of the guards came into the city, and told the chief priests all the things that had happened.

12 And when they had assembled with the elders, and had taken counsel, they gave a large sum of money to the soldiers,

13 Saying, You say, His disciples came by night, and stole him away while we slept.

14 And if this comes to the governor's ears, we will persuade him, and secure you.

15 So they took the money, and did as they were taught: and this saying is commonly reported among the Jews until this day.

11.15 Jesus appears to two disciples going to Emmaus Mark 16:12-13, Luke 24:13-35

Mark 16:12	Luke 24:13
12 After that he appeared in another form to two of them, as they walked, and went into the country.	13 And, look, two of them went that same day to a village called Emmaus, which was from Jerusalem about seven and one-half miles.

Luke 24:11-35

14 And they talked together of all these things which had happened.

15 And it happened, that, while they communed together and reasoned, Jesus himself drew near, and went with them.

16 But there eyes were shielded from recognizing him.

17 And he said to them, What manner of communications are these that you have with one another, as you walk, and are sad?

18 And one of them, whose name was Cleopas, answering said to him, Are you only a stranger in Jerusalem, and have not known the things which have come to pass there in these days?

19 And he said to them, What things? And they said to him, Concerning Jesus of Nazareth, who was a prophet mighty in deed and word before God and all the people:

20 And how the chief priests and our rulers delivered him to be condemned to death, and have crucified him.

21 But we trusted that he was to redeem Israel: and beside all this, today is the third day since these things were done.

22 Yes, and certain women also of our company made us astonished, who were early at the grave;

23 And when they did not find his body, they came, saying, that they had also seen a vision of angels, who said that he was alive.

24 And certain of those who were with us went to the grave, and found it even as the women had said: but him they did not see.

25 Then he said to them, O fools, and slow of heart to believe all that the prophets have spoken:

26 Ought not Christ to have suffered these things, and to enter into his glory?

27 And beginning at Moses and all the prophets, he expounded to them in all the scriptures the things concerning him.

28 And they drew near to the village, to which they were going: and he made as though he would have gone further.

29 But they constrained him, saying, Abide with us: for it is toward evening, and the day is far spent. And he went in to tarry with them.

30 And it happened, as he sat to eat with them, he took bread, and blessed it, and broke, and gave to them.

31 And their eyes were opened, and they knew him; and he vanished out of their sight.

32 And they said one to another, Did not our heart burn within us, while he talked with us by the way, and while he opened to us the scriptures?

33 And they rose up the same hour, and returned to Jerusalem, and found the eleven gathered together, and those who were with them,

34 Saying, The Lord is risen indeed, and has appeared to Simon.

35 And they told what things were done in the way, and how he was known of them in breaking of bread.

Mark 16:13	Luke 24:33-35
	33 And they rose up the same hour, and returned to Jerusalem, and found the eleven gathered together, and those who were with them,
13a And they went and told it to the residue:	
	34 Saying, The Lord is risen indeed, and has appeared to Simon.
	35 And they told what things were done in the way, and how he was known of them in breaking of bread.
13b neither did they believe them.	

11.16 Jesus appears to disciples sans Thomas (Jerusalem) Luke 24:36-48, John 20:19-25

Luke 24:36-40	John 20:19-20
36 And as they were speaking, Jesus himself stood in their midst, and said to them, Peace be to you.	19 Then the same day at evening, being the first day of the week, when the doors were shut where the disciples were assembled for fear of the Jews, Jesus came and stood in their midst, and said to them, Peace be to you.
37 But they were terrified and frightened, and	

supposed that they had seen a spirit.	
38 And he said to them, Why are you troubled? And why do thoughts arise in your hearts?	
39 Look at my hands and my feet, that it is I myself: handle me, and see; for a spirit does not have flesh and bones, as you see that I have.	
40 And when he had said this, he showed them his hands and his feet.	20a, b And when he had so said, he showed them his hands and his side.
	20c, d Then the disciples were glad, when they saw the Lord.

Luke 24:41-48

41 And while they yet did not believe for joy, and wondered, he said to them, Have you here any food?
42 And they gave him a piece of a broiled fish, and a honeycomb.
43 And he took it, and did eat before them.
44 And he said to them, These are the words which I spoke to you, while I was yet with you, that all things must be fulfilled, which were written in the law of Moses, and in the prophets, and in the psalms, concerning me.
45 Then he opened their understanding, that they might understand the scriptures,
46 And said to them, Thus it is written, and thus it was fitting for Christ to suffer, and to rise from the dead the third day:
47 And that repentance and remission of sins should be preached in his name among all nations, beginning at Jerusalem.
48 And you are witnesses of these things.

John 20:21-25

[97]21 Then Jesus said to them again, Peace be to you: as my Father has sent me, even so I send you.
22 And when he had said this, he breathed on them, and said to them, Receive the Holy Ghost:
23 Whose sins you remit, are remitted; and whose sins you retain, are retained.
24 But Thomas, one of the twelve, called Didymus, was not with them when Jesus came.
25 The other disciples therefore said to him, We have seen the Lord. But he said to them, Except I shall see in his hands the print of the nails, and put my finger into the print of the nails, and thrust my hand into his side, I will not believe.

---

[97] The disciple's power and authority 8 (of 10). Lu 24:44-48; Joh 20:21-22

11.17 Appears to the eleven (Galilee) Mark 16:14, John 20:26-31

Mark 16:14	John 20:26
14 Afterward he appeared to the eleven as they sat to eat, and upbraided them for their unbelief and hardness of heart, because they did not believe those who had seen him after he had risen.	26 And after eight days again his disciples were within, and Thomas with them: then Jesus came, the doors being shut, and stood among them, and said, Peace be to you.

John 20:27-31
27 Then he said to Thomas, Reach here your finger, and look at my hands; and reach here your hand, and thrust it into my side: and be not faithless, but believing.
28 And Thomas answered and said to him, My Lord and my God.
29 Jesus said to him, Thomas, because you have seen me, you have believed: blessed are those who have not seen, and yet have believed.
30 And many other signs truly did Jesus in the presence of his disciples, which are not written in this book:
31 But these are written, that you might believe that Jesus is the Christ, the Son of God; and that believing you might have life through his name.

11.18 Appears to seven disciples by sea of Tiberias John 21:1-25

John 21:1-25

1 After these things Jesus showed himself again to the disciples at the sea of Tiberias; and this is the way in which he showed himself.

2 There were together Simon Peter, and Thomas called Didymus, and Nathanael of Cana in Galilee, and the sons of Zebedee, and two other disciples.

3 Simon Peter said to them, I am going fishing. They said to him, We will also go with you. They went forth, and entered into a ship immediately; and that night they caught nothing.

4 But when it was morning, Jesus stood on the shore: but the disciples did not know that it was Jesus.

5 Then Jesus said to them, Children, have you any food? They answered him, No.

6 And he said to them, Cast the net on the right side of the ship, and you shall find some. They cast therefore, and now they were not able to draw it for the multitude of fishes.

7 Therefore that disciple whom Jesus loved said to Peter, It is the Lord. Now when Simon Peter heard that it was the Lord, he girded his fisher's coat to him, (for he was naked,) and did cast himself into the sea.

8 And the other disciples came in a little ship; (for they were not far from land, but as it were two hundred cubits, dragging the net with fishes.

9 As soon then as they were come to land, they saw a fire of coals there, and fish laid on it, and bread.

10 Jesus said to them, Bring some of the fish which you have now caught.

11 Simon Peter went up, and drew the net to land full of great fishes, a hundred and fifty-three: and for

all that many fish, the net was not broken.

12 Jesus said to them, Come and dine. And none of the disciples dared ask him, Who are you? Knowing that it was the Lord.

13 Jesus then came, and took bread, and gave them, and fish likewise.

14 This is now the third time that Jesus showed himself to his disciples, after he had risen from the dead.

15 So when they had dined, Jesus said to Simon Peter, Simon, son of Jonas, do you love me more than these? He said to him, Yes, Lord; you know that I love you. He said to him, Feed my lambs.

16 He said to him again the second time, Simon, son of Jonas, do you love me? He said to him, Yes, Lord; you know that I love you. He said to him, Feed my sheep.

17 He said to him the third time, Simon, son of Jonas, do you love me? Peter was grieved because he said to him the third time, Do you love me? And he said to him, Lord, you know all things; you know that I love you. Jesus said to him, Feed my sheep.

18 Very Truly, I say to you, When you were young, you girded yourself, and walked where you would: but when you are old, you shall stretch forth your hands, and another shall gird you, and carry you where you would not.

19 This spoke he, signifying by what death he should glorify God. And when he had spoken this, he said to him, Follow me.

20 Then Peter, turning about, saw the disciple whom Jesus loved following; who also leaned on his breast at supper, and said, Lord, who is he who betrays you?

21 Peter seeing him said to Jesus, Lord, and what shall this man do?

22 Jesus said to him, If I will that he remain till I come, what is that to you? You follow me.

23 Then this saying went abroad among the brethren, that that disciple should not die: yet Jesus did not say to him, He shall not die; but, If I will that he remain till I come, what is that to you?

24 This is the disciple who testifies of these things, and wrote these things: and we know that his testimony is true.

25 And there are also many other things which Jesus did, which, if every one of them should be written, I suppose that even the world itself could not contain the books that should be written. Amen.

11.19 The first great commission (Galilee) Matthew 28:16-20

Matthew 28:16-20

[98]16 Then the eleven disciples went away into Galilee, into a mountain to which Jesus had appointed them.

17 And when they saw him, they worshipped him: but some doubted.

18 And Jesus came and spoke to them, saying, All power is given to me in heaven and in earth.

19 Go therefore, and teach all nations, baptizing them in the name of the Father, and of the Son, and of the Holy Ghost:

---

[98] The disciple's power and authority 9 (of 10). Mt 28:16-20.

20 Teaching them to observe all things I have commanded you: and, look, I am with you always, even to the end of the world. Amen.

11.20 The second great commission and Ascension (Mount of Olives, Jerusalem) Mark 16:15-20, Luke 24:49-53

Mark 16:15-20	Luke 24:49-53
[99]**15** And he said to them, Go into all the world, and preach the gospel to every creature.	
16 He who believes and is baptized shall be saved; but he who does not believe shall be damned.	
17 And these signs shall follow those who believe; In my name they shall cast out devils; they shall speak with new tongues;	
18 They shall take up serpents; and if they drink any deadly thing, it shall not hurt them; they shall lay hands on the sick, and they shall recover.	
	49 And, look, I send the promise of my Father upon you: but wait in the city of Jerusalem, until you are endued with power from on high.
	50 And he led them out as far as to Bethany, and he lifted up his hands, and blessed them.
19 So then after the Lord had spoken to them, he was received up into heaven, and sat on the right hand of God.	51 And it happened, while he blessed them, he was parted from them, and carried up into heaven.
	52 And they worshipped him, and returned to Jerusalem with great joy:
	53 And were continually in the temple, praising and blessing God. Amen.
20 And they went forth, and preached everywhere, the Lord working with them, and confirming the word with signs following. Amen.	

---

[99] The disciple's power and authority 10 (of 10). Mr 16:15-20; Lu 24:49-53.

Dr. John Adeoye Olubobokun obtained a Ph.D. in Animal Science from Louisiana State University in 1987. He is an ordained minister, and founder, and president of Grace Capstone Ministries Inc., a non-profit religious and educational charity. John resides in Saskatoon, Saskatchewan, with his family.

John A. Olubobokun

John Olubobokun is available for speaking engagements and personal appearances. For more information contact:

John Olubobokun
C/O Advantage Books
PO Box 160847
Altamonte Springs, FL 32716

To purchase additional copies of this book or other books published by Advantage Books call our toll free order number at:

1-888-383-3110 (Book Orders Only)

Or visit our bookstore website at:
www.advbookstore.com

Longwood, Florida, USA
"we bring dreams to life"™
www.advbooks.com

① We have just finished our 15th year. It is clear we will not be doing this in 20 y

what will we leave her

② target developer not top 10's but kid fresh out o college not JAVA HTML5 — Java script? Use of higher level tools

③ Automation — 1 good hour per day Energy on

④ Doing as many Regattas as we like More tactical
① RC will survive (not certain but most logical Assumption Use as much of their stuff as possible
② Use their support

CPSIA information can be obtained at www.ICGtesting.com
Printed in the USA
BVOW09s1317160415

396478BV00001B/1/P